BEHIND THE SCENES
OF 911

Matt Drozd

Matt Drozd Books.com

I dedicate my book to all who serve and have served
in the military, especially those who gave their lives
to protect our freedoms

TABLE OF CONTENTS

PRELUDE

Before delving into the depths of our story, I thought it appropriate to explain how I started a military career when the thought never crossed my mind when growing up.

As a young boy living in the steel valley with two cousins and two Uncles serving in WWII, I never had an inkling that I would sign up for a stint in the military. When anyone asked me if I wanted to be in the military, I was quick to answer emphatically no. My older brother was drafted into the army in the sixties and my younger brother was commissioned as an officer in the Army.

Like many young men my age, I was given little choice but to sign up towards the end of the Vietnam war or be drafted involuntarily. I was only eighteen when my whole world seemed to fall apart. I needed to escape from a broken heart caused by my not being able to build a relationship with a young girl who lived in my neighborhood. At first, I tried to sign up as an army helicopter pilot at the latter part of the Vietnam war. I passed all the written tests but because my one eye was slightly below 20-20 vision, I was not accepted. As over 10% of all combat and support deaths in Vietnam occurred in helicopter operations (2,202 pilots, 2704 aircrew, and 1,26passengers), it was fortunate for me that I was not accepted. (*HueyVets*)

"Vietnam has been called America's "Helicopter War" because helicopters provided mobility throughout the war zone, facilitating rapid troop transport, close air support, resupply, medical evacuation, reconnaissance, and search and rescue capabilities. In addition, Arlington National Cemetery is the final resting place of helicopter crews whose remains were recovered many years after the end of the Vietnam War. The Vietnam Helicopter Pilots Association (VHPA) estimates that over 100,000 helicopter pilots and crew members served during the Vietnam War. Over 4,800 helicopter pilots and crew members were killed in action, and more than three hundred are buried at Arlington National Cemetery." *(Arlington National Cemetery)*

At the time, my older brother, Thomas, was drafted into the army and sent to South Korea. When my vision disqualified me for helicopter flying, he suggested that I enlist in an army military police reserve unit located in Pittsburgh where I was sent to Fort Knox for basic training.

Photo 1-Gold Depository at Fort Knox

The first building I confronted while reporting for basic training at Fort Knox is the gold depository vault. It was used in the film Goldfinger with Sean Connery. To me, it looked more like a mausoleum than a gold vault. Its ghost-like appearance left one to think it was an abandoned building rather than surrounded with the highest of security. Fort Knox Army Base "is a 109,000-acre military base that encompasses the United States federal gold reserve and the Fort Knox Human Resource Center of Excellence. The resource hub is a complex that houses 4,000 civilian and military personnel. President Franklin Roosevelt has gone down in history as the only president to have ever been allowed entry into the Gold Depository back in 1943.

The building that houses the gold is made up of over 16,000 cubic feet of granite, 4,200 cubic yards of concrete, 750 tons of reinforced steel, and 670 tons of structural steel. The Depository still serves its original purpose, holding 147.3 million ounces of gold, which is just over half of the U.S. Treasury's gold bullion." (1)

My most intimidating encounter was when I reached the welcome center for new army recruits. A sign above its entrance read "Welcome to the United States Army." There were many recruits from all levels of society, some having no choice because of their being drafted. Back then, there were four categories for military inductees. Those involuntarily drafted were listed as US's and three-year active military were classified as Regular Army (RA's). National Guard soldiers were categorized as NG's and then there was troops like me who were Enlisted Reserves (ER's). Some were easy going guys from Alabama and many draftees held advanced college degrees. I was the youngest recruit of the lot. When I asked many of those that were college graduates why they did not apply for a commission, the answer always came back that they were going to do their two years and get out.

Immediately after reporting, we were assigned to a platoon and a barracks. The barracks were structured from wood with two floors, each having two rows of open bunk beds. The in-processing started immediately, which consisted of haircuts, drawing of uniforms, and filling out paperwork. The barbers kiddingly asked each recruit how they would like their haircut and then shaved it all off. Immunizations were injected by air guns that tore many arms.

After being in-processed, we all laid around the barracks waiting for our drill instructors (DI's). "Most military training companies consisted of three or four squads with 20 to 50 soldiers and trained by a drill instructor." (2) The DI's that came to collect their troops were very intimidating with their eyes mysteriously covered by their smokey bear hats. Each of the DI's collected their respective troops and stood sternly in front of their new charges. Many of the DI's previously served in combat areas such as Vietnam. Some were on drugs, alcoholics, or suffered from combat stress.

If you got out of line, some DIs would hit you with the butt of a rifle in the head or gave you hardened chores. Because one of the recruits mouthed off to one of the cooks, he was chased around the mess hall with a knife.

The DI assigned to our platoon spoke elegantly and always addressing us as "gentlemen." His introduction was classic. "Gentlemen, I am your DI. My name is Sergeant Badcock. "Looking back on the graduation yearbook that I received upon completing basic training, his name was *Sergeant Badcock.* His name and initial demeanor frightened us all. You could hear moans and groans throughout the entire platoon. Badcock took immediate charge and marched us to our training company. When we reached the parade area in front of the barracks, Badcock told us to fall back into formation after picking out a bunk.

After falling back in formation, Badcock pointed to the other platoons. "Gentlemen, see these men over here." Our heads turned to the left looking at the platoon on our left. "Well gentlemen if you do what you are supposed to do and do it well, you gentlemen are going to be over there. drinking a beer with me under that tree. You could hear relieved sighs throughout the platoon.

8

Badcock kept his word during the entire training cycle. We woke at the scheduled time for morning reveille while the neighboring platoons were already outside standing in formation fully dressed in field packs. The good old boys from Alabama had lost their easy-going attitude and you could see the stress on their faces. There was one draftee that was suicidal. Instead of discharging him, the DI's forced him through the cycle. What disturbed me was that a DI had to accompany him through the assault courses, and he always ended up right next to me carrying a loaded M-16 rifle. He was throwing a grenade in a bunker next to me and shooting a loaded M-16 rifle while running down a hill. I kept thinking what if he threw the grenade in the air and blew us both up and accidentally shot an M-16 round my way.

Photo 2-Army Basic Infiltration Course

Two of our hair-raising training events was crawling through an assault course while three fixed machine guns were firing bullets above your head and explosives were going off in bunkers next to where you were crawling. You had to be careful not to get dirt in the muzzle of your rifle or they would make you do it again. Some of the recruits hid in the nearby woods and pretended they did the course.

The company commander felt it necessary to test our resolve by playing with our minds. When we were on the rifle range, he falsefully announced that we were at war with China.

On the way back to our barracks, you could not hear a pin drop. It was only later when we learned that we were not at war with China. One could only wonder why an officer would play with the minds of so many young and naive men. Luckily, Badcock never did the same. He led with respect and not with fear. As a result of his outstanding leadership and mentorship, our platoon finished in first place. I was able to apply what I learned from him when I later pinned on my bars as an officer.

As recently as 2024, I tried searching for SSGT Badcock. I was surprised and saddened to learn that he may have died in Vietnam. From what I found on a web site titled "Family Search," he may have died in Nam-Phan, Vietnam, at the young age of forty, and was buried in Washington DC. Someday, I hope to visit his grave site to pay my respects.

After completing boot camp, I returned home only to find that the first love of my life was now dating someone. This continued to tear at my heart for quite a long time. I returned to college, completed my degree, and took a job with General Motors Corporation. After serving three years in the Army reserve, I crossed over into the blue by enlisting in an Air Force National Guard unit to complete my last three years of my reserve military commitment. When I walked into the Air Force reserve recruiting office, an enlisted reserve member by the name of Rick Conwell greeted me.

Having the option as to which unit I wanted to join, he suggested one of them to me. The one that he suggested flew F-102 long-range interceptor fighter jets. On my way back home, a news station reported that one of the two Air Force units was activated. Not being able to recall which one I joined, I immediately returned to the recruitment office. Looking surprisingly at me, Rick exclaimed that he could not believe that I may have joined the unit that was activated and could be deployed into a high-risk combat zone. After frantically looking at the enlisted sheets, we discovered that I did not. Together, we had a good laugh and stayed close friends to this very day. Long thereafter, however, I felt guilty that I never stepped and went with the other unit that was deployed.

My ultimate dream was to earn a commission and become a fighter pilot. I tried joining the active Air Force as a fighter pilot but because I did not have 20/20 vision, I was disqualified. Years later, Rick and I both became officers, rising through the ranks to field grade officers.

To further escape the ongoing despair of losing the love of my life, I quit my first job at General Motors and tried to pursue a career in the motion picture industry. I wrote letters to the three main major motion picture companies. To my amazement, the acting CEO of Twentieth Century Fox wrote back telling me that he would see me. I left for California the next day.

Upon my arrival at the studios of Twentieth Century Fox, the receptionist showed me into the CEO's office. I was dressed in a business suit where he wore casual clothes. His office overlooked the production lots where top movies were filmed and famous actors once roamed. The CEO told me that he was willing to meet with me because I reminded him of when he started in the industry. He was a lawyer who became an agent for famous holly wood actors. Along with other movie moguls, he became acting CEO by ousting the former CEO who lost them millions. He noted that they were going to reduce costs by consolidating their New York operations and consolidating them in Hollywood. When doing so, he said that they would be hiring people with my background. After our meeting, the CEO gave me an open door to tour their movie lot. I was allowed to walk across the movie set "Hello Dolly," starring Barbara Streisand and Walter Matthau.

Upon returning home, I sent letters to the News programs of the three television networks in New York. The president of ABC News agreed to interview me when I was in

New York. After a lengthy interview, I was hired and pursued a once in a lifetime career in New York as the youngest Program Controller for ABC News. I was assigned to the world television and radio news programs and the ABC world News Bureaus. ABC's science editor, Jules Bergman, became my mentor. An excerpt from one of his space newscasts was featured in the movie Apollo XIII. I also worked on a documentary with Peter Jennings and Sam Donaldson. I was slated to become the Program Controller for the ABC News show 2020. With my now having an extensive background in television production, I again attempted to contact the CEO of Twentieth Century Fox. Sadly, I was told that he had died. This left me with no option but to return to Pittsburgh and finish my master's degree. Before leaving, I took an election graphic that appeared on national television with my press pass mounted on it.

Years later, I married and had two wonderful sons. At no fault of mine or my ex-wives, the marriage did not last. After dissolving a business partnership, I ended up as an administrator at a major university. Shortly thereafter, I volunteered for the Persian Gulf War, and this was when my second military career restarted, and my story Behind the Scenes of 911 begins.

CHAPTER 1

The Persian Gulf War

As the years went by, I dreamed that I would receive a commission and become a pilot. I realized, however, that I was too old to receive a commission in the military let alone become a pilot. Suddenly the Persian Gulf war broke out. My being patriotic, I contacted an Air Force recruiter to re-enlist.

After reviewing my background and education, the recruiter told me that there was a window for me to earn a commissioner even though I was beyond the age of commissioning. My age could be waived by gaining a slot in a unit as a Medical Service Corps officer. After extensive search, I found a unit that had an opening. With over a twenty-year break in military service, I may have a record of returning to military service. My brother, a Major in the Army, tried talking me out of it because I had two small sons. I told him that I could lose my children's respect if I did not accept the commission.

After a brief stint in the reserve unit, I transferred into the individual mobilization augmentee (IMA) program of the Air Force. "The Air Force's individual mobilization augmentee (IMA) program provides trained, equipped, and ready reservists when the service needs them to support an operational requirement. A significant change to the Reserves brought about by Operation Desert Storm continues to affect this program. These reservists are assigned to active-duty units rather than Reserve units, and their program's organizational structure is unique. The IMA program immediately augments active-duty units in time of war or national crisis by assigning reservists to them for training prior to such events. Instead of spending weeks or months trying to understand a unit's unique personalities and relationships, the IMA who has experience with the unit can step in and provide seamless support. "(3)

My first IMA assignment was serving at one of the largest medical centers in the Air Force, Wright Patterson. Fortunately, I served under one of the finest medical service officers I ever encountered, Colonel Gary Triche. His outstanding mentorship and command expertise enhanced my leadership skills.

After serving at the medical center for two years, I learned about an opening position at the Pentagon serving in the Medical Operations Center (MOC), Office of the Air Force Surgeon General at the Pentagon. Although I was reluctant to leave Wright Pat and Colonel Triche, I thought it would be fascinating to serve at the Pentagon. After making application, I was immediately accepted.

"The mission of the Air Force Medical Services (AFMS) supports the U.S. Air Force and Space Force through the provision of full spectrum medical readiness to the more than 200,000 Airmen and Guardians currently engaged in operations around the globe, while also delivering health care to 2.6 million patients." (4) One of my assignments was to help coordinate approval for the Secretary of the Air Force directed humanitarian response capability package, which provided the Service's first consolidated humanitarian relief capability.

While serving in the MOC, I had the opportunity to join in briefings with a two-star general and the three star surgeon general of the Air Force. After serving in the MOC

14

for one year, my interest turned to the possibility of being assigned to the Joint Chiefs of Staff.

"The Joint Chiefs of Staff (JCS) consists of the Chairman, the Vice Chairman, the Chief of Staff of the Army, the Chief of Naval Operations, the Chief of the Air Force, the Commandant of the Marine Corps, the Chief of the National Guard Bureau and the Chief of Space Operations. The collective body of the JCS is headed by the Chairman (or the Vice Chairman in the Chairman's absence), who sets the agenda and presides over JCS meetings. The Chairman of the Joint Chiefs of Staff is the principal military adviser to the President, Secretary of Defense, and the National Security Council (NSC). All JCS members are by law military advisers, and they may respond to a request or voluntarily submit, through the Chairman, advice or opinions to the President, the Secretary of Defense, or NSC.

The Goldwater-Nichols Department of Defense (DOD) Reorganization Act of 1986 identifies the Chairman of the Joint Chiefs of Staff as the senior ranking member of the Armed Forces. As such, the Chairman of the Joint Chiefs of Staff is the principal military adviser to the President.

Under the DOD Reorganization Act, the Secretaries of the Military Departments assign all forces to combatant commands except those assigned to conduct the mission of the Services, i.e., recruit, organize, supply, equip, train, service, mobilize, demobilize, administer, and maintain their respective forces. The chain of command to these combatant commands runs from the President to the Secretary of Defense directly to the commander of the combatant command. The Chairman of the Joint Chiefs of Staff may transmit communications to the commanders of the combatant commands from the President and Secretary of Defense but does not exercise military command over any combatant forces. In performing his duties, the Chairman of the Joint Chiefs of Staff consults with and seeks the advice of other members of the Joint Chiefs of Staff and the combatant commanders.

The Joint Staff is comprised of 2,000 civilians and service members from the Army, Navy, Marine Corps, Air Force, National Guard and Coast Guard--over eight hundred are civil servants. The men and women of the Joint Staff directly support the Chairman of the Joint Chiefs of Staff (CJCS), the highest ranking military officer in the U.S. Department of Defense and is the principal military advisor to the President of the United States. Their efforts have a direct impact on global operations and on our warfighters' ability to fight and win decisively in every domain - air, land, sea, cyber and space. Its main structure is comprised of eight Directorates that support the CJCS.

Directorate J1. Manpower and Personnel, fosters highly effective communication, cooperation, and collaboration within the J1, Joint Staff directorates, OSD, Services, and Combatant Commands to develop globally integrated solutions to joint manpower and personnel challenges. Additionally, the Directorate ensures comprehensive Joint Force readiness to meet warfighting requirements by monitoring, identifying, and predicting joint manpower and personnel challenges, and informing the resource prioritization, identification, and allocation.

J2 Directorate coordinates joint intelligence doctrine and architecture and manages intelligence for joint warfighting assessments. J-2 serves as the Intelligence Community manager for Support to Military operations and is the Director of the Joint Warfighting Capabilities Assessments for Intel, Surveillance, and Reconnaissance

J3 Directorate assists the Chairman in fulfilling responsibilities as the principal military advisor to the President and Secretary of Defense, developing and providing guidance to the combatant commanders and relaying communications between the President and the Secretary of Defense and the combatant commanders regarding current operations and plans.

J4 Directorate integrates logistics planning and execution in support of joint operations to drive joint force readiness, maximize the Joint Force Commander's freedom of action, and advises the Chairman of the Joint Chiefs of Staff on logistics matters.

J5 Directorate proposes strategies, plans, and policy recommendations to the Chairman of the Joint Chiefs of Staff to support his provision of military advice across the full spectrum of national security concerns to the President and other national leaders. J5 assesses risk in executing the National Military Strategy.

J6 Directorate represents the Joint Warfighter in support of the command, control, communications, and computer/cyber (C4) requirements validation and capability development processes while ensuring joint interoperability.

J7 Directorate supports the Chairman Joint Chiefs of Staff (CJCS) and the joint warfighter through joint force development (JFD) to advance the operational effectiveness of the current and future joint force, by focusing on joint training and exercising, education, doctrine, lessons learned, concepts, allies, and NATO.

J8 Directorate provides support to CJCS for evaluating and developing force structure requirements. J-8 conducts joint, bilateral, and multilateral war games and interagency politico-military seminars and simulations." (5)

After perusing the eight Directorates, I felt more suited for the logistics Directorate of J4, especially as this Directorate oversaw and wrote policy for the medical readiness of all the branches of the military and interacted closely with the three-star surgeon generals of all the military branches. Medical readiness ensures that uniformed service members are free of health-related conditions that limit their ability to achieve their assigned mission.

I felt the easiest and best way to be assigned was simply to knock on the door of the J4 at the Pentagon. When doing so, the security codes and cyber locks do not make it easy. Not having the code, I simply knocked. A Navy Captain (one rank lower than Admiral) answered the door.

His first question was "who was I and what did I want?" Reaching out to shake his hand, I held onto it steadfast. "I am an immobilized augmentee reservist that attaches to and supports the active duty. I want to support your mission." Perplexed, the Naval captain looked at me and then invited me in to explain how the IMA program works. After a lengthy discussion and a few weeks had passed, I was assigned to the Medical Readiness Division of the Joint Chiefs of Staff.

The first chairman that I would serve under on the Joint Staff would be the four-star army general, General Henry Hugh Shelton. "He was the first to possess a special operations background, expertise that fit well with Secretary of Defense William S. Cohen's interest in unconventional warfare. Shelton often stated that he did not believe in "fair fights" and endorsed the use of overwhelming force when committing American troops to combat. He believed the US military had to be prepared to undertake flexible missions with well-defined and limited objectives. Force readiness, therefore, was a top priority." (6)

CHAPTER 2

USS Cole Attack

Shortly after being assigned to the Joint staff, I was attached to a team that responded to a terrorist attack on a naval ship, the USS Cole. The USS Cole is 505 ft long with a 59-foot-wide beam. When fully loaded with crew and weaponry, it weighs 8900 tons.

"On 8 August 2000, Cole was deployed from Norfolk to the Mediterranean, Red Sea, Gulf of Aden, and Indian Ocean. On 12 October, while Cole refueled at Aden, Yemen, two al-Qaeda terrorists brought an inflatable Zodiac-type speedboat that carried a bomb alongside the destroyer, port side amidships, and detonated their lethal cargo. The explosion blew a 40-foot-wide hole in Cole, but the crew's valiant damage control efforts saved her." (7)

Photo 3-Hole in USS Cole caused by Terrorists

"The FBI instantly sent to Yemen more than one hundred agents from the Counterterrorism Division, the FBI Laboratory, and various field offices. Director Louis Freeh arrived soon after to assess the situation and to meet with the President of Yemen. The extensive FBI investigation determined that members of the al Qaeda terrorist network planned and carried out the bombing. The investigation also revealed that the USS Cole bombing followed an unsuccessful attempt on January 3, 2000, to bomb another U.S. Navy ship, the USS Sullivans. In this earlier incident, the terrorist boat sank before the explosives could be detonated; however, the terrorists salvaged the boat and the explosives. The boat was then refitted, and the explosives were reused in the USS Cole attack.

By the end of 2000, Yemeni authorities had arrested several suspects, the alleged masterminds of the USS Sullivans and the USS Cole plots who were known as al Qaeda operatives trained in al Qaeda camps in Afghanistan. They were later killed in air attacks." (8, 11)

Immediately upon the USS Cole being attacked, the Joint Staff Directorates sprang into action. All the Directorates stood up their crisis action centers. I was one of the officers sent to the J4 Crisis action center to work actions related to the bombing. Along with the Medical Operations Center, our task was to get medical personnel to the ship and stabilize the wounded.

"The resulting blast killed 17 Sailors, wounded thirty-seven others, and tore a hole forty by sixty feet in the ship's hull. In the aftermath of the explosion, the crew of USS *Cole* fought tirelessly to free shipmates trapped by the twisted wreckage and limit flooding that threatened to sink the ship. The crew's prompt actions to isolate damaged electrical systems and contain fuel oil ruptures prevented catastrophic fires that could have engulfed the ship and cost the lives of countless men and women. Skillful first aid and advanced medical treatment applied by the crew prevented additional death and eased the suffering of many others. Drawing upon their Navy training and discipline, the crew heroically conducted more than 96 hours of sustained damage control in conditions of extreme heat and stress. Deprived of sleep, food, and shelter, they vigilantly battled to preserve and secure and restore stability to engineering systems that were vital to the ship's survival. The crew of the Cole personified Honor, Courage, and Commitment."(9)

The commanding officer of our crisis action center assigned tasks to approximately twenty or more members that manned the center. When he came to me, I was tasked to arrange for medical care and provide air evacuation for the wounded. We arranged for the closest medical team from a neighboring country to stabilize the wounded. Air evacuation medical teams were deployed to transport the wounded.

After at least 24 hours had passed, our commander assigned me the task of arranging for the transport of the sailors, including the deceased members, back to Andrews Air Force Base. "Major Drozd, the Secretary of Defense (SECDEF) wants all the USS Cole sailors and its casualties back to Andrews ASAP. He wants to turn over the casualties to their families and to arrange accommodation for the crew and wounded, to be transported to the States." To arrange the return of the seventeen that paid the ultimate price, I had to contact Mortuary services at Dover AF Base.

"A solemn dignified transfer of remains is conducted upon arrival at Dover Air Force Base, Del., to honor those who have given their lives in the service of our country. Upon the return of the deceased from the theater of operations to the United States, their remains are transferred from the aircraft to an awaiting vehicle. The remains will then be transferred to the mortuary facility located at Air Force

21

Mortuary Affairs Operations, Dover AFB, Del. The dignified transfer is a solemn movement of the transfer case by a carry team composed of military personnel from the fallen member's respective service. A senior ranking officer of the fallen member's service presides over each dignified transfer. The sequence of the transfer starts with the fallen being returned to Dover AFB by the most expedient means possible typically includes a stop at Ramstein Air Base, Germany.

It is the Department of Defense's policy, and AFMAO's mission, to return America's fallen to their loved ones as quickly as possible. Once the aircraft lands at Dover AFB, service-specific carry teams remove the transfer cases individually from the aircraft and move them to an awaiting transfer vehicle. The vehicle(s) then transport the fallen to the mortuary facility for positive identification by the Armed Forces Medical Examiner System and for preparation to their final resting place." (10) Dover Mortuary Affairs give meticulous attention to making certain that the deceased are properly uniformed, and all medals properly placed.

To expedite the return of the fallen sailors to their families, I phoned the head of mortuary affairs at Dover. "I am sorry to bother you but the SECDEF wants the deceased transported to Andrews AFB so we can return them to their loved ones." I was surprised to hear from him that there would be no problem returning them in a timely manner. I asked him about the condition of the deceased. He informed me that because they were drawn into the water after the galley floor collapsed, they were in perfect condition. My heart sank when I heard the details. To this day, I question why the watch officer on the US Cole allowed the terrorists to get so close to their ship?

The next task of our team was to decide the fate of the USS Cole. We had two options. The first was to cannibalize the top-secret equipment, the armor, and the missiles, strip the ship down to its bare structure and sink it in the harbor. The other was to bring it back to a drydock area to repair it. I remember sitting in the crisis center with a team trying to ascertain what to do with the ship.

The replacement cost was one billion and repairs were estimated at $250 million. After comparing these costs, we decided to repair the ship and return it to service, but how and where do you repair an 8400-ton ship with a large gaping hole in its side? We knew that it would sink in route if we towed it in open seas from Aden Yemen to Ingalls Shipbuilding in Pascagoula, Mississippi, 8141 miles. The hole would quickly take in water, sinking it like the Titanic. The only way to transport it was to piggyback it on one of two salvage ships in the world capable of such a task.

Photo 4-Piggyback of USS Cole on USNS Tug Catawba

"The tug USNS Catawba towed the Cole out of the Yemen port into open sea where it was placed on the deck of the Norwegian heavy transport ship M/V Blue Marlin and transported back to the United States for repair." (12)

CHAPTER 3

American Under Attack

Photo 5 Pentagon-National Military Command Center

Next, I was assigned to fill the J4 desk of the Joint Staff, in the National Military Command Center.

"The NMCC is in the Joint Staff area of the Pentagon. The National Military Command Center is responsible for generating Emergency Action Messages (EAMs) to launch control centers, nuclear submarines, recon aircraft, and battlefield commanders worldwide. The NMCC is a Pentagon command and communications center for the National Command Authority (i.e., the President of the United States and the United States Secretary of Defense). The NMCC has three main missions, all serving the Chairman of the Joint Chiefs of Staff, the principal military advisor to both the Secretary of Defense and the President (also known as the National Command Authority).

- The primary task of the NMCC is to monitor worldwide events which may be of defense significance.
- The NMCC also has a crisis response component.
- A strategic watch component (e.g., monitoring ballistic missile launches and other nuclear activity).

The NMCC is operated by five teams on a rotating watch system. Each team typically has 17–20 personnel on duty performing a wide variety of functions. Teams are led by a deputy director for operations (DDO) and an assistant deputy director for operations (ADDO), and are divided into five duty officer positions: The DDO is typically a brigadier general or rear admiral, and the ADDO is typically a colonel or Navy captain. If the president convenes a conference with advisors to discuss options for launching a nuclear strike, the DDO would be a key participant in the meeting." (13)

When I was first assigned to the NMCC, it was one big room separated into modules, with each Joint Staff Directorate having an assigned desk. Later, it was reconfigured and more compartmentalized.

With all the monitor capabilities of the Pentagon, our world-wide intelligence had no advance notice of the "September 11 attacks, which triggered an enormous U.S. effort to combat terrorism. Some 2,750 people were killed in New York, 184 at the Pentagon, and 40 in Pennsylvania (where one of the hijacked planes crashed into the ground after the passengers attempted to retake the plane); all 19 terrorists died. Response departments in New York were especially hard-hit: hundreds rushed to the scene of the attacks, and more than four hundred police officers and firefighters were killed.

The terrorist attack plot: The September 11 attacks were precipitated in large part because Osama bin Laden, the leader of the militant Islamic organization al-Qaeda, held naive beliefs about the United States in the run-up to the attacks. Abu Walid al-Masri, an Egyptian who was a bin Laden associate in Afghanistan in the 1980s and '90s, explained that, in the years prior to the attacks, bin Laden became increasingly convinced that America was weak.

"He believed that the United States was much weaker than some of those around him thought," Masri remembered. Bin Laden believed that the United States was a "paper tiger," a belief shaped not just by America's departure from Lebanon following a marine barracks bombing, but by the withdrawal of American forces from Somalia in 1993, and the American pullout from Vietnam.

The key operational planner of the September 11 attacks was Khalid Sheikh Mohammed (often referred to simply as "KSM" in the later *9/11 Commission Report* and in the media), who had spent his youth in Kuwait. KSM became active in the Muslim Brotherhood, which he joined at age 16, and then went to the United States to attend college, receiving a degree from North Carolina Agricultural and Technical State University in 1986. Afterward he traveled to Pakistan and then Afghanistan to wage jihad against the Soviet Union, which had launched an invasion against Afghanistan in 1979.

"According to Yosri Fouda, a journalist at the Arabic-language cable television channel Al Jazeera who interviewed him in 2002, Khalid Sheikh Mohammed planned to blow up some dozen American planes in Asia, a plot that failed, "but the dream of Khalid Sheikh Mohammed never faded. And I think by putting his hand in the hands of bin Laden, he realized that he stood a chance of bringing about his long-awaited dream. "In 1996 Khalid Sheikh Mohammed met bin Laden in Tora Bora, Afghanistan.

Khalid Sheikh Mohammed dreamed up the tactical innovation of using hijacked planes to attack the United

States. Al-Qaeda provided the personnel, money, and logistical support to execute the operation, and bin Laden wove the attacks on New York and Washington into a larger strategic framework of attacking the "far enemy"—the United States—in order to bring about regime change across the Middle East.

The September 11 plot demonstrated that al-Qaeda was an organization of global reach. The plot played out across the globe with planning meetings in Malaysia, operatives taking flight lessons in the United States, coordination by plot leaders based in Hamburg, Germany, money transfers from Dubai, and recruitment of suicide operatives from countries around the Middle East—all activities that were ultimately overseen by al-Qaeda's leaders in Afghanistan.

Key parts of the September 11 plot took shape in Hamburg. Four of the key pilots and planners in the "Hamburg cell" who would take operational control of the September 11 attacks, including the lead hijacker Mohammed Atta, had a chance meeting on a train in Germany in 1999 with an Islamist militant who struck up a conversation with them about fighting jihad in the Russian republic of Chechnya. The militant put the Hamburg cell in touch with an al-Qaeda operative living in Germany who explained that it was difficult to get to Chechnya at that time, because many travelers were being detained in Georgia. He recommended they go to Afghanistan instead.

Although Afghanistan was critical to the rise of al-Qaeda, it was the experience that some of the plotters acquired in the West that made them simultaneously more zealous and better equipped to carry out the attacks. Three of the four plotters who would pilot the hijacked planes on September 11 and one of the key planners, Ramzi Binalshibh, became more radical while living in Hamburg.

Some combination of perceived or real discrimination, alienation, and homesickness seems to have turned them all in a more militant direction. Increasingly cutting themselves off from the outside world, they gradually radicalized each other, and eventually the friends decided to wage battle in bin Laden's global jihad, setting off for Afghanistan in 1999 in search of al-Qaeda.

One of the hijackers by the name of Atta and the other members of the Hamburg group arrived in Afghanistan in 1999 right at the moment that the September 11 plot was beginning to take shape. Bin Laden and his military commander Muhammad Atef realized that Atta and his fellow Western-educated jihadists were far better suited to lead the attacks on Washington and New York than the men they had already recruited, leading bin Laden to appoint Atta to head the operation.

The hijackers, established themselves in the United States, well in advance of the attacks. They traveled in small groups, and some of them received commercial flight training.

Throughout his stay in the United States, Atta kept Binalshibh updated on the plot's progress via e-mail. To cloak his activities, Atta wrote the messages as if he were writing to his girlfriend "Jenny," using innocuous code to inform Binalshibh that they were almost complete in their training and readiness for the attacks. Atta wrote in one message, "The first semester commences in three weeks...Nineteen certificates for private education and four exams." The referenced nineteen "certificates" were code that identified the nineteen al-Qaeda hijackers, while the four "exams" identified the targets of the attacks.

In the early morning of August 29, 2001, Atta called Binalshibh and said he had a riddle that he was trying to solve: "Two sticks, a dash and a cake with a stick down—

what is it?" After considering the question, Binalshibh realized that Atta was telling him that the attacks would occur in two weeks, the two sticks being the number 11 and the cake with a stick down a nine. Putting it together, it meant that the attacks would occur on 11-9, or 11 September (in most countries the day precedes the month in numeric dates, but in the United States the month precedes the day; hence, it was 9-11 in the United States). On September 5 Binalshibh left Germany for Pakistan. Once there he sent a messenger to Afghanistan to inform bin Laden about both the day of the attack and its scope.

September 11 attacks: Mohammed Atta

On September 11, 2001, groups of attackers boarded four domestic aircraft at three East Coast airports, and soon after takeoff they disabled the crews, some of whom may have been stabbed with box cutters the hijackers were secreting. The hijackers then took control of the aircraft, all large and bound for the West Coast with full loads of fuel. At 8:46 AM the first plane, American Airlines flight 11, which had originated from Boston, was piloted into the north tower of the World Trade Center in New York City. Most observers construed this initially to be an accident involving a small commuter plane. The second plane, Airlines flight 175, also from Boston, struck the south tower 17 minutes later.

At this point there was no doubt that the United States was under attack. Each structure was severely damaged by the impact and erupted into flames. Office workers who were trapped above the points of impact in some cases leapt to their deaths rather than face the infernos now raging inside the towers. The third plane, American Airlines flight 77, taking off from Dulles Airport near Washington, D.C., struck the southwest side of the Pentagon (just outside the city) at 9:37 AM, touching off a fire in that section of the structure. Minutes later the Federal Aviation Authority ordered a nationwide ground stop, and within the next hour (at 10:03 AM) the fourth aircraft, United Airlines flight 93 from Newark, New Jersey, crashed near Shanksville in the Pennsylvania countryside.

At 9:59 AM the World Trade Center's heavily damaged south tower collapsed, and the north tower fell 29 minutes later. Clouds of smoke and debris quickly filled the streets of Lower Manhattan. Office workers and residents ran in panic as they tried to outpace the billowing debris clouds. Several other buildings adjacent to the twin towers suffered serious damage, and several subsequently fell.

On the morning of September 11, President Bush had been visiting a second-grade classroom in Sarasota, Florida, when he was informed that a plane had flown into the World Trade Center. A little later Andrew Card, his chief of staff, whispered in the president's right ear: "A second plane hit the second tower. America is under attack." To keep the president out of harm's way, Bush subsequently hopscotched across the country on Air Force One, landing in Washington, D.C., the evening of the attacks.

At 8:30 PM Bush addressed the nation from the Oval Office in a speech that laid out a key doctrine of his administration's future foreign policy: "We will make no distinction between the terrorists who committed these acts and those who harbor them." Bush made one of the most memorable remarks of his presidency: *I can hear you. The rest of the world hears you. And the people who knocked these buildings down will hear from all of us soon.*

Bush's robust response to the attacks drove his poll ratings from 55 percent favorable before September 11 to 90 percent in the days after, the highest ever recorded for a president.

Unlike the relatively isolated site of the Pearl Harbor attack of 1941, to which the September 11 events were soon compared, the World Trade Center lay at the heart of one of the world's largest cities. Hundreds of thousands of people witnessed the attacks firsthand (many onlookers photographed events or recorded them with video cameras), and millions watched the tragedy unfold live on television. In the days that followed September 11, the footage of the attacks was replayed in the media countless times, as were the scenes of throngs of people, stricken with grief, gathering at "Ground Zero"—as the site where the towers once stood came to be commonly known—some with photos of missing loved ones, seeking some hint of their fate.

Moreover, world markets were badly shaken. The towers were at the heart of New York's financial district, and damage to Lower Manhattan's infrastructure, combined with fears of stock market panic, kept New York markets closed for four trading days. Markets afterward suffered record losses. The attacks also stranded tens of thousands of people throughout the United States, as U.S. airspace remained closed for commercial aviation until September 13, and normal service, with more rigid security measures, did not resume for several days.

The September 11 attacks were an enormous tactical success for al-Qaeda. The strikes were well coordinated and hit multiple targets in the heart of America. The attacks were magnified by being broadcast around the world to an audience of untold millions. The September 11 "propaganda of the deed" took place in the media capital of the world, which ensured the widest possible coverage of the event. Not since television viewers had watched the abduction and murder of Israeli athletes during the Munich Olympics in 1972 had a massive global audience witnessed a terrorist attack unfold in real time. If al-Qaeda had been an unknown organization before September 11, in the days after it became a household name.

After the attacks of September 11, countries allied with the United States rallied to its support, perhaps best symbolized by the French newspaper *Le Monde*'s headline, "We are all Americans now." Even in Iran thousands gathered in the capital, Tehran, for a candlelight vigil. Evidence gathered by the United States soon convinced most governments that the Islamic militant group al-Qaeda was responsible for the attacks. The group had been implicated in previous terrorist strikes against Americans, and bin Laden had made numerous anti-American statements. Al-Qaeda was headquartered in Afghanistan and had forged a close relationship with that country's ruling Taliban militia, which subsequently refused U.S. demands to extradite bin Laden and to terminate al-Qaeda activity there.

For the first time in its history, the North Atlantic Organization (NATO) invoked Article 5, allowing its members to respond collectively in self-defense, and on October 7 the U.S. and allied military forces launched an attack against Afghanistan Within months, thousands of militants were killed or captured, and Taliban and al-Qaeda leaders were driven into hiding. In addition, the U.S. government exerted great effort to track down other al-Qaeda agents and sympathizers throughout the world and made combating terrorism the focus of U.S. foreign policy.

Meanwhile, security measures within the United States were tightened considerably at such places as airports, government buildings, and sports venues. To help facilitate the domestic response, Congress quickly passed the USA PATRIOT Act (the Uniting and Strengthening America by Providing Appropriate Tools Required to Intercept and Obstruct Terrorism Act of 2001), which significantly but temporarily expanded the search and surveillance powers of the Federal Bureau of Investigation (FBI) and other law-enforcement agencies. Additionally, a cabinet-level Department of Homeland Security was established.

Despite their success in causing widespread destruction and death, the September 11 attacks were a strategic failure for al-Qaeda. Following September 11, al-Qaeda—whose name in Arabic means "the base"—lost the best base it ever had in Afghanistan.

Later some in al-Qaeda's leadership—including those who, like Egyptian Saif al-Adel, had initially opposed the attacks—tried to spin the Western intervention in Afghanistan as a victory for al-Qaeda. Al-Adel, one of the group's military commanders, explained in an interview four years later that the strikes on New York and Washington were part of a far-reaching and visionary plan to provoke the United States into some ill-advised actions: *Such strikes will force the person to conduct random acts and provoke him to make serious and sometimes fatal mistakes....The first reaction was the invasion of Afghanistan.*

But there is not a shred of evidence that in the weeks before September 11 al-Qaeda's leaders made any plans for an American invasion of Afghanistan. Instead, they prepared only for possible U.S. cruise missile attacks or air strikes by evacuating their training camps. Also, the overthrow of the Taliban hardly constituted an American "mistake"—the first and only regime in the modern Muslim world that ruled according to al-Qaeda's rigid precepts was toppled, and with it was lost an entire country that al-Qaeda had once enjoyed as a safe haven. And in the wake of the fall of the Taliban, al-Qaeda was unable to recover anything like the status it once had as a terrorist organization with considerable sway over Afghanistan.

Bin Laden disastrously misjudged the possible U.S. responses to the September 11 attacks, which he believed would take one of two forms: an eventual retreat from the Middle East along the lines of the U.S. pullout from Somalia in 1993 or another ineffectual round of cruise missile attacks similar to those that followed al-Qaeda's bombings of American embassies in Kenya and Tanzania in 1998. Neither of these two scenarios happened.

The U.S. campaign against the Taliban was conducted with pinpoint strikes from American airpower, more than 300 U.S. Special Forces soldiers on the ground working with 110 officers from the Central Intelligence Agency (CIA). In November, just two months after the September 11 attacks, the Taliban fell to the Northern Alliance and the United States. Still, it was just the beginning of what would become the longest war in U.S. history, as the United States tried to prevent the return of the Taliban and their al-Qaeda allies.

Faced with the problem of where to house prisoners as the Taliban fell, the administration decided to hold them at Guantánamo Bay, which the U.S. had been leasing from Cuba since 1903. As Secretary of Defense Donald Rumsfeld put it on December 27, 2001, "I would characterize Guantánamo Bay, Cuba, as the least worst place we could

Photo 6-Terrorist prisoners at GITMO Cuba

have selected." Guantánamo was attractive to administration officials because they believed it placed the detainees outside the reach of American laws, such as the right to appeal their imprisonment, yet it was only 90 miles (145 km) off the coast of Florida, making it accessible to the various agencies that would need to travel there to extract information from what was believed to be a population of hundreds of dangerous terrorists. Eventually, some eight hundred prisoners would be held there, although the prison population was reduced to less than 175 by the time of the 10th anniversary of the September 11 attacks." (14)

CHAPTER 4

Chaos and Uncertainty

Many a time I would stand the Watch in the National Military Command Center during holidays and weekends to give the active-duty members the time to spend with their families. I was scheduled to stand the Watch on September 11[th,] but the General called me to say that I did not have to report because the active duty was going to return the favor by standing the Watch for me.

Like many Americans, I was home on that fateful day when the planes struck the World Trade Centers and the Pentagon. I rushed to the television set when news came in about the attack on the World Trade Centers. Glued to the television, next came the attack on the Pentagon. Shortly thereafter, I received a phone call from the Pentagon asking if I would report for duty. My response was why would they even ask when any patriotic American would answer the call without hesitation.

The caller went on to say, "It will take time to cut orders on you to cover your travel and pay but we were hoping that you would come voluntarily as soon as possible. I responded by saying, "there is only one decision when my country calls and that is to report wherever and whenever called upon. Do not be concerned about cutting the order now sir, I will be there tonight." Regardless of having no orders, I knew that having no official orders, my family would not receive military benefits if I was killed in action.

I immediately packed my bags and left for Washington. As I made the four-hour drive to Washington, patriotic songs like "From a Distance" by Bette Midler and "Born in the USA" by Bruce Springsteen were being played repeatedly. Knowing that there was a good possibility that I may have been serving at the Pentagon when the plane hit, my sons, Matthew, and Stephen, repeatedly tried to contact me to see if I was one of the victims. They had no idea if I were alive until I could call them back several days later. While making the drive to the Pentagon, my thoughts turned to others in my division that may have lost their lives.

Even though the Pentagon has more floor space than the Empire state, the odds were great that it may have hit our side of the building and drive right through to the inner rings. "The plane hit the E Ring at the first deck level between Corridors 4 and 5. The plane's path of destruction ended in the alley between the C Ring and B Ring." (15)

Photo 7-Terrorist attack on the Pentagon

"The Pentagon has three times the floor space of the Empire State Building and can be daunting to navigate for newcomers. Positioned across the Potomac River from the nation's capital, the Pentagon is the nerve center for all things national defense. It is also one of the world's largest office buildings, made up of 23,000 military and civilian employees, including the secretary of defense and chairman of the Joint Chiefs of Staff. The five-sided structure is often seen as a universal symbol of America's strength and security, which made it a target that September morning. The shaking Miller, deputy assistant secretary of the Army for financial operations, felt was a 182,000-pound aircraft, still carrying thousands of gallons of fuel, colliding at full speed into the structure. The impact punched a hole through layers of limestone, brick, concrete, blast-resistant geotextiles, and reinforced steel columns. Flames burst through the roof and reached twice the size of the five-story target." (16)

"As no other event in U.S. history, not even Pearl Harbor, the deadly assaults on New York and Washington that took the lives of almost 3,000 people on11 September2001 shattered the nation's sense of security. The utter destruction of the Twin Towers in New York and the severe damage done to the Pentagon by Middle East terrorists signaled a changed world in the making, one that poses a constant threat of attack that the United States must guard against and defeat if its people are to live in freedom and safety. The nation responded first with stunned surprise and overwhelming grief, then with outrage and stern refusal to be intimidated. (17)

Shortly after the planes hit the Trade Centers and the Pentagon, the White House and Capitol were hurriedly evacuated. In New York, thousands of people poured into the streets, tying up transportation routes.

On the larger scene, in the skies above the Pentagon, Air Force F~16 fighters guarded the nation's capital as they had since 11 September, when at 9:30 a.m., only seven minutes before the Pentagon was hit, the first three armed Air National Guard fighters had taken off from Langley Air Force Base, Virginia, and via a circuitous route over the ocean headed for the Baltimore area to intercept Flight 11, mistakenly thought to be flying south toward Washington. Redirected to head for Washington because of an FAA report of another unidentified aircraft (Flight 77) six miles southwest of the city, the fighters flew at a maximum subsonic speed of 660 m.p.h. but were too late to intercept the airliner.

After the fighters arrived over the capital two of them established a combat air patrol at approximately 20,000 feet over the Pentagon. Warned that hijacked United Flight 93 was off course in the Cleveland area and presumed to be heading toward Washington, the two fighters set up a 20~mile racetrack pattern patrol over the area. The third Langley fighter, after investigating and identifying two aircraft near the Potomac as a military helicopter and a police helicopter, flew at low altitude around Washington, following instructions from the Secret Service to protect the White House.

The low flying Langley jet frightened many Pentagon evacuees who had been warned that another hijacked aircraft was on its way to the area. They heard the fighter before they saw it and mistook it for the dreaded second airliner. In the Center Court assisting firefighters, some people in the crowd walking from North Parking toward the Memorial Bridge ducked into the woods towards the river to hide from the fighter. Recognition of the plane as "friendly" brought relief and reassurance; people cheered.

Meanwhile in the president's absence on the 11th, Vice President Cheney directed actions from the White House. The threat of further attack on the nation's capital from the missing hijacked United Flight 93 and other yet unknown aircraft created the tragic dilemma of whether to authorize fighters to shoot them down. In a telephone conversation some time before 10:20 a.m. the president authorized Cheney to order the shootdown of hijacked planes, which he did by sending word to the National Military Command Center in the Pentagon which communicated the order to NORAD. At 10:39 the vice president informed Secretary Rumsfeld of the shootdown order." (18)

"Within the hour Air National Guard fighters from Andrews Air Force Base, Maryland, augmented the initial patrols by the Air Force fighters from Langley. Thereafter, during the day Air National Guard fighter aircraft came from air bases at Richmond, Virginia, and Atlantic City, New Jersey; at times as many as twelve fighters flew patrol over the capital area. Navy and Marine Corps aircraft also contributed to the improvised air defense on 11 September, as did Air Force tanker planes and E-3 Airborne Warning and Aircraft Control Systems

Combat air patrols (CAPs) of F-16s' flew over the Washington area, becoming a fixture until the spring of 2002. Thereafter, intermittent patrols were flown by fighters kept on alert. The extraordinary scale of Pentagon security after the attack was the product of immediate and ongoing cooperation among the federal, state, and local security agencies augmenting DPS and the military." (19)

Driving off the interstate onto the parkway going into Washington, I noticed many police vehicles parked along and facing the parkway with their emergency lights flashing. To this day, I do not know what they were trying to accomplish. I could only imagine that they were wanted to exhibit a show of force which would hopefully deter any terrorists coming into the capital.

Instead of going to Bolling Air Force base lodging, I went directly to the Pentagon. Both Bolling AF Base and the Pentagon were my homes away from home for six years. It was late at night by the time I arrived. Upon entering the

40

parking lot of the Pentagon, I was shocked to see the carnage caused by the terrorist. Flood lights were fixed on the gaping hole in the Pentagon's side and huge cranes were busy pulling out debris. Black smoke was bellowing high into the sky. You could almost imagine seeing the faces of those who perished in that smoke. Because the Pentagon was my home away from home and I considered those that perished part of my family, I took the attack very personal.

I froze in the parking lot staring at the rescuers working under glaring flood lights and smoke rising from the quelched fire. Many rescue people were scurrying all about the Pentagon frantically looking for survivors and clearing the rubble. I could only imagine what went on when the rogue aircraft crashed into the side of the Pentagon. Looking at where the plane entered the E ring further sparked my imagination to visualize where I may have been on that fateful day. Even though the NMCC was not caught in the line of fire, I suddenly had the eerie realization that I may have become one of the victims, especially as I kept thinking that I often walked the same destroyed corridors where the plane was demolished. Like a guided missile, the aircraft crashed through numerous rings of the Pentagon culminating in a corridor I frequently walked to enter the NMCC.

The wreckage of the aircraft was taken to one of the parking lots for forensic scientists to scan for evidence. Our leaders wanted to make certain who was responsible and who we had to go after. We wanted to make certain who was going to pay for causing this carnage, who we would be sending the war planes and our troops after, and who we had to punish. One might liken 911 to what a Japanese Admiral once termed when Pearl Harbor was attacked "we have awakened a sleeping giant and filled him with a terrible resolve." We were resolved to bring those responsible to justice!

"On 9/11, millions of Americans became glued to their televisions, watching in horror as hijacked planes attacked the World Trade Center and the Pentagon. But there was one critical group of people who, for a time, received only snippets of information—and misinformation—as the day unfolded. They were the passengers of Air Force One—including the president of the United States. Ann Compton, an ABC News correspondent, was on board Air Force One when it was in route back to Washington. She gave an accounting to History what transpired.

Flying on Air Force One (Photo 8), we were so far

moved from what was going on, the danger on the ground, and there was so little information, clear information coming in to us," a Secret Service agent who traveled with the president on 9/11, recalled to HISTORY, "I could tell you one thing emphatically, No one knew what was going on."

While the Secret Service believed the safest place for the president was in the skies on Air Force One, they were also constantly reacting to reports of perceived threats. The passengers and crew of Air Force One were in the dark on September 11, 2001.

President George W. Bush was in Sarasota, Florida visiting a school when news of the attacks reached his team. After delivering a brief statement to the nation ('Terrorism against our nation will not stand," he said), he and the rest of the passengers of Air Force One were rushed on board.

As they started to take off at 9:55 a.m., they received a report that someone with a stinger missile might be positioned at the end of the runway. (It turned out not true.)

Colonel Tillman, commander and pilot turned Air Force One around and took off in the opposite direction at a steep angle.

As Air Force One flew in a holding pattern over the Gulf of Mexico, the crew got word that the White House had received an anonymous threat saying, "Angel is Next." Angel was the codename for Air Force One. Uncertain if the threat had come from within the plane, or from the skies, Col. Tillman, and Master Sgt. Will Chandler, chief of security, ordered guards to take positions outside the plane's cockpit to the plane's front, where the president's quarters were. Air Force One's communications were spotty, possibly because Tillman dealt with external threats by flying the aircraft up to an unusually high altitude of 45,000 feet. "We're at such a height that it's like we're on a highway all to ourselves," Secret Service agent Wilkinson explained to HISTORY.

"So, if anyone starts to drive onto that highway, we'll know immediately they're up to no good." No One Knew Whether the Jet Fighters Approaching the Plane were Friends or Foes. At one point, Tillman received a warning from radio operators in Houston that an unidentified aircraft was on their tail. They spotted two fighters approaching, and for a moment, there was panic as the two planes could not be identified. Tillman recalled to HISTORY that he was thinking, "Okay, this may be how we're going to be attacked." Then he received a reassuring message. They explain to us they are a flight of two F-16s and are our cover.

No One Knew When They Could Go Back to Washington. Members of the media were asking where the president was during the national emergency. "I don't mean to say this in melodramatic terms, but where is the president of the United States?" ABC news anchor Peter Jennings said during the network's live broadcast. The CIA Knew Who Was Behind the Attacks Hours Before Informing the President. As the president's plane finally took off for

Washington at 4:33 p.m., he received another CIA report suggesting that the day's attacks were just the first of two waves—and that another one was coming. Thankfully, that would prove to be false. Air Force One arrived in Washington. At 8:30 p.m., Bush was finally able to address the nation from the White House." (20)

President Bush's father was quoted as saying: "The airborne terrorist attacks on the World Trade Center, the Pentagon, and the thwarted flight against the White House or Capitol transformed George W. Bush into a wartime president. The attacks put on hold many of Bush's hopes and plans, and Bush's father, the 41st president, declared that his son "faced the greatest challenge of any president since Abraham Lincoln." (21)

In times of emergency like 911, there is a bunker constructed under the East Wing of the White House. "The White House bunker, known officially as the Presidential unidentified Emergency Operations Center (PEOC), dates back to World War II, when officials set up a modest bunker for Franklin D. Roosevelt in the event of a surprise German attack on the capital. Harry Truman expanded the facility dramatically for the Cold War as part of a large White House renovation during his presidency. In the years since, the bunker has been updated technologically; and while officials and presidents had used it as part of drills and exercises, it had never been used for its intended purpose—until 9/11.

Still, the facility is staffed 24 hours a day, and that morning the team on duty had been gathering for its normal Tuesday morning staff meeting when the towers were struck. Within minutes, Vice President Cheney and other officials arrived. Navy Commander Anthony Barnes was on duty that morning, and in his first-ever interview, he recalls that he looked around and saw National Security Advisor Condoleezza Rice, White House Communications Director

Karen Hughes, Cheney aide Mary Matalin and Secretary of Transportation Norman Mineta: "Mr. Mineta put up on one of the TV monitors a feed of where every airplane across the entire nation was. We looked at that thing, there must have been thousands of little airplane symbols on it.

Barnes, who served on 9/11 as the deputy director of Presidential Contingency Programs, the deputy director of the nation's doomsday plans at the White House—explains, "The PEOC is not a single chamber; there are three or four rooms. The operations chamber is where my watch team was fielding phone calls. Then there is the conference room where Mr. Cheney and Condi Rice were, the room that had the TV monitors, telephones, and whatever else.

In those opening minutes of the crisis response, officials still struggled to understand what was happening—particularly as word came around 9:37 a.m. that the western face of the Pentagon had been hit too, targeted by American Airlines Flight 77, hijacked out of Dulles International Airport. "That first hour was mass confusion because there was so much erroneous information," recalls Barnes. "It was hard to tell what fact was and what wasn't. We couldn't confirm much of this stuff, so we had to take it on face value until proven otherwise."

Under the protocols for the secret system known as "continuity of government," meant to preserve the U.S. leadership and evacuate key officials to bunkers and mobile command posts around Washington in the event of an attack, Rumsfeld should have been immediately evacuated. Yet that day he found himself torn between his official duties and the unfolding human tragedy. His actions that morning, where he helped carry stretchers of wounded personnel out of the impact zone, would long endear him to the military. But placing himself in danger and out of communication in a moment of true crisis was precisely the wrong action from an official standpoint.

That vacuum—with the "Secretary of Defense" beyond reach and the president himself being hustled aboard Air Force One in Florida—meant that Cheney faced the critical hour from 9:30 a.m. to 10:30 a.m. almost entirely alone. They struggled to piece together what was happening. As Barnes says, "Every one of my guys in the watch room has at least two phones to their ears.

One of the most critical questions to arise was how to manage the remaining hijacked planes—no one from air traffic control or the military was sure how many planes in the air were still under the control of terrorists, but they feared the number might be a dozen or more.

Then, at 9:59 a.m., the morning went from bad to worse as the South Tower collapsed in a rolling cloud of dust. A decisive moment arrived sometime shortly thereafter, around 10 a.m. The Pentagon thought there was another hijacked airplane, and they were asking for permission to shoot down an identified hijacked commercial aircraft. Barnes asked the Vice President that question and he answered it in the affirmative. Barnes asked again to be sure. 'Sir, I am confirming that you have given permission?' For me, being a military member and an aviator—understanding the absolute depth of what that question was and what that answer was, I wanted to make sure that there was no mistake whatsoever about what was being asked. Without hesitation, in the affirmative, he said any confirmed hijacked airplane may be engaged and shot down.

A question, though, has lingered ever since: The vice president is not part of the military chain of command and, in theory, does not have authority to order fighters into battle—let alone to take an unprecedented step of shooting down a commercial domestic airliner filled with civilians.

46

According to standard protocols, such an order should only come from the president.

It is not clear—and years of extensive investigation has never definitively determined—whether Cheney had spoken to President Bush to get such an authority. Both men have hinted that they had spoken prior to Cheney's order, but there's little concrete evidence they did. In fact, the preponderance of evidence appears to show that VP Cheney unilaterally gave the order." (21)

"The plane hit the outer wall between the first and second floors and smashed through three of the Pentagon's five concentric rings. The jet fuel exploded into a fireball, and about half an hour later a section of the building above where the plane hit collapsed. By that time, most people working there had been evacuated. However, 125 people working in the building were killed, as were the sixty-four crew, passengers, and hijackers on the plane. The Pentagon had recently been upgraded in response to the 1995 Oklahoma City bombing, and this likely prevented worse damage and a higher death toll. The impact, fire, and collapse of the affected part of the building destroyed most of the aircraft, leaving only a few pieces of wreckage." (22)

"Sixty-four people were onboard American Airlines Flight 77 flying from Dulles International Airport in Virginia across the country to Los Angeles. On that flight were five Saudi terrorist men, linked to al-Qaida, who hijacked the jet somewhere over eastern Kentucky. The westbound plane deviated from its flight plan, turning south at 8:54 a.m. Air traffic controllers knew something was wrong, but pinpointing AA 77 was impossible. There were hundreds of planes already in the sky, each one indicated by a speck on a radar board. Roughly 30 minutes after the Twin Towers were hit, AA 77 was back in the D.C. area. The Boeing 757 airliner went full throttle across Washington Boulevard, the expressway that separates the Pentagon from Arlington National Cemetery. The plane was flying near ground-level, slicing through streetlights in the parking lot along the way. Its nose pierced the first floor of the Pentagon's outermost ring, between corridors four and five, at 9:37 a.m. The deafening explosion rocked the western side of the 28-acre complex as if it were completely lifted from its foundation."

"Flight 77 struck the western side of the Pentagon at the 1st Floor level just inside Wedge 1 near Corridor 4 and proceeded diagonally at an approximate 42-degree angle towards Corridor 5 in the most vacant and unrenovated Wedge 2. Flight 77 had taken off with a total weight of over ninety tons, 25 percent of it in fuel.

Allowing the hour-and-a-quarter flight from Dulles Airport to Kentucky and back, Flight 77 still had most of its original 7,256 gallons of fuel on board, the greater part of it in the wings, when it hit the Pentagon. Traveling at 530 miles per hour, the aircraft, and the subsequent fuel explosion, delivered enormous destructive power. The destruction and, more importantly, the loss of life, would have been worse without the reinforcement of the exterior wall and installation of blast-resistant windows and fire suppression systems made during the recent renovations." (23)

I normally walk in the same corridor where the plane flew into the Pentagon. If I had been there that day as planned, I could have been one of the casualties.

"A truck delivery driver who witnessed everything, said, "I was just here to deliver my load, when I heard a noise and looked up and I saw the plane coming in." "Then he said the pilot just gunned it. The next thing he said took us by surprise. He said he could see the faces of the people in the windows of the airplane as it flew into the Pentagon." (23)

"There were also many speculations about why the terrorists would sacrifice their lives by committing suicide attacks. "According to a report from The Program on Terrorism and Low Intensity Conflict at Tel Aviv University's Institute for National Security Studies, "In 2019, 149 suicide bombings were carried out in 24 countries by 236 suicide bombers, among them 22 women. In these suicide bombings, 1,850 people were killed and 3,660 were wounded. "More than 80 percent of these suicide bombings were committed by Salafi-jihadist groups."

The concept of martyring oneself to achieve forgiveness of sins and to obtain access to paradise is applicable to both male and female suicide bombers. The role of the recruiter cannot be underestimated in these circumstances. A Muslim man or woman, or any potential convert, is first located as a suicide bomber by a recruiter, and the recruiter then establishes a relationship with them. With time and trust, a relationship develops, and the person divulges their sins to the recruiter, with admission of guilt and shame. The recruiter may already be aware of the sins if the person is a target. Eventually, the recruiter talks the person into becoming a martyr to find forgiveness from Allah and entrance into paradise. In life, the most perfect aim is for *istishadi* through jihad, and the martyr will receive bountiful gifts in paradise. Men will receive seventy-two virgins." (24)

Later, many of us surmised that the intention of the terrorist who piloted the plane was that the path that he took to hit the Pentagon was the path Muslim's pray to Allah. He may have believed that he was going straight to heaven and receive his reward of seventy-five virgins!

CHAPTER 5

Devastation and Carnage

After snapping out of my fixation on the devastation before me, I started towards one of the unscathed entrances to the Pentagon. As I walked towards the entrance, I could see the burning flames and the smell of smoke and what may have been burning fuel coming from the airplane buried deep inside the Pentagon. My thoughts turned to what may have gone through the passengers' minds when they realized their fate and what motivated the terrorists to sacrifice their lives and those of the sixty-four passengers.

The report of the delivery driver seeing the terrified faces of passengers pressed against the windows of the aircraft was corroborated by what the guards told me.

After regaining my composure, I entered one of the heavily guarded doors leading into the Pentagon. Normally, the guards at the door carry only pistols. When it becomes heightened security, however, there are guards surrounding the perimeters of the Pentagon brandishing fully automatic weapons and bandolier of bullets crisscrossing their chest. Military members and civilian workers at the Pentagon are issued badges that they swipe upon entering the Pentagon. Most of the interior doors have cyber locks with combinations, hand IDs, and eye IDs. Military members cannot carry their cell phones into the NMCC, depositing them at the door before allowing them to enter. To have access to the NMCC and top-secret documents, you must have a need-to-know basis and have the necessary top-secret clearances. Most that serve in the National Military command center possess systems established sensitive compartmented information (SCI), a type of United States classified information concerning or derived from sensitive intelligence sources, methods, or analytical processes. All SCI must be handled within formal access control by the Director of National Intelligence. Some areas also require NATO clearance. I was cleared for all.

Upon entering the Joint Staff's office of medical readiness, the whole area was abuzz with my colleagues working on a myriad of actions of great importance to the Joint Staff. By the tense atmosphere that permeated throughout the Pentagon, you could sense that war was imminent. You could see in the faces of all I passed in the hallways that everyone was geared up to avenge those that lost their lives and had a strong desire to protect America even if it meant sacrificing their own lives.

The military personnel assigned to the Joint Staff were in high tempo, gearing up for what would be asked of them. "The "Joint Staff" is composed of equal numbers of officers from the Army, Navy and Marine Corps, and Air Force. The Marines make up about 20 percent of the number allocated to the Navy." (25) The Chairman of the Joint Chiefs of Staff must provide reliable information to key decision makers throughout Washington including the Secretary of Defense and the President. I could not even fathom what stress and anxiety he may be undergoing. Standing alongside him as time moved on, I would soon find out.

Desperately trying to stay out of the way, I just stood there watching history unfold. Not since Pearl Harbor has there been a direct attack on the United States, and I found myself in the center of what became one of the main targets.

Despite what next may befall any one of us and the turmoil that enveloped us, all we could think about was doing our best to protect our country and bring the perpetrators to justice.

Everyone was frantically doing their part to protect our country and its people. "During the September 11 attacks, Secretary of Defense Donald Rumsfeld ordered the DEFCON level be increased to three, and a stand-by for an increase to DEFCON 2. It was eventually lowered to DEFCON 4 on September 14." (28) As of January 2023, our current DEFCON level is estimated to be at 3 due to the Russian conflict, according to OSINT (*Open-Source Intelligence*)

"The alert system operated under several levels of what is known as DEFCON levels, Defense Readiness Condition. DEFCON, short for Defense Readiness Condition or simply Defense Condition, is the U.S. military's ranking system for defense readiness for a potential nuclear attack. The system of ranking the perceived threat to national security was created during the Cold War, when fear of communism was at a high. DEFCON 5 is in effect for the lowest perceived threat, while DEFCON 1 is the highest threat level and readiness for a state of war.

- DEFCON 5 is "peacetime normal," the default state of readiness for the United States military.
- DEFCON 4 describes the everyday operating procedures for fighting units. At DEFCON 4, the U.S. military complex ramps up intelligence gathering and shores up security.
- DEFCON 3, Two steps from war, is seen as a standby level of alert, and it is the highest level of alert during peacetime.
- DEFCON 2, one step from nuclear war, is implemented when an enemy attack is

52

expected. Troops are poised for combat at this time.

- DEFCON 1 represents the highest level of readiness for nuclear war.

The DEFCON level is controlled primarily by the U.S. president and the U.S. Secretary of Defense through the Chairman of the Joint Chiefs of Staff and the Combatant Commanders; each level defines specific security activation and response scenarios for the personnel in question. The United States has never been at DEFCON 1 – at least not to the public's knowledge – since the system began." (26)

Despite the secretary of defense' showing compassion for leaving his office to help the injured being treated outside the Pentagon, he received some follow-up critique for not staying at his post. "One of the reasons Cheney was left on his own during that first hour of the crisis was because Defense Secretary Donald Rumsfeld, officially the second person in the military chain of command, rushed out of his Pentagon suite in the moments after the attack and went to the crash site personally.

Under the protocols for the secret system known as "continuity of government," meant to preserve the U.S. leadership and evacuate key officials to bunkers and mobile command posts around Washington in the event of an attack, Rumsfeld should have been immediately evacuated. Yet that day he found himself torn between his official duties and the unfolding human tragedy. His actions that morning, where he helped carry stretchers of wounded personnel out of the impact zone, would long endear him to the military. But placing himself in danger—and out of communication in a moment of true crisis—was precisely the wrong action from an official standpoint." (27)

After my commander assigned tasks to others, it was now my turn to do my part. Looking intently at me, he outlined what was expected of me. "Because you have no specific actions to work on, I am sending you to the NMCC to represent the J-4 on the crisis action teams (CAT)."

My being new on the Joint Staff and knowing being assigned to the NMCC was the innermost sanctity of the military, I stood there like a deer in the headlights. I could not believe that he was assigning me to perform what would be one of the most demanding duties of the military. I would be surrounded by seasoned high ranking officers and along with other CAT team members, I would be in the section where a three-star general is responsible for assisting the Chairman in fulfilling his responsibilities as the principal military advisor to the President and Secretary of Defense.

Looking at my commanding officer, I exclaimed. "But sir, I am new to the Joint Staff and the NMCC demands seasoned CAT team members." At first, I stood silent while trying to rationalize why the Joint Staff would entrust me, a new and untested member, to serve at the highest levels of military command. Upon gaining my composure, I quickly replied to my commanding officer. "Sir, I am new to the Joint Staff and am not confident that I can effectively perform the services that would be required of me." He assured me that the J-4 Directorate would support me whenever needed. Without further discussion or explanation, he just looked at me and spoke. "You need to report to the NMCC." Looking at his watch, "That will be twelve o'clock midnight." Looking at mine, that would only give me the opportunity to catch a couple of hours' sleep. Knowing that I could not make it to the base lodging and back in time, I decided to return to catch a couple of hours sleep in my car and later change in the Pentagon Gym. The only problem was that the floodlights of workers extracting plane wreckage and casualties from the pentagon kept me awake most of the time.

At fifteen minutes until midnight, I reported for duty in the NMCC. The general on duty was preparing to brief our team on our assignments and overall mission. He started by informing us that there would be two teams, each serving twelve hours daily and the need to stay an extra half hour before and after our twelve-hour shifts. The shifts started at 12:00 midnight to 12:00 noon the next day seven days a week, and the two teams would take turns rotating every other week. As I looked around the room, I kept thinking how the team members with young families would balance such a hard schedule and maintain a normal family life at the same time. Some of them even went back to their normal duty stations after serving their twelve hours to catch up on unfinished work. To alleviate their load, I took additional Watches including holidays.

My team was briefed on our responsibilities and the operating procedures of the NMCC. We were told that "the NMCC has three main missions, all serving the Chairman of the Joint Chiefs of Staff in his role as the principal military advisor to both the Secretary of Defense and the President (also known as the National Command Authority).

- "The primary task of the NMCC is to monitor worldwide events which may be of defense significance.
- The NMCC also has a crisis response component (e.g., response to the bombing of the *USS Cole*, the September 11 attacks, the attack on the USS *Liberty*}
- A strategic watch component (e.g., monitoring ballistic missile launches and other nuclear activity).

"The duty in the CAT requires personnel to monitor operations 24 hours a day. Two twelve-hour shifts are scheduled between two teams. CAT members must possess

Top Secret (TS) and Sensitive compartmented information (SCI) clearance.

The crisis action team (CAT) of the Pentagon is intended to provide intense management of "limited" crisis situations beyond the capabilities of an operations team. The crisis action team has been the Joint Staff organization of choice for crisis management. The CAT mission is to support "the Director for Operations (DJ-3) who assists the Chairman in carrying out responsibilities as the principal military advisor to the President and Secretary of Defense, developing and providing guidance to the combatant commanders and relaying communications between the President and the Secretary of Defense and the combatant commanders regarding current operations and plans." By managing a crisis effectively, a CAT team can minimize the adversities that can impact the coordination of resources, personnel, strategies, and the national security of the United States." (28)

While we were being briefed, the military and civilian workers throughout the Pentagon were rehearsing exit drills should the Pentagon be attacked again. The Pentagon was receiving anonymous phone calls threatening us with another attack. One such threat was the detonation of an atomic bomb, like the one that was dropped on Hiroshima Japan during WWII.

Photo 9-Little Big Boy Atomic Bomb

"The atomic bomb used at Hiroshima, Japan, on August 6, 1945, was "Little Boy". The bomb was dropped by a USAAF B-29 bomber, Enola Gay, piloted by U.S. Army Air Force Colonel Paul Tibbets, Jr. The bomb weighed 9,000 pounds and had a diameter of only twenty-eight inches and 120 inches long." "By the end of 1945, the bomb had killed an estimated 140,000 people in Hiroshima, and a further 74,000 in Nagasaki. A slightly larger plutonium bomb

exploded over Nagasaki three days later levelled 6.7 sq km. of the city and killed 74,000 people by the end of 1945. Ground temperatures reached 4,000 C and radioactive rain poured down." (29)

A bomb the size of an atomic bomb could take out a five-mile radius of Washington DC. That would include the Pentagon, the White House,

Photo 10 Atomic Bomb Cloud

and the Capital. The entire seat of government. For months after the attack on the Pentagon, the police cars with their blinkers on stayed in place along the main roads leading into Wahington DC. A bomb the size of an atomic bomb could be transported in by simply using a small box van and the terrorist intruders who brought it could get freely away after parking it in the center of Washington and detonating it on a timer.

It did not even have to be an atomic bomb that could do major damage. The explosive device that was detonated in Oklahoma city was improvised from ammonium nitrate fertilizer and nitromethane, which were put into the back of the truck and left to explode. It was the worst terrorist attack on U.S. soil up to that time, killing 169 people. (30) Multiply that number if several trucks laden with explosives were strategically placed around Washington DC.

Realizing that the Pentagon could be attacked again, security was given instructions to those that worked there as to where they should escape if we were slimed again. One of the CAT members on our team raised his hand with a question. "Sir, where do we go if we are hit again?" The general looked at him with no emotion. "You go nowhere. You stay at your duty station and if necessary, die in place. The other CAT team who is off duty will replace you at an alternative site."

One of our first tasks was to source units that may be needed on an all-out assault on Afghanistan. We needed to make sure the units were intact and 100% staffed and equipped.

Whenever we had a break, we would ascend out of the Command Center to the courtyard of the Pentagon or outside to grab a bite to eat. The Red Cross and many other Humanitarian Non-governmental organizations (NGOs) set up their tents in one of the Pentagon parking lots. They were there to support the military while we worked on a myriad of issues to protect our country. They prepared all types of food that were of the highest quality and comparable to that which was prepared by the finest restaurants in Washington. Every shift that began their Watch in the NMCC could partake in endless servings of breakfast food prepared by McDonalds and waiting for us at the entrance to the NMCC.

Besides working day-to-day actions for the Chairman and Secretary of Defense, our CAT teams were responsible to build and daily update a power point presentation that monitored ongoing global events impacting the national security of our nation. Some of the slides also summarized our progress on the Afghan war and other conflicts of interest. One slide that was always inserted was the number of prisoners held at Guantanamo Bay. "The facility became the focus of worldwide controversy over alleged violations of the legal rights of detainees under the Geneva Conventions and accusations of torture or abusive treatment of detainees by U.S. authorities." (31)

Prior to launching our attack on Afghanistan, we were tasked to build a coalition of military components from various countries. The reason was to show an overpowering force and that other countries agreed and support of our invading another country to clean out the terrorists. We simply did not want to look like the "ugly American."

"The terrorism of September 11th was not just an attack on the United States, it was an attack on the world. Citizens from more than eighty countries died that day - innocent men, women, and children from across the globe. Within hours of the tragedy, coalitions involving many nations assembled to fight terrorism - hundreds of countries have contributed to a variety of ways - some militarily, others diplomatically, economically, and financially. Some nations have helped openly; others prefer not to disclose their contributions. Our coalition partners contributed nearly 6,000 troops to Operation Enduring Freedom *(the official name given to the war in Afghanistan)*, and to the International Security Assistance Force in Kabul - making up more than half of the 11,000 non-Afghan forces in Afghanistan. The war against terrorism is a broad-based effort that will take time. Every nation has different circumstances and will participate in different ways. This mission and future missions will require a series of coalitions ready to take on the challenges and assume the risks.

There was always a high-ranking officer in command of the NMCC and a smaller cadre of military members that manned it when not fully staffed with action officers. While the CAT teams were going about their duties for the

Chairman and SECDEF, they would on a regular basis exercise and simulate nuclear command launches. Because we were not included, we were not fully aware of what went on behind the secure compartment of the NMCC. Even though all of us had top secret clearances, access for us was not granted because the exercise came under the basic security principle of "Need to know."

"Planning for the potential employment of U.S. nuclear forces goes through a deliberate and methodical process. It includes elements such as identification of objectives and guidance, target development, weaponizing, force planning, force execution, and battle damage assessment (BDA). To meet these objectives, U.S. Strategic Command (USSTRATCOM) and geographic combatant commands nominate, vet, and select adversary strategic facilities and capabilities as targets. This process cannot succeed without command and control, and U.S. policy states that the nuclear deterrent is only as effective as the command-and-control network that enables it to function. The United States ensures this effectiveness through the Nuclear Command and Control System (NCCS), a combination of capabilities necessary to: ensure the authorized employment and termination of nuclear weapon operations under all threats and scenarios; secure against the accidental, inadvertent, or unauthorized access to U.S. nuclear weapons; and prevent the loss of control, theft, or unauthorized use of U.S. nuclear weapons. The NCCS is broken into two main components: nuclear command, control, and communications (NC3) and nuclear weapons safety, security, and incident response.

NC3 requires rigorous procedures and processes to support the President and the Secretary of Defense in exercising command authorities in the areas of situation monitoring, decision-making, force direction, force management, and planning to direct the actions of the people who operate nuclear systems. The National Military Command Center (NMCC) which is the primary facility, provides daily support to the President, the Secretary of Defense, and the CJCS, on the monitoring of nuclear forces and ongoing conventional military operations. (33)

After a long night in the NMCC with little sleep, I drove to the Air Force Base to check into a room. Upon my arrival, I learned there were no space. I showed my orders to the base lodging manager and insisted that I needed to be close to the Pentagon. I could have checked into a hotel in Washington but wanted to be on an Air force base and on top of operations, It was approximately 2:00 in the afternoon when I arrived.

Photo 11-President's Marine One Helicopter

Bolling AFB is the base where they housed Marine one, the President's helicopters. Standing on the steps of Base housing, I could see a series of the President's helicopters circling the area doing touch and goes (continually landing and taking off). I surmised that in view of the terrorist attacks, they were either exercising their Operation Plans or simply performing diversionary tactics.

Marine One is the call sign for any Marine Corps aircraft carrying the President. The fleet of helicopters is operated by the HMX-1 "Nighthawks." HMX-1 uses two unique aircraft types: the Sikorsky VH-3D *Sea King* and VH-60N

Blackhawk, in support of Presidential missions. Marine One can be distinguished by its high-gloss, green and white paint scheme, referred to as "White Tops." The *Sea King* can transport fourteen passengers while the *Blackhawk* seats eleven passengers. The *Blackhawk* helicopters fold easily and can be loaded onto an Air Force C-17 transport aircraft. When the President travels, either domestically or internationally, the helicopters travel with him. Marine One always flies in a group with identical helicopters, sometimes as many as five. One helicopter carries the President, while the others serve as decoys for would-be assassins on the ground. Upon take-off, these helicopters begin to shift in formation regularly to obscure the location of the President. Every Marine One is equipped with state-of-the-art security and technology. Every time Marine One lands, the President is greeted and received by an armed Marine guard wearing a Marine Blue Dress uniform.

Marine One is often used as an alternative to motorcades, which can be expensive and logistically difficult. When the President leaves Washington D.C., he takes the helicopter from the White House South Lawn to Andrews Air Force Base where his plane, Air Force One, is waiting. He also uses the helicopter to get to Camp David, the Presidential retreat in Western Maryland. While Air Force One flies the President to an airport, Marine One is often used to transport the President around the area in which he is traveling, especially if the helicopters are more conducive to what he is doing, as viewing areas in the aftermath of disasters." (34)

"The White House uses Sikorsky helicopters known as Marine One when the president is aboard, as well as custom Boeing 747s that are immediately recognizable as the iconic humpback Air Force One. Sometimes the president uses a more modified 757 if his destination is nearby or if a runway is not long enough to accommodate the bigger plane.

Marine One costs between $16,700 and almost $20,000 per hour to operate, according to Pentagon data for the 2022 budget year. Air Force One is even more expensive: roughly $200,000 per hour.

But those figures only scratch the surface of the real cost. There also are military cargo planes that travel ahead of the president to make sure his armored limousines are in place, not to mention the enormous security apparatus that follows the president everywhere.

New aircraft are in the works because the current versions are decades old. Sikorsky is producing 23 updated helicopters to serve as Marine One. Boeing is building two new Air Force One planes, and they are scheduled to be finished by 2028. According to the Pentagon, the planes will come with all enhancements, including "a mission communication system," a "self-defense system" and even "autonomous baggage loading." (35)

"When the president flies for political purposes, the campaign is supposed to pay the bill. But during an election year, the line between governing and campaigning can be fuzzy.

It is up to the White House counsel's office to figure out what percentage of the president's travels are campaign related. That determines how much the federal government should be reimbursed. Sometimes the calculations are not straightforward, such as when the White House adds an official event to an otherwise political trip.

No matter what, taxpayers end up on the hook for most of the cost. Campaigns do not pay for all the Secret Service agents and the rest of the security apparatus. In fact, they usually only cover the cost of Air Force One passengers who are flying for explicitly political purposes — like buying a ticket on a particularly exclusive private jet.

As an example, "Biden's campaign and his joint fundraising committee have been stockpiling travel cash in an escrow account maintained by the Democratic National Committee. From January 2023 until the end of last month, they deposited $6.5 million. Some of that money goes to general campaign logistics, such as staff expenses and advance work. The account is also used to reimburse the federal government for official aircraft used to transport the president, the first lady, the vice president and the second gentleman when they travel for the reelection effort.

So far, not much money has found its way back to the U.S. Treasury. As for the latest data available, just $300,000 has been provided.

It is safe to assume that Biden's campaign will end up forking over much more than that once the campaign is over. Trump's team reimbursed the federal government $4.7 million for travel expenses during the 2020 race.

President Obama flew to Israel to attend the funeral of former Prime Minister Shimon Peres. With this unscheduled visit, Obama is now in second place for most international presidential travel behind Bill Clinton who made fifty-five treks abroad.

By the latest estimate, it costs over $180,000 per flight hour to operate the President's aircraft, which is a modified military version of a Boeing 747. "(36)

CHAPTER 6

Battle of Logistics

George W. Bush coalesced around a strategy of first ousting the Taliban from Afghanistan and dismantling al-Qaeda, though others contemplated actions in Iraq, including long-standing plans for toppling Saddam Hussein. Bush demanded that Taliban leader Mullah Mohammed Omar"deliver to the United States authorities all the leaders of al-Qaeda who hide in your land," and when Omar refused, U.S. officials began implementing a plan for war. (37)

The next day in the NMCC was a nonstop flurry of deployment orders and laying the groundwork for an assault on the Taliban in Afghanistan. There was many negotiations with operatives inside the country and we wanted to make certain that all was in place before we started our assault. Much was going on behind the scenes.

A major concern was taking care of the noncombatant people of Afghanistan. We needed to not only make certain that they had ample food supplies but with the onslaught of winter, we wanted to make certain that they had winter clothing and blankets. To accommodate them, we air dropped blankets and meals ready to eat (MRE). The photos that came back to us were of people using the blankets to pick up the MRE's. The terrain looked like a moon scape. What we did not expect was that the color of the MRE's were offensive to their religion. We had to change the color.

Unbeknownst to us at the time, the Secretary of Defense had already communicated with the Commander of our Central Command (CENTCOM), Tommy Franks, about his intake. The commander of CENTOM oversees our military forces in the areas that include Afghanistan and Iraq. CENTCOM's Area of responsibility (AOR) covers twenty-one nations in the Middle East, Central and South Asia, and the strategic waterways that surround them. Prior to the 2008 UCP, CENTCOM had seven African nations in its AOR. When AFRICOM was established, all but Egypt were transferred from CENTCOM to AFRICOM. Nations in the CENTCOM AOR share borders with nations in the AFRICOM, EUCOM and INDO-PACOM AORs.

CENTCOM is one of eleven combatant commands that defends the United States and its interests. In a major crisis such as 9-11, all eleven combatant commands go on high alert to protect our national interests, each having a major role to play:

- Africa Command defends U.S. interests in Africa
- Cyber Command unifies cyberspace operations
- European Command works with NATO
- Indo Pacific Command enhances security
- Northern Command prioritizes homeland defense
- Southern Command enhances peace, promotes human rights, and deters illegal activities
- Space Command conducts operations in, from and to space to defend U.S. vital interests
- Special Operations Commands oversees the special operations components of our armed forces
- Strategic Command operates globally to deter and detect attacks against the United States
- Transportation Command provides transportation capabilities for our military

The President, through the Secretary of Defense, establishes and prescribes the force structure of combatant commands. The Unified Command Plan (UCP) assigns missions, responsibilities, and geographic areas of responsibility to combatant commands. (38)

One would wonder what would have gone through the mind of Tommy Franks, the CENTCOM commander, finding out that he was to put forth a plan of action to bring those responsible for 911 to justice. In an interview with PBS, Tommy Franks revealed some of his most inner thoughts during 9-11 and his conversation with the Secretary of Defense:

"My thoughts were about the same as a great many Americans. When the first plane hit the one trade tower, I looked at it and wondered what would cause that. But obviously, in my line of work, and being responsible for the region that I am responsible for, my first thought was "I wonder if this is a terrorist attack? It is. Then as we watched live and saw the second plane hit the other tower, there was of course no question in my mind, and I think not in the minds of a great many Americans.

We thought, "This is a terrorist act." Almost immediately I was speaking with Secretary Rumsfeld and talking about it. Of course, the conclusion, I think, by a great many of us at that time was related to Al Qaeda, at least some form of sponsorship. There was immediate consideration, beginning on Sept 12, of operations that we might need to undertake in Afghanistan. Secretary Rumsfeld told me on Sept 12, 'Prepare credible military options and bring them to me. We do that [by] being blessed by the service of a great many very, very smart people who were operating from here in Tampa and several other locations. They were putting their heads together; considering time-distance factors, scoping the mission, so that we could describe the appropriate mission to the secretary; and ultimately, the president --

thinking their way through everything from the application of kinetics, and what size force would be required to do what -- the normal approach to military planning.

The options that we prepared were presented to the secretary. He approved them. We took them to the president on, if my memory serves, Sept. 21, and the president approved the options. We described what we thought was the appropriate approach to the mission in Afghanistan. The president approved it in concept and said, "Move out and set conditions to begin operations in Afghanistan. Let me know when you are ready.

I think a great many people know for some 10 or 11 years of experience in Afghanistan, they introduced 625,00 people on the ground and had 15,000 of them killed and 55,000 of them wounded. So, we took as instructive, as a way not to do it."

To assure success in Afghanistan, we not only needed to formulate a consortium of countries, but we had to look for insurgent forces in Afghanistan that were willing to assist our efforts. Most logical would be the warlords.

A point put forth to Tommy Franks was that "The war begins with the bombing. Then, at some point, there is the insertion of Special Forces with the warlords of the Afghan Allies." He in turn emphasized that "Recognize that when we started combat operations, about 80 percent or so of Afghanistan was under the control of the Taliban. The standing military forces that opposed the Taliban were called the Northern Alliance, because where these enclaves were located, the ones who turned out to be friendly to us. Since about 20 percent of Afghanistan was controlled by the Northern Alliance, it made perfect sense to us that this would be a place to see what we could leverage, which opposition forces we could support, link up with, provide assistance to gain leverage with, in order to accomplish our mission." (39)

Next, we had to establish a credible logistics system to support our assault and solve the Afghan logistics problem. We do not have for that country a major logistics hub akin to the one we have in Kuwait," Mullen says. "We don't have in Afghanistan, anywhere near the number of runways or rail hubs or road networks that exist in Iraq. And we do not have quite frankly the same ground to cover. As one soldier told me on the first visit to Afghanistan back in 2007, the terrain itself is the enemy."

Afghanistan has a landscape of dirt roads and narrow mountain passes. There are no railroads. The nearest seaport is Karachi, Pakistan, five hundred miles from the closest major Afghan city, Kandahar.

"This is going to be a tough operation," says retired Army Lt. Gen. Gus Pagonis. "It doesn't mean it can't be done but it's going to take a lot of troops and a lot of innovation. "Pagonis should know. He ran logistics for the 1991 Gulf War, when he was lucky enough to have two large ports in Saudi Arabia and a network of modern highways to move vehicles and equipment to supply depots.

The biggest headache, I would say if we're squeaking anywhere, is probably on airfields," he admits, pointing to only three major airfields in the country: Bagram Air Base, just north of the capital city of Kabul; Camp Bastion in the southern province of Helmand; and in the neighboring province, Kandahar Airfield. Required more use of ground vehicles and helicopters.

Demand for combat-enabling supplies such as subsistence, fuel, ammunition, and repair parts, can be difficult to forecast because of the nature and unpredictability of conflict.

The topography in Afghanistan also heavily influences the need to store supplies. Dominated by mountains in the middle of the country and along the eastern border with Pakistan, the populated valleys and flatlands are often isolated in the winter months because of snow accumulation in mountain passes.

Photo 12-Equipment Airlift Afghanistan

Just twenty percent of the supplies come in by air. That includes ammunition, sensitive military gear like radios and some armored vehicles. The rest of the supplies, everything from plywood to lettuce comes over land, including two routes through Pakistan." (40)

"Having the ability to supply and sustain an army is the difference between a professional organization and a well-organized militia. The U.S. military operates one of the most sophisticated supply and distribution systems in the world. Soldiers can leave their bases in the United States and arrive in a foreign country ready to execute operations in less than 48 hours. As supplies arrive, the military maintains momentum to continue the push forward.

Since Afghanistan is a landlocked country, supplies had to pass through other countries in order to reach it, or else be delivered by air. Air transport was prohibitively expensive, so NATO forces tended to rely on ground routes for non-lethal equipment. This was principally accomplished either by shipping goods by sea to the Pakistani port of Karachi in the southern Sindh province, or by shipping them through Russia and the Central Asian states.

All munitions, whether small arms ammunition, artillery shells, or missiles, were transported by air." (41) Airlifting supplies cost up to ten times as much as transporting them through Pakistan. There were two routes from Pakistan to Afghanistan, but both were closed in November of 2011 by Pakistan due to incident. (42) In order to reduce costs, these goods were often shipped by sea to ports in the Persian Gulf and then flown into Afghanistan. The air supply effort at the beginning of the war was the third largest in history, after the Berlin Airlift and the 1990 airlift for the Gulf War.

CHAPTER 7

Building a Coalition

After the attacks of September 11, countries allied with the United States rallied to its support, perhaps best symbolized by the French newspaper *Le Monde*'s headline, "We are all Americans now." Even in Iran thousands gathered in the capital, Tehran, for a candlelight vigil. Evidence gathered by the United States soon convinced most governments that the Islamic militant group al-Qaeda was responsible for the attacks. The group had been implicated in previous terrorist strikes against Americans, and bin Laden had made numerous anti-American statements. Al-Qaeda was headquartered in Afghanistan and had forged a close relationship with that country's ruling Taliban militia, which subsequently refused U.S. demands to extradite bin Laden and to terminate al-Qaeda activity there.

"For the first time in its history, the North Atlantic Organization (NATO) invoked Article 5, allowing its members to respond collectively in self-defense, and on October 7 the U.S. allied military forces launched an attack against Afghanistan. Within months, thousands of militants were killed or captured, and Taliban and al-Qaeda leaders were driven into hiding. In addition, the U.S. government exerted great effort to track down other al-Qaeda agents and sympathizers throughout the world and made combating terrorism the focus of U.S. foreign policy. Meanwhile, security measures within the United States were tightened at such places as airports, government buildings, and sports venues. The terrorism of September 11th was not just an attack on the United States, it was an attack on the world. Citizens from more than eighty countries died that day, innocent men, women, and children from across the globe. Within hours of the tragedy, coalitions involving many nations assembled to fight terrorism, hundreds of countries have contributed to a variety of ways, some militarily, others diplomatically, economically, and financially. Some nations have helped openly, others prefer not to disclose their contributions.

In Afghanistan alone, our coalition partners contributed 6,000 troops to Operation Enduring Freedom and the International Security Assistance Force in Kabul, making up more than half of the 11,000 non-Afghan forces in Afghanistan. The war against terrorism is a broad-based effort that will take time. Every nation has different circumstances and will participate in different ways. This mission and future missions will require a series of coalitions ready to take on the challenges and assume the risks associated with such an operation.

Coalition forces made important contributions in the war against terrorism across the spectrum of operations. Contributions included, but are not limited to, providing vital intelligence, personnel, equipment, and assets for use on the ground, in the air and at sea. Coalition members also have provided liaison teams, participated in planning, provided bases, and granted over-flight permissions - as well as making sizable contributions of humanitarian assistance." *(The White House, President George W. Bush)*

Whenever possible, America never wants to go it alone. By doing so, it would look like we are ganging up on another country and we are the only country that has a grievance.

The following is just a fraction of the support provided by other countries:
- Australian Special Operations Forces (SOF) performed SOF missions.

- Bahrain maintained fighter units provided defensive Combat Air Patrol
- Belgium led the largest multinational humanitarian mission.
- Canada contributed the first coalition Task Group to arrive in CENTCOM.
- Czech Republic performed local training as well as Consequence Management
- Danish Air Force provided one C-130 aircraft with seventy-five crew and support personnel.
- Egypt had three personnel at CENTCOM.
- Finland assisted Humanitarian Assistance organizations in Afghanistan.
- French Air Force, deployed aircraft to Tajikistan provided humanitarian assistance.
- German Special Operations Forces performed the full spectrum of SOF missions.
- Britain's Royal Air Force provided aircraft throughout the region.
- Greeks offered one frigate and one engineering company.
- Italian personnel have been committed to Operation enduring freedom.
- Japan dispatched three Destroyers and two supply ships (about 1200 personnel)
- Jordan has provided basing and overflight permission for all U.S. and coalition forces.
- The Netherlands deployed one C-130 aircraft to Manas.
- New Zealand provided logistic and HA airlift support with Air Force C-130 aircraft.
- Norwegian cleared more than 180,000 square meters of mines on Qandahar airfield.

- Poland has also planned for twenty soldiers to deploy to Kuwait to support MIO operations.
- Portugal has personnel at CENTCOM.
- South Korea has transported forty-five tons of humanitarian supplies valued at $12 million.
- Romania approved basing and overflight permission for all U.S. and coalition forces.
- Russia has supported HA operations by transporting tons of food commodities.
- Spain deployed one P-3B to Djibouti, three C-130s to Manas and two naval frigates.
- Turkey provided basing and overflight permission for all U.S. and coalition forces.
- United Arab Emirates provided basing and overflight permission.
- Uzbekistan sent five personnel at CENTCOM" (43)

CHAPTER 8

Call in the Calvary

"There were two routes from Pakistan to Afghanistan (both were closed in November 2011 following the Salala incident. Afghanistan also borders Turkmenistan, Uzbekistan, and Tajikistan, so alternate supply routes, termed the Northern Distribution Network, existed to move supplies into Afghanistan through these countries. However, these routes were longer and costlier than the routes through Pakistan.

For military aircraft to fly over some countries, a particular country must secure air rights from that country. We learned that one of the countries wanted extortion size money for that right. Because their money demands were so high, we decided to reroute our refueling tankers around that country. Because our country had a hostile relationship with Iran and Turkmenistan, so we had to focus on other countries such as Karachi and Pakistan.

For the next days leading up to the invasion of Afghanistan, our teams were collecting information and working through problems and strategies. Each of us were relaying information sent back to our respective duty sections and preparing daily briefs from information that we collected around the globe. Our briefs were top secret, and each major issue was depicted on a slide so decisions makers could quickly decipher and initiate actions. The briefs went to all offices that had a need to know as well as the Secretary of Defense, the Chairman of the Joint Chiefs of Staff, and the

President. Before distributing them, each crisis action team would meet in the tank's conference room and thoroughly scrub them to make certain there was no incorrect information. Each section had their own slide(s) and were responsible for making certain that they were accurate.

While we were conveying information sent to us around the globe, the Combatant commanders, especially CENTCOM, were readying their troops and waiting for the word to implement their respective war plans.

The Afghanistan campaign started covertly on September 26, with a Central Intelligence Agency (CIA) team known as Jawbreaker arriving in the country and, working with anti-Taliban allies, initiating a strategy for overthrowing the regime. U.S. officials hoped that by partnering with the Afghans they could avoid deploying a large force to Afghanistan. Pentagon officials were especially concerned that the United States was not drawn into a protracted occupation of Afghanistan, as had occurred with the Soviets more than two decades prior. The United States relied primarily on the Northern Alliance, which had just lost Massoud but had regrouped under other commanders. The Americans also teamed with anti-Taliban Pashtuns in southern Afghanistan, including a little-known tribal leader named Hamid Karzai. (44)

We received continual photographs in the NMCC of operations on the ground. After laying the groundwork for the invasions of Afghanistan, we anxiously awaiting any word or photos if our work succeeded or not. Suddenly, cheers went through the command center when a picture of a special ops guy on horseback appeared on the screen.

Photo 13-U.S. soldiers on Horseback

One would think that he would have been riding in a Humvee instead of on a horse. As the special ops guys were trying to organize the warlords and their mode of transportation was horseback, it only seemed appropriate for our people to do the same mode of transportation. Otherwise, the warlords may not relate to us.

Before the 9/11 attacks, then-Capt. Mark Nutsch never expected he would use horseback riding — a skill he learned growing up on a Kansas cattle ranch. But weeks later, on Oct. 19, 2001, Nutsch, and a team of eleven other Green Berets with the 5th Special Forces Group's Operational Detachment Alpha 595 were inserted into Afghanistan to liberate the region from the Taliban without tanks or trucks. Just horses.

"We did not know horses were going to be involved until about 48 hours prior to our insertion when we were given the phrase 'be prepared to use indigenous animals for transportation,'" Nutsch told Military Times. "No one had horse saddles ready to go, so we just...figured it out on the ground and we rode the local horses with local saddles and equipment," Nutsch said.

ODA 595 was one of several Special Forces teams sent into Afghanistan to topple the Taliban weeks after the 9/11 attacks as part of an unconventional mission known as *Task Force Dagger*. The insurgent group had provided a safe haven for al-Qaida leader Osama bin Laden in Afghanistan.

Although Nutsch said they were not expected to survive the mission, the team had earned a reputation as an experienced group familiar with combat. Five out of the twelve men were combat veterans who had served in Somalia, Bosnia, or the First Gulf War. "We had a great amount of experience on that team," Nutsch said.

"Our average age was 32, we averaged eight years' time in service at that point already, and we just were considered a very senior, mature unconventional warfare-focused team."

Alongside Central Intelligence Agency counterparts and anti-Taliban ethnic leaders, ODA 595 and several other Green Beret teams helped pull Afghanistan from Taliban leadership just months after planes struck the Twin Towers and the Pentagon.

"My team was informed that we were going to be the first Special Forces team deployed from the Special Forces Group into a mission that we didn't fully know what it was going to be at that point," Nutsch said. "But they had set us aside and said, 'start planning.'"

To prepare for Task Force Dagger, ODA 595 poured over National Geographic, and tourist maps as they studied up on the regional personalities. Specifically, Nutsch said the team identified the anti-Taliban leaders of the Tajiks, Uzbeks, and Hazaras who formed the Northern Alliance. The Green Berets and CIA counterparts worked to unite these groups to form a militia with 5,000 fighters. ODA 595 first headed to Uzbekistan on Oct. 5, 2001, before crossing into Afghanistan on Oct. 19 in an MH-47 Chinook helicopter and connecting with Gen. Abdul Rashid Dostum and his Uzbek militia.

Dostum was a former communist general who had earned some notoriety for changing his allegiance in previous Afghan conflicts. We knew nothing about these guys," retired Lt. Gen. John F. Mulholland, former U.S. Army Special Operations Command commander said, according to the Associated Press. "All of these guys have blood on their hands. None of these guys are clean actors." "There were a lot of unknowns," Mulholland added. "That's being gentle."

Upon arrival, the team had a lot to learn — including how to ride the horses the locals rode within hours of touching down in Afghanistan. "We are figuring out; how do you carry your rifle? What gear do I keep on my body? What can I put on the horse? What do I leave behind? You know, can I trust the guys next to me? Is there an ambush up ahead?" Nutsch said. "There's a whole lot of things going on besides having this half-wild animal that you're trying to figure out how to ride," Nutsch said.

According to Nutsch, it was "pure fate" that he grew up on a cattle ranch and already knew his way around horses. Not everyone was as experienced as Nutsch. One of the other men on the team had ridden horses a little in high school, and it was a completely new experience for the other ten members. The men received a horseback riding crash course involving hours on the horses as soon as they arrived in Afghanistan — a painful process that demanded using new muscles. Furthermore, the saddles and riding gear wasn't designed to accommodate the Americans, who were larger and heavier than their Afghanistan counterparts, according to an Army news release. Broken stirrups were repaired with parachute cargo straps.

Although Nutsch said there was a steep learning curve at first, the men adapted well, and the horses provided them with some flexibility. For example, they could ride at any time during the day or night, in all terrain types. Meanwhile, the Taliban and al-Qaida had limited mobility using in the tanks left over from when the Soviet Union exited Afghanistan in the 1980s.

"The horses allowed us to get in around them and behind them, and cut them off basically from reinforcement and retreat," Nutsch said. This was possible because the special forces teams worked in three-man cells, along with their Afghan allies, and could view the enemy from various vantage points in adjacent districts, Nutsch said.

Although Nutsch said there were several close calls, no one on his team was seriously injured during Task Force Dagger. On Nov. 10, ODA 595 and militia allies liberated the city of Mazar-e-Sharif from the Taliban, marking a huge victory that paved the way for future success. Weeks later, Taliban surrendered in other areas of Afghanistan.

"Our American presence on the ground gave them hope and emboldened them that they can have a little better future," Nutsch said about the Afghan allies. "And I'm proud to say that 18 years later, those groups are still united and trying to be part of the political solution." (45)

The CIA team was soon joined by U.S. and British special forces contingents, and together they provided arms, equipment, and advice to the Afghans. They also helped coordinate targeting for the air campaign, which began on October 7, 2001, with U.S. and British war planes pounding Taliban targets, thus marking the public start of Operation Enduring Freedom. In late October, Northern Alliance forces began to overtake a series of towns formerly held by the Taliban. The forces worked with U.S. assistance, but they defied U.S. wishes when, on November 13, they marched into Kabul as the Taliban retreated without a fight.

Afghanistan assault consisted of three phases. "The first phase of the war in Afghanistan entailed small teams of Special Forces soldiers working on the ground with local militia forces opposed to the Taliban. Here, the U.S. soldiers describe what it was like to fight side by side with the Afghan commanders. The war begins with the bombing. The second phase, from 2002 until 2008, was marked by a U.S. strategy of defeating the Taliban militarily and rebuilding core institutions of the Afghan state. The third phase, a turn to classic counterinsurgency doctrine, began in 2008 and accelerated with U.S. Pres. Barack Obama's 2009 decision to temporarily increase the U.S. troop presence in Afghanistan. The larger force was used to implement a strategy of protecting the population from Taliban attacks and supporting efforts to reintegrate insurgents into Afghan society. The strategy came coupled with a timetable for the withdrawal of the foreign forces from Afghanistan; beginning in 2011, security responsibilities would be gradually handed over to the Afghan military and police. The new approach failed to achieve its aims. Insurgent attacks and civilian casualties remained stubbornly high, while many of the Afghan military and police units taking over security duties were ill-prepared to hold off the Taliban. By the time the U.S. and NATO combat mission formally ended in December 2014, the 13-year Afghanistan War had become the longest war ever fought by the United States. American military casualties included some 2,400 service members killed, and 20,700 others wounded. (46)

Meantime, military actions were being implemented at the Pentagon. Soon after we were given the green light to bomb enemy targets in Afghanistan, we received photos of missiles being loaded onto aircraft (Photo 13).

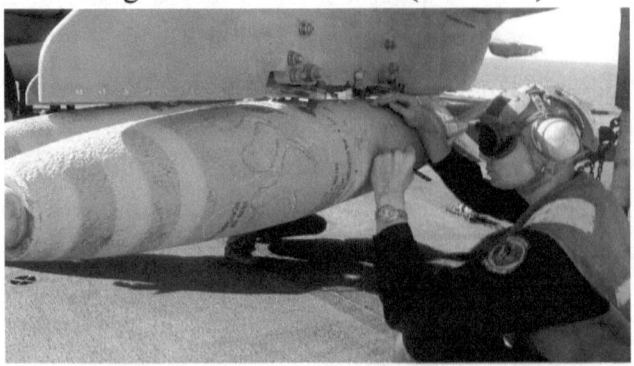

Photo 14-Writing messages on bombs to Afghanistan

The munition loaders would write messages on the bombs such as "this is for all Every day, one senior officer reported on the number of, and type of bombs dropped. There was a time that we considered dropping one of the largest non-nuclear bombs in Afghanistan, call the "mother of all bombs" or what we also called "Big Bertha." It was dropped in 2017 during the Trump administration.

President Donald Trump said he authorized the military. Targeting an ISIS cave complex in eastern Afghanistan, the U.S. dropped "the mother of all bombs." While the MOAB is the largest non-nuclear bomb ever used in

combat, it is not the largest non-nuclear bomb in the U.S. military's arsenal. That is the massive ordnance penetrator (MOP), which is 30,000 pounds. A MOAB

Photo 15-Largest non-nuclear bomb

is a 30-foot-long, 21,600-pound, GPS-guided munition. The US and Afghan forces were unable to advance because ISIS mined the area with explosives. The bomb was dropped to clear the tunnels. (47)

We received photos from Afghanistan depicting how the war was progressing. There are two that sticks out in my mind. The first was one of our missiles striking a truck filled with Taliban's who were evidently either going to or coming from wreaking havoc on our soldiers. One of our fighters swooped down towards the truck like an eagle going after its' prey. After scoring a perfect hit, the pilot pulled a lot of G forces to bring his plane out of the dive. You could see his face from a camera that he had mounted on his instrument panel. As he pulled out of the dive, you could see men being blown out of the truck.

Another involved the pilot of a fighter plane, the A10 Warthog. The A-10C Thunderbolt II is the first Air Force aircraft specially designed for close air support of ground forces. They are simple that can be used against light maritime attack aircraft and all ground targets, including tanks and other armored vehicles. The photo depicted the aircraft riddled with anti-aircraft shrapnel after it returned from making a low flying bombing run hitting numerous enemy targets. Normally an aircraft hit that many times would crash, thus the reason it being surrounded by pilots staring in wonderment as to how the pilot was able to drop all its bombs and make it back safely. The pilot of the aircraft was standing in the middle of the other pilots. She was a young woman about five feet five.

CHAPTER 9

Hunt for Bin Laden

The joint U.S. and British invasion of Afghanistan in late 2001 was preceded by over two decades of war in Afghanistan (see Afghan War). On December 24, 1979, Soviet tanks rumbled across the Amu Darya River and into Afghanistan, ostensibly to restore stability following a coup that brought to power a pair of Marxist-Leninist political groups—the People's (Khalq) Party and the Banner (Parcham) Party. But the Soviet presence touched off a nationwide rebellion by fighters—known as the mujahideen—who drew upon Islam as a uniting source of inspiration. These fighters won extensive covert backing from Pakistan, Saudi Arabia, and the United States and were joined in their fight by foreign volunteers (who soon formed a network, known as al-Qaeda, to coordinate their efforts). The guerrilla war against the Soviet forces led to their departure in 1989. In the Soviets' absence, the mujahideen ousted Afghanistan's Soviet-backed government and established a transitional government.

The mujahideen were politically fragmented, however, and in 1994-armed conflict escalated. The Taliban emerged and in 1996 seized Kabul. It instituted a severe interpretation of Islamic law that, for example, forbade female education and prescribed the severing of hands, or even execution, as punishment for petty crimes. That same year, al-Qaeda leader Osama bin Laden was welcomed to Afghanistan (having been expelled from Sudan) and established his organization's headquarters there. With al-Qaeda's help, the Taliban won control of over 90 percent of Afghan territory by the summer of 2001. On September 9 of that year, al-Qaeda hit men carried out the assassination of famed mujahideen leader Ahmad Shah Masoud, who at the time was leading the Northern Alliance (a loose coalition of mujahideen militias that maintained control of a small section of northern Afghanistan) as it battled the Taliban and who had unsuccessfully sought greater U.S. backing for his efforts (48)

"One would ask why Bin Laden hated American and was willing to take his holy war to the very heart of America.

In a never-published interview with a French journalist in April of 1995, Osama bin Laden says that his decision to fight alongside Afghan mujahedeen dated from "the time when the Americans decided to help the Afghans fight the Russians."

In August of 1995, Bin Laden issued a communiqué called "an Open Letter to King Fahd." He outlines major grievances against the Saudi regime: lack of commitment to Sunni Islam, inability to conduct viable defense policy, the squandering of public funds and oil money, and the dependence on non-Muslims for protection. He calls for a campaign of guerilla attacks to drive U.S. forces out of the Saudi Kingdom.

In July 0f 1996, The British newspaper *The Independent* quotes bin Laden as saying: What happened in Riyadh and [Dhahran] when 24 Americans were killed in two bombings is clear evidence of the huge anger of Saudi people against America. The Saudis now know their real enemy is America." [From *The Washington Post* 8/23/98]

Several months after being expelled from the Sudan, in August of 1996, bin Laden issues his "Declaration of War

Against the Americans Who Occupy the Land of the Two Holy Mosques." It reads, in part: "Muslims burn with anger at America. For its own good, America should leave [Saudi Arabia.] ...

Bin Laden is quoted in October/November issue of *Nida'ul Islam* magazine as saying: "As for their accusations of terrorizing the innocent, the children, and the women, these are in the category of 'accusing others with their own affliction in order to fool the masses.' The evidence overwhelmingly shows America and Israel killing the weaker men, women, and children in the Muslim world and elsewhere.

In a CNN interview with Osama bin Laden, he says: "We declared jihad against the US government, because the US government is unjust, criminal and tyrannical. It has committed acts that are extremely unjust, hideous and criminal whether directly or through its support of the Israeli occupation." Bin Laden issued an edict calling for attacks on all Americans, including civilians, and announces the creation of the International Islamic Front for Jihad Against the Jews and Crusaders, in association with extremist groups from Egypt, Pakistan and Bangladesh." (49)

"The hunt for Osama Bin Laden started immediately upon, we received intel reports that he had health issues such as a failing kidney and needed dialysis.

"Over the last ten years conflicting reports on Osama Bin Laden's health have filled the headlines. Some say he had serious kidney problems and needed access to dialysis technology, while others mention an enlarged heart, hypotension (low blood pressure), shrapnel injuries, kidney stones, and even diabetes type 1. Can we separate fact from fiction, or will we never know? Many of us have had an image of a frail man with failing organs wandering through the mountains. Pakistan's ex-president, Pervez Musharaff, in

2002 said he had kidney problems. One story had him seeking kidney care in a Dubai hospital in 2000. But the words were never supported by compelling evidence.

We had numerous reports that Bin Laden was holed up in a cave somewhere inside the Pakistani border which proved wrong. Bin Laden was still at large and could pose another serious threat in the near or long term. "In fact, a report by the FBI noted his long history of terrorist attacks. Osama bin Laden—also known as Usama bin Laden—was a violent terrorist and mass murderer who used bombings and bloodshed to advance his extremist goals. After founding the terrorist organization al Qaeda, he engineered a series of attacks in multiple countries that killed thousands of men, women, and children, often ordinary citizens just going about their daily lives." (50)

"In September 2001, President Bush announced that he wanted Osama bin Laden captured—dead or alive—and a $25 million bounty was eventually issued for information leading to the killing or capture of bin Laden. Bin Laden evaded capture, however, including in December 2001, when he was tracked by U.S. forces to the mountains of Tora Bora in eastern Afghanistan. Bin Laden's trail subsequently went cold, and he was thought to be living somewhere in the Afghanistan-Pakistan tribal regions." (51)

"An intensive manhunt for Omar, bin Laden, and al-Qaeda deputy chief Ayman al-Zawahiri was undertaken. Prior to the killing of bin Laden by U.S. forces in 2011, the Americans were believed to have come closest to bin Laden in the December 2001 battle of Tora Bora (bin Laden's mountain stronghold). But bin Laden was thought to have managed to have slipped into Pakistan with the help of Afghan and Pakistani forces that were helping the Americans. Critics later questioned why the U.S. military had allowed Afghan forces to lead the assault on the cave complex at Tora Bora rather than doing it themselves. (Indeed, Democratic presidential candidate Sen. John Kerry made this criticism repeatedly during the 2004 general election campaign.) Al-Qaeda subsequently reestablished its base of operations in the tribal areas that form Pakistan's northwest border with Afghanistan.

Omar and his top Taliban lieutenants settled in and around the Pakistani city of Quetta, in the remote southwestern province of Balochistān. One of the final major battles of the first phase of the war came in March 2002 with Operation Anaconda in the eastern province of Paktia, which involved U.S. and Afghan forces fighting some eight hundred al-Qaeda and Taliban militants. The operation also marked the entrance of other countries' troops into the war: special operations forces from Australia, Canada, Denmark, France, Germany, and Norway participated."(*Britannica, Afghanistan War, 2001-2014*)

The capture of Bin Laden occurred after I left the Joint Staff and President Bush left office. Therefore, we did not have privy to the details but a story by CNN World and an account by the CIA summarizes his capture:

"While Bin Ladin had been a key focus of the IC since the 1990s, shortly after the September 11, 2001, terrorist attacks on the United States, the CIA began collecting information on key individuals connected to or providing support to Bin Ladin. Reporting identified a key courier by his kunya, or operational pseudonym. It would be years later that the kunya was matched to a real name.

By late 2010, further intelligence linked the courier to a compound in Abbottabad, a town in Pakistan's Khyber-Pakhtunkhwa Province (formerly the Northwest Frontier Province), about thirty-five miles north of Islamabad. The compound and its main residence had extensive security features unusual for the area: high walls topped with barbed wire, double entry gates, opaque windows, no apparent internet or telephone connections, and all trash was burned rather than collected. Moreover, the two registered owners did not appear to work or have an income that would allow them to afford such a large residence. This, along with other intelligence, led the IC to assess that the compound was being used to hide Bin Ladin, as well as the courier.

Intense training for the raid began, including the building of an exact life-size replica of the compound with movable interior walls to prepare the assault teams for any internal layout they might encounter.

The operation, authorized by the President on April 29th, was a surgical raid by a small team of special operations forces chosen to minimize collateral damage, to pose as little risk as possible to noncombatants on the compound or to Pakistani civilians in the neighborhood, and to increase the likelihood of confirming the identity of Bin Ladin. (52)

"The CIA informs President Obama that bin Laden may be living in the Abbottabad compound in Pakistan. April 29, 2011 - At 8:20 a.m. ET, President Obama gives the order to raid bin Laden's compound."

The helicopters arrived at the Abbottabad compound at 0030-Pakistan time on May 2; one crashed, but the assault continued without delay.

- They arrive outside the compound in two Black Hawk helicopters.
- The operation takes 40 minutes in total.
- US Special Forces breached the outer walls of the compound before fighting their way through the ground floor of the three-story building. The firefight then moves to the second and third floors.
- In the last 5-10 minutes of the firefight, bin Laden is killed by a gunshot.
- Wound to the head.

- Three men, including a son of bin Laden, are killed as well as one woman.
- Bin Laden's body is identified by one of his wives. Facial recognition is also used.
- Bin Laden is buried at sea off the deck of the USS Carl Vinson in the Arabian Sea. He is buried within 24 hours according to Islamic law." (53)

"A news story by ABC News, however, seems to support the contention of Obama's administration that no one received the bounty for the capture of Osama bin Laden. According to a news report by ABC News in May 19, 2011, however, "no one will receive the $25 million reward for the capture of Osama bin Laden, say U.S. officials, because the raid that killed the al Qaeda leader in Pakistan on May 2 was the result of electronic intelligence, not human informants. We do not expect a reward to be paid," said a senior U.S. official familiar with the bin Laden hunt, meaning that the $25 million bounty offered by the U.S. under the Rewards for Justice program after the 9/11 terror attacks will probably remain uncollected.

The reason is simple, say officials involved in or knowledgeable about the hunt for the world's most wanted man: the CIA and the military never had an al Qaeda operative as an informer willing to give him up. Instead, what killed bin Laden was electronic surveillance, and an operational mistake by one of his closest associates. After a slow drip of intelligence year after year, and then a final flurry of data collection and analysis brought a team of SEALs to bin Laden's Abbottabad compound on a moonless night. Electronic intel and a mistake by a bin Laden courier led to the raid." (54)

My theory has always been that the powers to be did not want to take him alive. They preferred to have any physical being of him eliminated from the face of the earth.

If there was a burial site for people to visit and the visitors were terrorists, his burial site may incite terrorists to take revenge by performing terrorist acts. One might liken it to the burial site of JFK in Arlington cemetery which fills one with inspiration and admiration rather than despair and a desire for vengeance.

An account written on the web site HISTORY gives credence to my theory:

"After identifying his body, the military brought him aboard the USS *Carl Vinson* and buried him in the northern Arabian Sea the same day.

"The U.S. took political, religious, and practical factors into consideration when deciding how to bury bin Laden's body. There was concern that if he were buried on land, his grave could become a shrine for his followers. There was a need to observe Islamic funeral practices, including the custom of burying a body within 24 hours of a person's death. And there was the question of whether the U.S. should take photos or provide some sort of visual proof that he was dead.

US Officials Feared His Grave Would Become a Shrine. When U.S. forces killed Osama bin Laden, who was 54, the U.S. government's explanations for why it didn't bury him in the ground were a little inconsistent. News articles quoted American officials both on and off the record who said that the U.S. didn't want him to have a physical grave because it might become a shrine, but also because an unnamed country had declined to accept his body. Articles speculated that the country was Saudi Arabia, where bin Laden was born.

The Saudis are inclined toward a form of Islam called Wahhabism," he says, which rejects shrines of prominent people. The fact that Saudi Arabia would not want his grave to become a shrine in their country, combined with the fact that bin Laden was extremely critical of Saudi Arabia, makes Ahmed think that if U.S. officials asked the country to receive bin Laden's body, "they asked out of ignorance." Burying bin Laden in northwest Pakistan, where Special Forces killed him, would not be ideal from a U.S. perspective either, since shrines are considered powerful symbols in that region, Ahmed says. To avoid bin Laden's grave becoming an important symbol to his followers, the U.S. made the decision to bury him at sea. Although this deviates from the way most Muslim burials occur, U.S. officials insisted it still took steps to bury him according to Islamic funeral practices.

This was offensive to many Iraqis because the U.S. was deliberately disrespecting the bodies of Muslims. Even if a person is executed for crimes, Islamic scholars argue that the person should receive a respectful burial. U.S. officials say the burial of bin Laden, criticized though it was an attempt to honor that principle." (55)

In the NMCC, we had been privy to several other bounties which I will discuss later but could not corroborate an article that appeared in THE ATLANTIC about other bounties. According to THE ATLANTIC, "Whatever the truth, bounties like this one remain an offer for terrorists all over the world. Up to $25 million is available for "information that brings to justice" Ayman al-Zawahiri, bin Laden's successor as leader of al-Qaeda. Zawahiri now tops the list of most-wanted terrorists sought under the State Department Bureau of Diplomatic Security's Rewards for Justice program. Taliban chief Mullah Omar, Islamic State leader Abu Bakr al-Baghdadi, and Haqqani Network head Sirajuddin Haqqani occupy a lower tier—they are worth up to $10 million apiece. Prior to recent unconfirmed reports of the death of ISIS's purported second-in-command, Abu Alaa al-Afri, the State Department offered $7 million for information leading to his whereabouts. Some forty-six terrorists are valued at $5 million each. And so, on down to the modest $1 million bounty for Radullan Sahiron, a leader of the Filipino terrorist organization Abu Sayyaf Group. It's unclear whether a little-known ISIS official with the nom de guerre Abu Sayyaf (no relation), who was killed in a rare raid into Syria by U.S. Special forces over the weekend, was on the list." (56)

Another bounty was offered on the capture of Bin Laden's son, Hamza. "According to a BBC news story March of 2019, Hamza Bin Laden is emerging as a leader of the Islamist militant group, officials say. He is thought to be based near the Afghan Pakistani border. In recent years, he has released audio and video messages calling on followers to attack the US and its Western allies in revenge for his father's killing. In 2011, US special forces killed Osama Bin Laden in a compound in Abbottabad, Pakistan. He approved the attacks on the US on 11 September 2001, in which 3,000 people were killed." Hamza Bin Laden, who is believed to be about 30 years old, was officially designated by the US as a global terrorist two years ago. The US state department says he married the daughter of Mohammed Atta, who hijacked one of the four commercial aircraft used in the 2001 attacks, and crashed it into one of the World Trade Center towers in New York. Letters from Osama Bin Laden seized from his compound indicated that he had been grooming Hamza, thought to be his favorite son, to replace him as leader of al-Qaeda." (57)

Hamza bin Laden was killed in a U.S. counterterrorism operation, President Trump confirmed. "He was killed in an operation in the Afghanistan-Pakistan region, the White House said in a statement. His death will not only deprive al Qaeda of important leadership skills and the symbolic connection to his father, but undermines important operational activities of the group," He was responsible for planning and dealing with terrorist groups." (58)

One of the many photos we received from our troops on the ground was a photo what appeared to be Bin Laden's son-in-law fleeing Afghanistan on a motor bike. Because of him being so tall, it was a comical site to see his feet dragging on the ground. "Later he was arrested in Jordan and his trial took place amid extra security measures at the U.S. District Court in Manhattan. The assistant director in charge of the FBI's New York field office, likened Abu Ghaith to "a consigliere for the mob or the chief of staff to a corrupt foreign leader" and said he was a "spokesman, confidant and senior adviser" to bin Laden's organization. He was sentenced to life in prison." (59)

CHAPTER 10

Protecting our Government

Another major concern that confronted the Pentagon and the White House was to make certain that the government and defense of the country would continue if another major catastrophic attack leveled our seat of government (The White House and The Capital) and the higher command of the military (The Pentagon). To guard against this, plans are in place to make certain that there is continuity of the government. As the current events unfolded, it was imperative for us to implement the plans. There are numerous locations where the axis of power would be re-established if such an event occurred.

"Continuity of Operations (COOP) is the initiative that ensures that Federal Government departments and agencies are able to continue operation of their essential functions under a broad range of circumstances including natural, man-made, and technological threats and national security emergencies." (60)

Further defined by FEMA, "Continuity of Operations (COOP), as defined in the National Continuity Policy Implementation Plan (NCPIP) and the National Security Presidential Directive 51/Homeland Security, is an effort within individual executive departments and agencies to ensure that their Primary Mission Essential Functions (PMEFs) continue to be performed during a wide range of emergencies, including localized acts of nature, accidents and technological or attack-related emergencies." (61)

"The president has numerous places he or she can go in the event of emergency should Washington DC be attacked again.

President's emergency Operations Center (PEOC): under the East Wing of the White House, is the first place the president will go in the event of a catastrophic emergency. The underground bunker is designed to withstand a nuclear blast and is where Vice President Dick Cheney met the National Security Council during the 911 attacks. This is one of many bunkers located in the Washington DC area and was originally built for FDR during World War II. (After addressing the nation, President Bush met with his National Security Council in the PEOC.

High Point Special Facility (Mount Weather-*Photo 15*)

Built into Mount Weather in Bluemont, VA, the High Point Special Facility is an evacuation point for high-level officials in the event of an emergency. Constructed between 1954 and 1958 by the Eisenhower Administration, it was initially designed to protect the president and his aides from a nuclear attack. In addition to the above-ground facilities, there is an underground system of tunnels and bunkers designed to keep the government functioning for as long as needed in the event of a catastrophe.

The Doomsday Plane. The E-4B is a plane designed as a mobile communications center for the president and his/her staff during a catastrophic event. A crew stands by 24/7, ready to go at a moment's notice. The plane is a modified 747 capable of traveling 620 miles per hour, 40 mph faster than a normal 747. It can refuel in midair and stay airborne for days. The plane is covered in an electromagnetic pulse shield to prevent its system from being fried in the event of a nuclear blast. It also has a thermo-radiation shield.

Offutt Air Force Base. During the 9/11 attacks, then-President George W. Bush left Florida, briefly touched down in Louisiana to address the nation and get out of the air while more attacks may have been imminent, then flew to Offutt Air Force Base, just south of Omaha, NE, smack dab in the middle of the United States. Offutt is home to the E-4 series doomsday planes (there are four of them), the US Strategic Command, and the 55th Wing of the Air Combat Command.

Raven Rock Mountain Complex. Raven Rock Mountain Complex, also known as Site R, is an underground bunker designed to be the US command center in the event of World War III, as a backup for the Pentagon. Located near Blue Ridge Summit, PA, the facility is built into a mountain and designed to withstand a nuclear blast. It is entirely self-sufficient, with two power plants, multiple underground water reservoirs, and a sophisticated ventilation system. It can operate for 30 days with no access to the outside world and can accommodate 3,000 people.

The Greenbrier Resort Bunker. Hiding beneath the luxurious Greenbrier Resort near White Sulfur Springs, WV is a bunker designed to handle doomsday scenarios. It was built to house all of Congress in the event of a nuclear strike. The facility was code named Greek Island and is encased in three feet of steel-reinforced concrete. It could operate fully self-sustained for a month. Greek Island was retired before it was ever used, when its secrecy was blown in a 1992 *Washington Post* article.

Cheyenne Mountain Complex. Carved into the Rocky mountains of Colorado, the Cheyenne Mountain Complex military base is very close to NORAD (North American Aerospace Defense Command) HQ. Designed to withstand a nuclear blast, the facility monitors the skies constantly for threats. It is owned and operated by the Air Force Space Command, and is completely self-sustaining, with its own power plant, heating, and cooling system, and water supply. It is a level one security designation, more secure than the Pentagon.

As to other Washington DC components, "The **Federal Relocation Arc** is a network of facilities surrounding Washington, D.C. designed to ensure the survival of non-military components of the United States government in the event the capital city of Washington is rendered uninhabitable during a war or other serious emergency, such as a nuclear attack. Departments participating in the Federal Relocation Arc are primarily agencies that might not themselves be military targets but could have their operations disrupted should a serious event occur in the capital." (62)

To my surprise, I was assigned to a Pentagon's continuity of operation team. The team included high ranking officers. We were sent to a site that housed an underground nuclear bunker. A building was built deep into the mountain that was fully equipped that could sustain a large entourage of Army, Navy, Air Force, and Marine Corps. It also had apartments for high level officials including the President, Vice President, and Secretary of Defense. Access to the facility requires top secret clearances and sensitive compartmented information (SCI). Until 911 struck, the facility had a skeleton crew and was not utilized that much.

When we pulled up to the site, we had to pass a series of clearances before gaining access. We then boarded a bus that rode us down a long tunnel in the mountain. Reaching the first door we discovered

Photo 16-Double Vault Door Entrance

it was not just a door. Like other hardened underground facilities, it was a large vault door heavily guarded. After we passed through the first door, we encountered another vault door. The second vault door was not opened until the first door was closed. Once inside, we stepped across a road laid throughout the mountain. We went straight to our command center and quarters. The building was equipped with living quarters as well as high tech electronic equipment. The look of the interior reminded me of scenes from a James Bond movie.

Inside the mountain, we had our own water supply and gym. To stay in shape, I would use the gym and run back and forth on the road which was built inside the mountain. Our quarters had all the comforts of home including a sauna. When the lights went out, you felt like you were in a bat cave. The interior of the mountain was one large cave with all the amenities of offices and sleeping rooms. Our part of the building housed a full suite of rooms in case the President and the Secretary of Defense needed to seek the safety of the bunker which would withstand a nuclear hit. Kiddingly, I laid down in the Presidents bed. The complex also accommodated a fully equipped cafeteria.

Our quarters inside the building deep in the mountain were reserved for Generals but as Action officers from the Pentagon, we were given access to them. Each of us had our separate room with bath. The apartments even had a Sauna. For exercise, the building had a gym with tread mills and weights. I used weights but for cardiovascular, I ran on the road that was built inside the mountain. We had a reserve water supply in the mountain as well as a cafeteria. Once we settled into our quarters, our commander called us together to brief us on our mission. The primary purpose of our mission was to continue military operations and help establish a seat of government if Washington was destroyed in another attack. We will be monitoring events throughout the globe and duplicate the operations at the Pentagon should the NMCC be eliminated. This will guarantee that the baton can be picked up if either the Pentagon or White House is attacked and destroyed.

Our orders were not to leave this facility until we receive an all clear from the Pentagon. None of us may see daylight for weeks. The plan is that if the White House were also destroyed, the President and the SECDEF would relocate to our facility or one of the alternative designated sites. We were then given a tour of the facility. The apartments the President and the SECDEF. The apartments were never updated and were still in an outdated motif of the 1950s. When touring the President's apartment, I could not resist lying down on top of the bed. I was surprised to learn that it was not that comfortable and needed cleaning.

We then went to our operations center where we would gather and monitor events transpiring throughout the world (Photo 16).

Photo 17-Operrations Center Monitoring World

Our combatant commands across the world would report in through monitors mounted on the wall in a large conference room like the NMCC. Each screen was designated for incoming information from the Combatant commands located throughout the globe and responsible for their respective geographical locations. There were no actions for us to work on, our mission was to simply stay in place and implement our continuity of operations if called upon. Daily we followed the briefing slides that were being generated by the NMCC.

"A unified combatant command, also referred to as a combatant command (CCMD) or (COCOM), is a joint military command of the United States Department of Defense that is composed of units from two or more service branches of the United States Armed Forces, and conducts broad and continuing missions. There are currently 11 unified combatant commands, and each is established as the highest echelon of military commands, in order to provide effective command and control of all U.S. military forces, regardless of branch of service, during peace or during war time. Unified combatant commands are organized either on a geographical basis (known as an "area of responsibility", AOR) or on a functional basis, e.g., special operations, force projection, transport, and cybersecurity. Currently, seven combatant commands are designated as geographical, and four are designated as functional. Unified combatant commands are "joint" commands and have specific badges denoting their affiliation.

The Unified Command Plan (UCP) establishes the missions, command responsibilities, and geographic areas of responsibility of the combatant commands. Each time the Unified Command Plan is updated, the organization of the combatant commands is reviewed for military efficiency and efficacy, as well as alignment with national policy Africa Command-Protects and defends U.S. Interests by strengthening the defense capabilities of African nations.

- Central Command Builds cooperation among nations throughout the Middle East, responding

102

to crisis, deterring, and defeating threats, and increasing regional stability.

- Cyber Command-Defends and advances national interests.
- European Command Works with NATO and partner nations to address security and defense in Europe and parts of the Middle East and Eurasia
- Indo-Pacific Command Works with its partners to promote development, enhance security, deter aggression, and provide humanitarian assistance.
- Northern Command-defers, detects, detect, defeats to the United States, conducts security cooperation with allies and partners, and supports civil authorities, Northcom's top priority is homeland defense.
- Southern Command works with allies and partners across central and south America to enhance peace, promote human rights, deter illegal activities, and conduct multinational military exercises.
- Space Command-conducts operations in, from, to space to deter conflict, and if necessary, to defeat aggression, deliver space combat power for the joint/combined force, and defend U.S. vital interests with allies and partners.
- Space Operations Command-oversees the various special operations components of the armed forces.
- Strategic command-operates globally to deter and detect strategic attacks against the United States
- Transportation command-provides transportation capabilities for the military (63)

Every NMCC power point briefing included one slide about the number of Taliban prisoners at Guantanamo Ban. One day while we were monitoring the daily NMCC briefing fed to us from the Pentagon, the prisoner slide came up. The Chairman or the Director of Joint Operations (three-star general) would ask us for input. When it came to reporting the number of prisoners at GITMO, I leaned over to our commanding officer and whispered in his air that he should kiddingly include our remote team. Our commander interjected our numbers into the prisoner slide. Everyone laughed, and thought a bit of humor was appropriate for how worn out everyone was from serving long and arduous Watches. After a couple of weeks, we were given the green light to go outside from the command center. It felt good after living like a bat deep inside a mountain.

During our briefings over the next two weeks, I had the opportunity to point out some areas that could compromise the security of the facility and our communications. After a few weeks went by, our team was relieved by another team. We then returned to the NMCC at the Pentagon to re-join the action officer teams at the NMCC.

While serving at the Pentagon, my life was not my own. I rarely had the opportunity to see my two sons, deploying wherever and whenever asked. For six years, I had no personal life and lost touch with family and friends. My significant other broke off our long-term relationship. Whenever I had a couple of days off and not deployed overseas, I would travel between Washington and my home in Pittsburgh to see my two sons.

CHAPTER 11

Homeland Defense

We knew that there was a need for more advanced and ongoing protection of our country. A team of us hunkered down in a conference room of the Joint Staff and started to formulate security protection plans that would give birth to Homeland Security. "A marine Lieutenant who was highly respected by the Joint Staff, Lt. Colonel Robert Salesses, was appointed to be in charge. Bob would later serve in a civilian capacity as Deputy Assistant Secretary of Defense for Defense Continuity and Mission Assurance. "(64)

"Department of Homeland Security (DHS) was created through the combination of all or part of twenty-two different federal departments and agencies into a unified, a more effective, integrated Department, creating a strengthened homeland security enterprise and a more secure America that is better prepared to confront the range of threats we face. With the passage of the Homeland Security Act by Congress in November 2002, the Department of Homeland Security formally came into being as a stand-alone, Cabinet-level department to further coordinate and unify national homeland security efforts." (65)

"It was during this same time, that the birth and code name Noble Eagle also came about. Operation NOBLE EAGLE is the name given to all North American Aerospace

Defense Command (NORAD) aerospace warning, control, and defense missions in North America. Through Operation NOBLE EAGLE, NORAD deters, detects, and defeats potential threats to U.S. and Canadian airspace 24/7/365.

The Chairman of the Joint Chiefs of Staff designated military operations supporting homeland security as Operation NOBLE EAGLE, following the terrorist attacks of September 11, 2001. While NORAD's mission has always been to defend the airspace of the U.S. and Canada, prior to 9/11 NORAD was primarily postured to look outward.

Over the last two decades, NORAD's mission has changed to include a focus on threats that may originate within the U.S. and Canada, and the addition of a maritime warning mission. NORAD has three subordinate regions: the Alaskan NORAD Region (ANR), the Canadian NORAD Region (CANR), and the Continental U.S. NORAD Region (CONR). Together, the three NORAD regions provide airspace surveillance and control, and directs air sovereignty activities for their respective airspace." (66)

After returning to the rejoin the action officers on the Watch at the Pentagon, I learned more about what our pilots were facing on the day the planes hit the World Trade Centers and the Pentagon. Besides some of our fighter pilots faced with the possibility of having to shoot down an American passenger airplane, there was talk of their risking their own lives if their weapon systems failed to shoot them down.

"New York Air National Guard Maj. Jeremy Powell was a 31-year-old tech sergeant taking part in Exercise Vigilant Guardian when 9/11 occurred. He was the first military person to learn about the hijackings, having taken the initial call from the Federal Aviation Administration's Boston center. Master Sgt. Stacia Rountree was a 23-year-old senior airman working as an identification technician.

Vigilant Guardian was her first major NORAD exercise. Like everyone else, Powell and Rountree remember that day vividly.

The fighters were meant only to shadow potentially hijacked planes, but Rountree said there was discussion of those pilots making the ultimate sacrifice. "In case their weapons were out, and if we had to use force, they were discussing whether or not those guys would have to go kamikaze," she said, meaning some pilots were considering risking their own lives by using their planes to stop hijacked jetliners. "It was scary, when you thought about the possibility of them having to do that.

Back then, our primary focus was that we were looking at the possibility of terrorists attacking us from the outside the United States," tech sergeant Jeremy Powell of the NY National Guard said. We were not really focused on the inside.

Nobody thought that somebody would go ahead and utilize planes that were in the U.S. to do something, so our radar coverage was indicative of that, the military has been monitoring the skies over the U.S. ever since. "A lot of people didn't even realize that we were probably there, or what we even do, which could be a good thing," said Powell. "It reinforces the idea that somebody's always watching you, especially in the sky. The FAA's there, it is their airspace, but the military is, too." (67)

Realizing a similar attack could happen when large audiences of people were assembled at such sporting events as the Super Bowl, we tasked F16's to fly over the events. Every day in briefing, one of the slides reported how many and where Combat Air Patrol (CAPs) were going to be flown.

"Combat air patrol (CAP) is a type of flying mission for fighter aircraft. A combat air patrol is an aircraft patrol

provided over an objective area, over the force protected, over the critical area of a combat zone, or over an air defense area, for the purpose of intercepting and destroying hostile aircraft before they reach their target. Combat air

Photo 18-Combat Air Patrols over sea

patrols apply to both overland and overwater operations, protecting other aircraft, fixed and mobile sites on land, or ships at sea. Known by the acronym CAP, it typically entails fighters flying a tactical pattern around or screening a defended target, while looking for incoming attackers. Effective CAP patterns may include aircraft positioned at both high and low altitudes, to shorten response times when an attack is detected." (68)   We made sure all major events were protected by F16 CAPs. The aircraft flew so high that the attendees did not even know they were flying above.

Each day, the CAT team members and the three star directorates of the Joint Staff would meet in the NMCC briefing room to review the briefing that provided key global information for the top decision makers. Those receiving our briefs included the Chairman of the JCS, the SECDEF, and the President. The three star generals and admirals along with the Chairman of the JCS would sit at the main conference table while a senior officer gave the brief standing at a podium. The CAT team members would sit behind the Generals. After the brief was given and updated for any additions or corrections, the Director of the Joint Staff would point to the Directorates and to each of us and ask if we had any input. I decided to provide input. My expertise in chemical, biological, radiological, nuclear, and energy lent credibility to what I said. "We are focusing on the weapons of mass destruction such as Explosive Devices but glossing over other weapons of mass destruction, CBRNE. We must better protect our water supplies and guard against a biological attack. IEDs are more contained where CBRNE, especially viruses, will spread like wildfire throughout our entire country."

Upon giving my input, I had to leave early for another meeting. The senior officer in charge of giving the briefing later told me that there was a great show of support for what I said among the senior staff and the action officers. Comments came that they never pondered in detail what I proposed could happen and needed to place more emphasis on it. I did bring it up several times later to make certain that it did receive a high priority.

During my time in the NMCC, I was challenged numerous times to make life changing decisions. Everyone in Washington thought they were going to save the world. Most of the people on capitol hill were in a frenzy trying to play a major role in saving America. Two instances that came to mind was a phone call from a congressman and another was the decision to shoot down a little Cessna aircraft.

The first was a call from a Congressman who had missed his flight to the middle east. He told me that he and another congressman was going to Saudi Arabia to meet with a prince. Because he missed his flight, he frantically told me that he would like to board one of our military flights that was going to Saudi Arabia. Before passing his request up the chain of command, I knew that the answer would be no, but I wanted to at least give him the courtesy of an answer. We could not be transporting civilians on our military aircraft when America was preparing for war. In addition, the threat risk was high, and he could very well be captured by terrorists and held hostage. Upon contacting the general, he confirmed what I thought. The general did however direct me to offer him a lift to Spain, but he would have to find his own transportation to Saudi. I relayed our decision to the congressman and that was the last I heard from him.

Another time is when I received a radio call from an F16 who informed me that there was an unidentified Cessna flying in the airspace of POTUS. POTUS is the call name we used for the President of the United States. The F-16 pilot could not make radio contact with the pilot of the small Cessna aircraft and wanted to know what his orders was.

Flight Restrictions in the Proximity of the Presidential and Other Parties (14 CFR Section 91.141)

"Temporary flight restrictions (TFRs) are issued with respect to airspace over presidential and other parties. A TFR may be requested by the Washington headquarters office of the U.S. Government agency responsible for the protection of the person concerned. This agency will contact FAA Headquarters in accordance with the established procedures and request the necessary regulatory action. TFRs may be issued by the ATO Director of System Operations Security (or designee). No person may operate an aircraft over or in the vicinity of any area to be visited or traveled by the President, the Vice President, or other public figures contrary to the restrictions established by the FAA. Flight restrictions in the proximity of the President, Vice President, and other parties must be in accordance with Special Operations." (FAA.gov)' (69)

Immediately, the thought crossed my mind that this small aircraft could simply be an innocent day flyer with a family. Even though the orders were to shoot down any unidentified aircraft, I did not have the authority to do so and wanted to avoid it at all costs. The procedure was to call the ranking general officer on duty and he or she would pass it up the line. Before calling the ranking duty officer, I directed the F-16 pilot to get as close to the Cessna as possible and get his attention by waving his wings and giving him a thumbs down if he could make visual contact. I anxiously waited to see if the F-16 pilot was successful. After fifteen minutes, I received the call saying that he was able to make contact, and the Cessna quickly left the President's air space. The F-16 pilot said you could see the surprise look on the pilot's face of the Cessna and was certain that he was shocked when he saw an F-16 that came close to his aircraft.

CHAPTER 12

HEROES NOT FORGOTTEN

While serving on the NMCC Watch, we learned about a sad event that happened during the Watch. It was sadly reported during our Watch that very evening that one of our Rangers, Pat Tillman, was killed in Afghanistan and it was likely from friendly fire. I was especially surprised and saddened to learn that weeks later that Tillman's family learned his death had been accidental rather than from friendly fire. It was difficult for me to fathom that someone in the Army gave Pat's family wrong information. "His parents publicly criticized the Army, saying they had been intentionally deceived by military officials who wanted to use their son as a patriotic poster boy. They believed their son's death was initially covered up by military officials because it could have undermined support for the wars in Iraq and Afghanistan.

Pat Tillman, who gave up his pro football career to enlist in the U.S. Army after the terrorist attacks of September 11, was killed by friendly fire while serving in Afghanistan on April 22, 2004. Tillman turned down a three-year, multi-million-dollar deal with the Cardinals and instead, prompted by the events of 9/11, joined the Army along with his brother Kevin, a minor-league baseball player.

The Tillman brothers were assigned to the 75th Ranger Regiment in Fort Lewis, Washington, and did tours in Iraq in 2003, followed by Afghanistan the next year. The news that Tillman, age 27, was mistakenly gunned down by his fellow Rangers, rather than enemy forces, was initially covered up by the U.S. military. I was surprised and disappointed to learn later that the Army initially maintained that Tillman and his unit were ambushed by enemy forces. Tillman was praised as a national hero, awarded the Silver Star and Purple Heart medals, and posthumously promoted to corporal. While commemorating Pat, we should remember that his brother Kevin also sacrificed himself to serve our country. Both were true American heroes who unselfishly put their country before themselves. They put their lives on hold and foregone considerable money to answer the call to service in a far-off land." (70)

"The subject of friendly-fire casualties burst upon the national psyche in the wake of Operation Desert Storm as grim details of tragic accidents were reported in the media. To provide so-called analysis and to give a sense of perspective, news reporters seized upon an historical norm: that, typically, only 2% of all battlefield casualties could be expected from friendly fire. Early news items contrasted this low rate with a 9% friendly fire casualty rate on the Kuwait-Iraq battlefield, but the percentage grew even higher as data became more complete; a later tally showed one out of every four combatants had been killed by friendly weapons. The official friendly fire casualty rate is 17% for Desert Storm: 613 battle casualties, 146 killed or died of wounds, 467 wounded. Of the 146 killed, thirty-five were fratricide, and of 467 wounded, 72 were caused by Coalition forces." (71)

There are many other Americans that did what Pat, and his brother Kevin sacrificed, putting their lives on hold, leaving their families behind, and putting themselves in harm's way. There were many that went before and came after. Just to name a few others, three conscientious objectors were awarded the highest military medal of the military, the medal of honor. Two fought in the Vietnam war and the third in WWII. Being conscientious objectors, they could have been excused from dawning a military uniform. The US allowed conscientious objectors during World War II to serve in noncombat roles; most worked as medics in the Army. This allowed them to serve without carrying a weapon. Because of their religious beliefs of not taking up arms against their fellow man, however, they agreed to serve as Medics. One that I accidentally stumbled across was a graduate of West Virginia University, Corporal Thomas Bennett. My one son Matthew, a division one athlete, was housed in a dormitory named after him. Another of the men, Desmond Doss, had his story translated to the silver screen in "Hacksaw Ridge," directed by Mel Gibson.

"The Medal of Honor is the nation's highest medal for valor in combat that can be awarded to members of the armed forces. The medal was first authorized in 1861 for Sailors and Marines, and the following year for Soldiers as well. Since then, more than 3,400 Medals of Honor have been awarded to members of all DoD services and the Coast Guard. Medals of Honor are awarded sparingly and are bestowed only to the bravest of the brave; and that courage must be well documented." (72)

Photo 19-Medal of Honor Medals

"During the waning days of December 1861, President Abraham Lincoln signed a Congressionally approved bill (Public Resolution 82) creating two hundred "medals of honor," specifically for enlisted Navy personnel. In July 1862, President Lincoln authorized 2,000 Army medals. Like the Navy medals, these were to be "presented, in the name of the Congress" to enlisted personnel who "distinguish themselves by their gallantry in action, and other soldier-like qualities" during the Civil War." (73)

Many a long night while on the 10:00 PM to 10:00 AM Watch, I would walk the abandoned halls of the Pentagon during my break. The hallways of the Pentagon are adorned with history from many wars gone by. I would frequent the Hall of Heroes where the names of the Medal of Honor awardees are etched upon displays of honor.

Photo 20-Medal of Honor recipient-Hall of Heroes

The room is dedicated for people to honor the brave service members who have received the Medal of Honor. I would scan the names and find the names of the three conscientious objectors who I now had a desire to learn more about them.

When doing so, I saw some had two stars next to their name, indicating that they were awarded the Medal of Honor more than once. I knew that they had to survive the first to be awarded the second, but I always wondered which did not survive the second. It was obvious that one of the recipients, George Armstrong Custard, did not. He led his men in one of U.S. history's most controversial battles, the Battle of the

Little Bighorn, on June 25, 1876. As a result of what was thought a heroic action, he was awarded the medal of honor. He distinguished himself in the American Civil War (1861–65) but later led his men to death in the battle of the little big horn. Standing before his name, I thought it would have been far more appropriate to award his men medals for their bravery and court martial Custard for his wrongful action of slaughtering his men needlessly.

When older veterans found out that I served at the Pentagon, they asked me if I would check on a medal that their commander told them he was nominating them for, but they never received, especially those who fought in WWII. Upon making a formal inquiry into the Army, I learned that many army companies were on the move so fast that their commander either did not have the time to write the award or did not properly submit it. A fire at St. Louis where many documents were destroyed could have housed the necessary paperwork to award the medals. Whatever the case, I was sadly told that without documentation, there was nothing they could do about awarding the medal.

Another bizarre story I came across is when a Lt Colonel who was responsible for reviewing inquiries from family members trying to locate decorations their loved ones never received. He told me that there was one inquiry he received that really stood out for him. After much research, he discovered that the soldier in question single handily took out 750 Japanese soldiers who were gunning down our soldiers. Not only did he do this heroic act, but he also did another similar one. The soldier was never decorated for his bravery. Hollywood made a movie about it. The Lt Colonel told me that not only should the soldier have received a medal, he should receive a congressional medal of honor.

Military members serving at the Pentagon, including myself, would frequently exercise on their break by running from the Pentagon, across the Arlington Memorial Bridge, and around the monuments. Every time I ran across the bridge, I could almost hear the drums in my mind that I heard as a little boy long ago when I was glued to the TV watching President Kennedy's funeral procession. When it was raining and I was on the night Watch, I would sometimes run the halls inside the Pentagon. The guards had no problem with me doing so if it was after 10:00 PM when most of the troops went home. Some of the four-star generals, however, remained in their offices working late at night when I ran past their offices. I asked them to join me. All were gracious and never complained about me. I was probably the only person to ever run inside all the halls of the Pentagon.

Another part of mine would be walking around the military monuments or visiting Arlington cemetery to bring myself to reality as to the importance of my continuing to volunteer for active duty. While walking solemnly past the Vietnam wall one day, I stopped to talk to one of the park Rangers about the many precious memorabilia that people so lovingly left in front of a name. They included medals, letters, flowers, etc. I asked the ranger how many items had been left at the wall and what was the most unusual item that was left. Years ago, he told me that there were approximately 50,000 items and they were kept in a warehouse and that someday they may put them on display someday. He then began to tell me a story about the most unusual

"The story goes that there were two best friends that lived in a small town and right next door to one another. They considered themselves brothers and each of their mothers were like their own. For story's sake, we will call them Johnny and Jimmy. One day, Jimmy came over to tell Johnny that he was enlisting in the Army and was going to Vietnam. Hearing this, Johnny quickly replied, "you are my brother Jimmy, where you go, I go!" Johnny enlisted with Jimmy, and both were sent off to serve in Vietnam. Jimmy was killed in action. At the end of the war, Johnny immediately went over to Jimmy's mother. He was broken hearted and sobbed in front of Jimmy's mother exclaiming that "I cannot believe that my brother is gone." Holding Johnny in her arms, she told him about a new Harley Davidson motorcycle that Jimmy bought before leaving for Vietnam. It was his intention to ride it about the countryside when he returned. Looking intently at Johnny, she said that she could not sell or give it away to just anyone so Johnny would have to take it. Johnny exclaimed that he could not because every time he rode it, it would sadly remind him of his brother Jimmy. After much urging from Jimmy's mother, Johnny took the motorcycle. After riding it for two weeks, he took it to the Vietnam wall where it is now in the warehouse."

Another heartfelt story about the Vietnam wall involved the youngest person to serve and be killed in Vietnam, Dan Bullock. "When he was just 14 years old, Bullock walked into a U.S. Marine Corps recruitment station. He falsified the date on his birth certificate to read December 21, 1949, so he could pass as 18 years old. Bullock enlisted in the U.S. Marine Corps on September 18, 1968. His family was unaware of his decision until he came home with papers in his hand. On June 7, 1969, Bullock was killed by small arms fire while on night watch. He was 15 years old and had been in-country for only one month. He was the youngest soldier to be killed in the Vietnam War." (74)

Least us not forget those heroes that served in other wars. Three close friends of mine, my cousin, and my uncles served in WWII. My one friend Franz told me the story that when he was leaving for boot camp on a train, he did not have enough money to buy food. When his wife came to see him off, she slipped him what little change she had to buy something. Franz was eventually deployed to the front in

Africa. Because of his being one of the larger soldiers, he always carried the biggest weapon which was quite heavy. One of his fellow comrades in arms insisted on relieving him for a while. When his platoon came to a mountain they had to scale, the Platoon leader ordered the soldier with the big gun to stay behind to cover them as they climbed the mountain. Upon reaching the top to join up with a larger force, they heard gunfire from below. A patrol went back to retrieve the one soldier only to find he was killed by enemy gunfire. Franz always lamented that he should not have let his friend carry the big gun.

Another unsung hero was Jerry, a highly decorated soldier including a Silver Star. Jerry was a member of a bombardier crew that flew many missions over enemy territory. On one mission, a bomb got stuck in the bomb door. Jerry had to climb down while holding on for dear life to chop the bomb loose. If he had not done it, the plane and their crew would have been blown up when trying to land.

A third unsung hero was my good friend Phil. Phil flew B17s during the war. Over one-third of B17 bombers were lost in combat. Some of them were destroyed by their own bombs when they skipped bombed targets "About one percent of bombs dropped were hitting their targets. Clearly a better way had to be found such as skipping the bombs across the water. Approaching the target at 200 mph, aircraft released bombs at two hundred feet or lower, about three hundred yards from the hulk. The bombs would skip across the water into the side of the ship." (75) Phil told me that that many a time, one of the bombs would deflect off the water back up into the belly of a plane, demolishing the aircraft and killing the crew.

CHAPTER 13

Wearing Several Hats

During one of my long night Watches, a Colonel came by my NMCC duty station. He informed me that he was also called to active duty and was serving in Secretary Rumsfeld's Executive Support Center and he was getting little sleep because they were short staffed. After expressing my concerns, he asked me if I could provide any time. I pointed out that I am serving fourteen-hour watches with little time to spare. "Besides, you need to be a full bird Colonel to serve in the Rumsfeld's Executive Center." I am only a Major. The Colonel was quick to reply. "No problem, I will get you assigned. I merely shrugged my shoulders.

A day later, the Colonel came back and said the executive support center put me on the roster as an additional duty. I could start the first day I was off duty in the NMCC.

At that time, the Executive Support center (ESC) was aligned with the Under Secretary of Defense for policy. "The mission of the Office of the Under Secretary of Defense for Policy is to consistently provide responsive, forward-thinking, and insightful policy advice and support to the Secretary of Defense, and the Department of Defense, in alignment with national security objectives." (76)

Most of our duties involved fielding questions that came in for the Secretary of Defense. We would set up the SCIF (Sensitive compartmented information facility) for the

Office of the Secretary of Defense. A sensitive compartmented information facility (SCIF/skɪf/), in United States military, national security/national defense and intelligence parlance, is an enclosed area within a building that is used to process sensitive compartmented information (SCI) types of classified information. SCIFs can be either permanent or temporary and can be set up in official government buildings (such as the Situation Room in the White House), onboard ships, in private residences of officials, or in hotel rooms and other places of necessity for officials when traveling" (77)

"Because of the operational security (OPSEC) risk they pose, personal cell phones, smart watches, computer flash drives (aka, "thumb drives"), or any other sort of personal electronic device (PED), cameras (analog or digital) other than those that are U.S. Government property and which are used only under strict guidelines, and/or any other sort of recording or transmitting devices (analog or digital) are expressly prohibited in SCIFs." (78)

"Similarly, the President has a room in the west wing of the white house that he uses for directing operations of the military, called the White House Situation room.

Photo 21-President's Situation room in White House

The Situation Room is an intelligence management complex on the ground floor of the West Wing of the White House. While the name suggests it is a single room, it is in fact a 5,000 square feet operations suite consisting of a duty watch station and three secure conference rooms. It is run by about 130 National Security Council staff for the use of the president of the United States, chief of staff, national security advisor, homeland security advisor, and other senior advisors for monitoring and dealing with crises, as well as conducting secure communications with outside (often overseas) persons. The Situation Room has secure, advanced communications equipment for the president to maintain command and control of U.S. forces around the world." (79)

Our duties in the ESC also included reviewing top secret faxes that came in and forwarding them to the pertinent offices, including the White House. One lady that came into our office to pick up the faxes for her office was rude. At times, she ripped them out of the hands of one of the officers.

When I was on duty, we received a phone call from an individual that claimed he was Henry Kissinger. The young enlisted that took the call was not sure it was him.

Kiddingly, I mimicked how Henry Kissinger would talk and the enlisted said that did sound like him. It turned out that Mr. Kissinger simply wanted to change the date of a luncheon appointment.

Another time was when an Under Secretary of Defense was giving his family a tour of the Pentagon and asked me if I had the code to open his office. The reason he did not have it is because most higher-ranking secretaries rely on their staff to open the office. I could see he was disappointed that he could not gain access to his office. To not disappoint him, I asked if he would like to see the offices used by the Secretary of Defense. For the undersecretary, it was not that exciting because he was in that office daily. It was, however, a treat for his family.

We had access to the office of the secretary of defense and would have to go in on occasion if called upon. The office had a huge conference room and a separate little room in case the secretary wanted some privacy. The cabinet members could loan artifacts or art from the Smithsonian. Rumsfeld had General Pershing's huge oak desk. He only used it for a conversation piece. The desk sat unused in his office with a bronze buffalo stature on its center. Instead, he used a podium. He wanted to work standing and free to move around the room. When he finished working at the end of the day, his staff would take photographs of the papers on the desk and put them back exactly as he left them when he returned to the office.

To retain my serving in the Executive Support Center, its director wrote the following memorandum to retain me.

"The Increased operation tempos generated by the Global War on Terrorism and Homeland Security continues to generate a host of policy issues that must receive expert attention in an efficient and timely manner. Major Drozd has

played a key role in helping to alleviate this workload and has become a valued member of our team by working key organizational and policy issues in both the Executive Support Center and the National Military Command Center. He is vital to OSD's mission of waging the war on terrorism and enhancing homeland security.

Major Drozd has always stood ready to serve OSD with unconditional dedication and commitment. He has made himself available on a moment's notice and has never refused whatever may be asked of him. We will require his skills and expertise for a long time to come and would therefore appreciate everything you can do to solidify his retention"-Robert Coombs, Director Executive Support Center, Office of the Secretary of Defense

OFFICE OF THE ASSISTANT SECRETARY OF DEFENSE
1200 DEFENSE PENTAGON
WASHINGTON, DC 20301-1200

HEALTH AFFAIRS

September 19, 2002

MEMORANDUM FOR HQ ARPC/SGE

SUBJECT: Retention of Major Matthew J. Drozd

The increased operational tempo generated by the Global War on Terrorism and Homeland Security continues to generate a host of policy issues that must receive expert attention in an efficient and timely manner.

Major Drozd has played a key role in helping to alleviate this workload and has become a valued member of our team by working key operational and policy issues in both the Executive Support Center and the National Military Command Center. He is vital to OSD's mission of waging the war on terrorism and enhancing homeland security. He brings to our organization extensive expertise as a program director in the Office of the Assistant Secretary of Defense for Health Affairs and as a former member of the J-4/Health Services Support on the Joint Staff. He possesses critical security clearances and expertise that are crucial to carrying out our day-to-day operations.

Major Drozd has always stood ready to serve OSD with unconditional dedication and commitment. He has made himself available on a moment's notice and has never refused whatever may be asked of him. We will require his skills and expertise for a long time to come and would therefore appreciate everything that you can do to solidify his retention.

Thank you for your consideration.

Robert W. Coombs, Jr.
Director, Executive Support Center
Office of the Secretary of Defense

While on duty in the SECDEF's Executive Support Center, an invitation came in from the Mayor's office of New York, Mayor Michael Bloomberg. The Mayor was holding a training exercise to prepare New York for any future terrorist attacks that may occur and invited the Department of Defense to send a representative. The SECDEF's office tasked me to attend. "911: Fixing the Lifeline for the City That Never Sleeps. Mayor Bloomberg Plans to Integrate New York City's Antiquated Emergency Systems; Implementation Date Still Unknown" (80)

Upon reaching New York City, I set my GPS for the address given to us. It was under the Brooklyn bridge. Upon walking in, I was surprised to see Mayor Michael Bloomberg in the middle of administrators from his office giving a mock news conference. After a welcome from the Mayor and an explanation on what was to transpire, the training exercise commenced. I was surprised to see that most of it centered around how to respond to the press more than the issues related to modifying their 911 response system.

As soon as a break was called, I approached the mayor to introduce myself as a representative of the Secretary of Defense. The mayor was most gracious. He told a humorous story and why he did not live in the Mayor's mansion. He said that he chose not to live in the mansion provided at no cost to the mayors of New York. Instead, he chose to live in a high-rise apartment building that he owned. He further joked about whether he needed bullet proof glass following 911. He called someone that was once not fond of him and asked if they still felt the same. Because they did not, he said that he did not need bullet proof glass.

Photo 22-New York Mayor's Home

"Ever since Gracie Mansion became the official residence for New York mayors, in 1942, very few of the ten eligible tenants have turned up their noses at the chance to live, rent free, in the stately riverside home. Well, one, to be precise— Michael R. Bloomberg. He was keen to tell the future mayors that they should sleep somewhere else, on their own dimes, just as all city employees do, and as he has done himself since he took office in 2002. Of course, he is the only one of the past ten mayors who could hang his baseball cap anywhere in 12,500 square feet of town house right down the street from Central

Park, in a walled estate in Bermuda or in a grand residence in London. Not that he does not appreciate the place." (81)

On another weekend while serving in the Executive Support Center of the SECDEF, I received a call from a new Chief of Staff for the Chairman. He was a Rear Admiral. He summoned me to the Chairman's office to discuss an action they were about to perform. Upon reporting to his office, he told me that we were sending aircraft to the Middle East.

I knew that we had to procure air passages when flying military aircraft over another country. "By international law, a state has complete and exclusive sovereignty over the airspace above its territory", which corresponds with the maritime definition of territorial waters as being 12 nautical miles (22.2 km) out from a nation's coastline." (82) I advised the admiral that there were some airspace issues that could cause us problems and asked if I could make a phone call before he authorized the action. He retorted that he had both the Chairman's and SECDEF's approval. He secured their approval over a phone call. After I insisted to phone the Undersecretary of defense for policy, the admiral acquiesced. The undersecretary agreed with me and said that he would take care of it. After waiting for fifteen minutes, I returned to the Chairman's office where the admiral was waiting for me. He said that the action was somehow stopped and directed me to sit at the conference table while he summoned some of our legal people. Looking intently at me, he quietly said that we need to rework the action. If we had gone through with the initial plan, it would have caused an international incident.

While I was still assigned to the Joint Chiefs of Staff, I was also supporting Rumsfeld's Executive Support Center. Officers who once served alongside me in the medical readiness division of the Joint Staff and left to support Health and Human Services became shorthanded. To provide them with some support, I took an additional assignment to join them. I was now serving additional duties in three different areas.

Maj Matt Drozd,USAF
With appreciation of your service to the Nation

Chairman of the Joint Chiefs of Staff

Military members who leave the Joint Staff for another assignment receive a letter from the Chairman, take a photograph with them. Because the first Chairman I served under left not long after I joined the Joint Chief of Staff, I did not have the opportunity to take one with him. I not only took one with General Myers, but he sent me a letter of gratitude for my service. With my status as an IMA reservist and volunteering to go on active duty, I was afforded the opportunity to serve in more than one area as an additional duty. I also received one of his military coins which is minted for high-ranking officers.

"I'd like to express my appreciation for your great work. You contributed immeasurably to the success of the Joint Staff during a critical period in the Nation's history. You coordinated and directed crucial joint, Service, and interagency support actions for a myriad of contingency, disaster relief, and humanitarian assistance operations in support of national security interests around the globe. As a result of your efforts, the Chiefs and I were better able to carry out our responsibilities of providing military advice to the President and the Secretary of Defense-Richard B. Myers, Chairman of the Joint Chiefs of Staff"

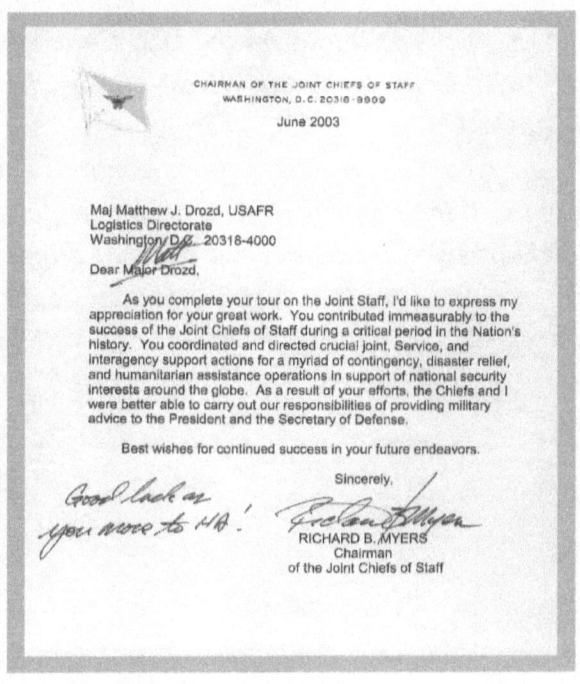

I also received a defense Meritorious Service Medal for helping to save injured sailors aboard the USS Cole and volunteering to deploy to an alternate site to assure that our government would go on (continuity of operation) if Washington was wiped off the face of the earth as the result of another terrorist attack. The Medal Read:

"Major Matthew J. Drozd distinguished himself by exceptionally meritorious service while serving as Action Officer, Health Service Support Divion, Logistics Directorate, Joint Staff. Working a myriad of medical and logistics issues, his accomplishments include providing critical technical support as a member of several National Military Command Center Crisis Action Teams. He was instrumental in providing critical and timely coordination for immediate medical care and evacuation of sailors injured during the terrorist attack on the USS Cole, which resulted in the saving of numerous lives. Major Drozd further distinguished himself by volunteering for a crisis action team that deployed to an alternate command site from the Pentagon. While on-site, the exemplary performance of Major Drozd and his team ensured Joint Staff continuity of operations and provided support for key leaders from the Office of the Secretary of Defense." – Richard Meyers, Former Chairman of the Joint Chiefs of Staff

Citation
TO ACCOMPANY THE AWARD OF THE
Defense Meritorious Service Medal
TO

MATTHEW J. DROZD

Major Matthew J. Drozd, United States Air Force Reserve, distinguished himself by exceptionally meritorious service while serving as Action Officer, Health Service Support Division, Logistics Directorate, the Joint Staff, from September 1999 to June 2002. Major Drozd's tireless efforts and exceptional leadership skills proved invaluable to the Logistic Directorate, while serving as an Individual Mobilization Augmentee assigned to the Health Service Support Division. Working a myriad of medical and logistics issues, his accomplishments include providing critical technical support as a member of several National Military Command Center Crisis Action Teams. He provided readiness guidance to the supporting and supported combatant commands during Operations ENDURING FREEDOM and NOBLE EAGLE. He was instrumental in providing critical and timely coordination for immediate medical care and evacuation of sailors injured during the terrorist attack on the USS Cole, which resulted in the saving of numerous lives. Major Drozd further distinguished himself by volunteering for a crisis action team that deployed to an alternate command site from the Pentagon. While on-site, the exemplary performance of Major Drozd and his team ensured Joint Staff continuity of operations and provided support for key leaders from the Office of the Secretary of Defense. The singularly distinctive accomplishments of Major Drozd reflect great credit upon himself, the United States Air Force Reserve, and the Joint Staff.

Years later I had the opportunity to meet up and take another photo with General Myers at an international conference, U.S Global Impact Forum, in Washington DC. The Forum brings together distinguished leaders including former Cabinet officials, members of Congress, and every living Secretary of State. The National Security Advisory Council also includes more than two hundred retired three- and four-star generals and admirals.

"Following the terrorist attacks of 9/11, letters laced with anthrax began appearing in the U.S. mail, causing great fear and anxiety throughout government offices in Washington DC. It is critical to monitor medical and health issues, both physical and mental, when it comes to terroristic threats. Unfortunately, the military focused more so on the physical adversity caused by terrorist attacks.

According to the National Library of Medicine, "the mental effects of Terrorism is intended to provoke collective fear and uncertainty. This fear can spread rapidly, enhancing the psychological effects of terrorism, and is not limited to those experiencing the event. Included are family members of victims and people who view broadcast images. Psychological suffering is usually more prevalent than the physical injuries from a terrorism event. Understanding these psychological consequences is critical to the nation's efforts to develop intervention.

The effect of traumatic events on human functioning has been a subject of study for many years. An abundance of research has examined traumatic events ranging from individual events such as motor vehicle crashes and sexual assaults to community-wide events such as natural disasters, commercial airplane crashes, and community violence, as well as global events such as war." (83)

As a result of the anthrax attacks, five Americans were killed and seventeen were sickened in what became the worst biological attacks in U.S. history. The ensuing investigation by the FBI and its partners—code-named "Amerithrax"—has been one of the largest and most complex in the history of law enforcement. The Amerithrax Task Force—which consisted of 25 to 30 full-time investigators from the FBI, the U.S. Postal Inspection Service, and other law enforcement agencies, as well as federal prosecutors from the District of Columbia and the Justice Department's Counterterrorism Section—expended hundreds of thousands of investigators work hours on this case. Their efforts involved more than 10,000 witness interviews on six different continents, the execution of eighty searches, and the recovery of more than 6,000 items of potential evidence during the investigation." (84)

In response to the attacks, Deputy Secretary of Defense Paul Wolfowitz established the Pentagon Force Protection Agency, which assumed the role of providing basic law enforcement and security for the Pentagon." (85)

Upon checking the stockpiles of anthrax vaccine, we discovered that we only had enough vaccine to protect critical medical people and medical responders. In addition, we had to reserve enough vaccine to protect those troops that we deployed into high-risk areas.

"Following the terrorist attacks of September 11, anthrax and the anthrax vaccine became national concerns. During the 1991 Gulf War, concerns that Iraq had prepared anthrax spores for use as a biological weapon motivated the U.S. military to administer anthrax vaccine to an estimated 150,000 service members. After the war, admission by Iraq that it had indeed produced weapons containing anthrax spores confirmed fears of the potential use of anthrax as a biological weapon. Secretary of Defense William Cohen announced a plan to vaccinate all U.S. service members. The universal vaccination plan was to be phased in gradually, starting with service members scheduled for deployment to areas considered to be "high risk. As more service members received the vaccines, however, some raised concerns about the safety and the efficacy of the vaccine." (86)

CHAPTER 14

Assignment State Department

After a brief stint in Health Affairs, I noticed that there was a small group of military personnel serving at the State Department, the Pol Mil Bureau. There are a select group of uniformed military officers that serve in the POL Mil Bureau, approximately fifty plus or minus. The Bureau of the Political-Military Affairs (PM) builds enduring security partnerships to advance U.S. national security objectives. "The PM is the Department of State's principal link to the Department of Defense. The PM Bureau provides policy direction in the areas of international security, security assistance, military operations, defense strategy and plans, and defense trade." (87)

As I always wanted to see the inner workings of the State Department, I applied for an IMA position in the Pol Mil Bureau. Fortunately, the officer, Colonel Chuck Wilson, felt he could use me in his Political Military Action Team (PMAT). He was the officer in charge of political-military affairs, national security policy, defense acquisition, and business development. Prior to joining the PolMil Bureau, he commanded four different military units and performed operational testing of the prototype S1034 pressure suit and flew the first operational mission of the Lockheed U-2S spy plane. He is a rated US Air Force command pilot with over 3,800 flight hours. (88)

Colonel Wilson was a visionary and showed great insight by creating the PMAT. The PMAT, like the NMCC gathered information around the globe and built it into a brief to be distributed to other departments throughout the State Department.

During and following 9/11, the PMAT briefs proved to be of great value in combatting the war on terrorism. Colonel Wilson's duties at the PMAT were to interface with the Department of Defense. Many a day he would find himself in high level meetings at the Pentagon and briefing the Under Secretary of State on issues that can impact our relations with countries across the globe.

"The PMAT maintains a 24/7 watch center and is staffed by personnel with extensive diplomatic and military expertise to provide various functions, to include:

- Coordinating military operations with the National Joint Operations and Intelligence Center, geographic combatant command centers, and the State Department Operations Center.
- Providing diplomatic information to military command centers and to Foreign Policy Advisors.
- Publishing the twice-daily Political-Military Situation Report
- Processing diplomatic aircraft and ship clearance applications or amendments, and handling related interagency inquiries
- Serving as the initial point of contact for unresolved radiological alarms for the Nuclear Trafficking Response Group (NTRG).
- Serving as the PM Bureau Representative to State Department task forces." (89)

While serving in the PMAT, I had the opportunity to attend the indoctrination and training school for Foreign Service Officers.

Included in the class were briefings by former ambassadors and leaders of agencies like the Jewish Federation. One of the former Ambassadors gave an interesting lecture on how the Islamic movement Wahhabi, of which some members subscribe to using terroristic acts to preserve what they believe to be the teachings of their religion, Wahhabism. "Wahhābism is prevalent in Saudi Arabia and Qatar and was founded by a Muḥammad ibn ʿAbd al-Wahhāb and started in the 18ᵗʰ century. It was later adopted in w1774 by the Saudi family before they discovered the vast oil reserves." "Wahhabism advocates a purification of Islam, rejects Islamic theology and philosophy developed after the death of the Prophet Muhammad, and calls for strict adherence to the letter of the Koran. It eschews "innovations," including practices viewed as polytheistic, such as the worship of saints, mysticism, and decoration of graves. It prohibits dancing and music." (90)

"Fifteen of the 19 September 11 hijackers were from Saudi Arabia, and all of them are believed to have been Wahhabis. In the United States, Wahhabism has been equated with radicalism and terrorism in some newspaper articles, books, and public discourse. For instance, in his 2002 book, *The Two Faces of Islam*, journalist Stephen Schwartz wrote that, "Wahhabism exalts and promotes death in every element of its existence: the suicide of its adherents, mass murder as a weapon against civilization, and above all the suffocation of the mercy embodied in Islam. However, not all experts agree that "Wahhabism" and "Salafism" are inherently synonymous with violence, terrorism, or radicalism. For example, FBI counterterrorism officials told us that Wahhabism is not inherently violent or terroristic but

136

has been manipulated for violent or terroristic ends. In addition, representatives from the Commission noted that many Wahhabis/Salafis throughout the world are doctrinally rigid, but peaceful." (91)

Another speaker put forth an interesting scenario. He said that when you were a child, your mother may have said that "if you did not eat your porridge, the boogie man was going to get you." In the middle east today, the mother of a mid-eastern child might say, "if you do not eat your dinner, the Crusaders are going to get you!" That is because the Crusaders were trying to force their religion on people of the Middle East who in turn may envision the Crusaders as what we would perceive today as terrorists.

From the PMAT, I was transferred over to the Consequence Management (CM) section of the Political Military Bureau. "The Foreign Consequence Management Program provides a critical element in a layered defense in depth against WMD Terrorism. The WMD Terrorism Office is responsible for the security policy framework that integrates foreign consequence management activities of the U.S. Government into a strategic architecture for planning and response. In this capacity, the office maintains the following portfolios: Foreign Consequence Management (FCM) covers the U.S. efforts to assist partner nations in their preparation to recover and mitigate casualties from a terrorist attack. FCM strengthens political and operational capability of international partners to deter, detect, defeat, and respond to terrorists and their facilitators. Upon request by the host nation, FCM will lead an interagency team to conduct a survey and an assessment of CM response capabilities. They also provide recommendations to improve response capacity, as well as how to integrate international assistance." (92)

One of the first actions I undertook was to interpret a message from a foreign ship steaming towards a port that housed one of our embassies and a large population of people. The message we received was not very legible, it was seriously broken and written in a foreign language unfamiliar to us in Consequence Management. I thought that there should be no problem for one of our language experts to translate the message. In about an hour or two, the word came back from our people that it would take two to three days for them to interpret the message. Not believing what I heard, I took it upon myself to piece the message together and used a language conversion site to translate it.

The message was from a ship asking permission to drop a body off that was infected with a deadly virus. I could not believe what I heard. I instructed our people to order the ship captain that he was not permitted to drop the body off and to turn his ship out to sea immediately. I then said that if he did not comply, we would have to take forceful messages.

This August, Vaccine Nation, the organizer of the World Vaccine Congress, released its list of the 10 most important infections with no vaccine: (93)

- Chagas disease (American trypanosomiasis)
- Chikungunya
- Dengue
- Cytomegalovirus
- HIV/AIDS
- Hookworm infection
- Leishmaniasis
- Malaria
- Respiratory Syncytial Virus
- Schistosomiasis

The Director of Consequence management at the State Department wrote to me commending me for my service.

CHAPTER 15

IRAQ War

While the Afghan war waged on, the dictator of Iraq Hussein, kept rearing his ugly head. "Because Iraq had a history of using chemical weapons, and giving up its weapons of mass destruction was a requirement of the U.N. Security Council resolutions, Iraq initially promised to cooperate with the U.N. Special Commission on Iraq (UNSCOM). The United Nations expected that disarmament would proceed smoothly and wrap up quickly. Instead, inspectors said that Iraq undermined and circumvented inspections from the beginning and continued to develop weapons of mass destruction. The inspectors were withdrawn in 1998.

Among other things, U.N. inspectors located hundreds of tons of chemical weapons agents and thousands more tons of the chemicals used to make them; a major biological weapons production facility; machines for separating out radioactive isotopes that could be used to fuel a nuclear bomb; and dozens of missiles, launching pads, and missile warheads for both conventional and chemical munitions. Inspectors were stunned by the volume of information and material they found, and surprised that Iraq's weapons programs were much more advanced than they had expected." (94)

On Feb. 5, 2003, U.S. Secretary of State Colin Powell sat in front of members of the U.N. Security

Council. He had been a staunch critic of U.S. intervention against Iraq's authoritarian leader, Saddam Hussein. But with the world watching, Powell made a case for war.

"My colleagues, every statement I make today is backed up by sources — solid sources," he said. "These are not assertions. What we're giving you are facts and conclusions based on solid intelligence."

Powell used information that intelligence officials assured him was credible. There were reconnaissance photos, elaborate maps, and charts, and even taped phone conversations between senior members of Iraq's military.

"Saddam Hussein has chemical weapons," Powell said. "Saddam Hussein has used such weapons. And Saddam Hussein has no compunction about using them again, against his neighbors, and against his own people."

Powell repeatedly used one phrase during his hour-long speech: "weapons of mass destruction." He said those words a total of seventeen times. It was the phrase the Bush administration kept publicly using to help justify invading Iraq." (95)

In anticipation of reprisals on embassies overseas should the president order an attack on Iraq, the Pol Mil Bureau decided to deploy a team to help implement plans to protect our embassies in case there were reprisals against them. Upon entering the conference room of the Pol Mil Bureau, I found a group of our people reviewing plans and a map. I was told that I was going to be deployed to Kuwait in two days and should go home to say goodbye to my family. I was handed a check list that is normally given to military members when they are deployed and told to contact the State Department's travel agency to make travel arrangements. A standout on the check list was to make certain that my WILL was up to date.

My first phone call was to my family to tell them I was coming home to say goodbye. For security reasons, I did not tell them where I was being deployed. My second call was to the travel agency. The travel people informed me that because of the distance to Kuwait, I was eligible fly Business Class which would cost over $3,000 more than economy   Even though no one would have known, I instructed the travel agent to save taxpayer money by booking me an economy fair. While driving to Pittsburgh to say goodbye, I was dictating my Will on a recording when I was pulled over by a State Trooper. He asked why I was going so slow. After explaining I was going home to tell my family goodbye because I was being deployed overseas. Showing him my orders, he bade me good luck and sent me on my way.

After spending a day with my children, I returned to Washington to pack my bags and get ready to board the airplane. The airline was Lufthansa and flying economy was great. Upon landing in Kuwait, I was met by other team members who took me straight to the Embassy. After spending the remainder of the day evaluating their security, I checked into the hotel. The hotel was five-star rated and had all the services we needed without leaving the hotel. With the next day being a holiday, it gave me the opportunity to take a tour of the city. Before getting into our vehicles, we had to check under the car and hood to make certain a terrorist did not wire our vehicles with a bomb.

As I drove around Kuwait, I noticed that their houses were comparable to our large mansions and two of the ones side by side were the same. I was told that a Kuwait man can have more than one wife, but they must give each the same lifestyle. "Kuwait has the highest rate of polygamy amongst the Gulf Arab states, along with over a quarter of them marrying their cousins, a new study has shown. The study revealed that Kuwait topped the rate of polygamy with 8.13 percent, followed by Qatar with a rate of 7.88 percent and Bahrain at 5.16 percent." (96)

While we waited for President Bush's decision on invading Iraq, the president gave a follow-on speech to the case Colin Powell made before the UN for war against Iraq. President Bush "argued that the vulnerability of the United States following the September 11 attacks of 2001, combined with Iraq's alleged continued possession and manufacture of weapons of mass destruction (an accusation that was later proved erroneous) and its support for terrorist groups renewed the priority on Iraq. UN Security Council Resolution 1441, passed on November 8, 2002, demanded that Iraq readmit inspectors and that it comply with all previous resolutions. Iraq appeared to comply with the resolution, but in early 2003 President Bush and British Prime Minister Tony Blair declared that Iraq was actually continuing to hinder UN inspections and that it still retained proscribed weapons. Other world leaders, such as French Pres. Jacques Chirac and German Chancellor Gerhard Schröder, citing what they believed to be increased Iraqi cooperation, sought to extend inspections and give Iraq more time to comply with them. However, on March 17, seeking no further UN resolutions and deeming further diplomatic efforts by the Security Council futile, Bush declared an end to diplomacy and issued an ultimatum to Saddam, giving the Iraqi president 48 hours to leave Iraq. The leaders of France, Germany, Russia, and other countries objected to this buildup toward war.

"When Saddam refused to leave Iraq, U.S. and allied forces launched an attack on the morning of March 20; it began when U.S. aircraft dropped several precision-guided bombs on a bunker complex in which the Iraqi president was

142

believed to be meeting with senior staff. This was followed by a series of air strikes directed against government and military installations, and within days U.S. forces had invaded Iraq from Kuwait. Despite fears that Iraqi forces would engage in a scorched-earth policy—destroying bridges and dams and setting fire to Iraq's southern oil wells, little damage was done by retreating Iraqi forces; in fact, large numbers of Iraqi troops simply chose not to resist the advance of coalition forces. In southern Iraq the greatest resistance to U.S. forces as they advanced northward was from irregular groups of Baath Party supporters, known as Saddam's Fedayeen. British forces which deployed around the southern city of Basra faced resistance from paramilitary and irregular fighters." (97)

"In central Iraq, units of the Republican Guard—a heavily armed paramilitary group connected with the ruling party—were deployed to defend the capital of Baghdad. As U.S. Army and Marine forces advanced northwestward up the Tigris-Euphrates river valley, they bypassed many populated areas where Fedayeen resistance was strongest and were slowed only on March 25 when inclement weather and an extended supply line briefly forced them to halt their advance within 60 miles (95 km) of Baghdad. During the pause, U.S. aircraft inflicted heavy damage on Republican Guard units around the capital. U.S. forces resumed their advance within a week, and on April 4 they took control of Baghdad's international airport. Iraqi resistance, though at times vigorous, was highly disorganized, and over the next several days, army and Marine Corps units staged raids into the heart of the city. On April 9 resistance in Baghdad collapsed, and U.S. soldiers took control of the city." (98)

Kuwait was used as the staging area for our military. "Even without the use of Saudi Arabia's vast desert expanses to launch a ground invasion of Iraq, the U.S.

143

military would have plenty of room to operate from tiny Kuwait and elsewhere, defense experts say.

There already are more than 12,000 U.S. forces in Kuwait - mostly Army soldiers - training in desert warfare. At least another 14,000 are in other Persian Gulf nations, and the Navy has an aircraft carrier, the USS Lincoln, in the northern Persian Gulf with more than 5,500 sailors and dozens of warplanes aboard." (99)

Regarding medical personnel and their patients, they are to be treated differently than combatants according to the Geneva Convention. "International humanitarian law provides specific rules to safeguard combatants, or members of the armed forces, who are wounded, sick or shipwrecked, prisoners of war, and civilians, as well as medical personnel, military chaplains, and civilian support workers of the military.

"Article 37 of the Geneva convention constitutes that if religious, medical, and hospital personnel fall into the hands of the enemy, they must be respected and protected; they may continue to perform their duties as long as necessary for the care of the wounded and sick. When they are performing those functions, the occupying power cannot compel these personnel to give priority to the treatment of any person, except on medical grounds. The personnel cannot be compelled to conduct tasks that are not compatible with their humanitarian mission.

Photo 23-Army Combat Field Support Hospital

Article 37 would apply to an Army Combat support hospital (CSH), field hospital that were deployed to Iraq. The end state once all field hospital units are deployed forward is to provide HSS and hospitalization with a 240-bed hospital; the hospital center provides medical mission command with up to two field hospitals (32-bed), one medical detachment surgical (24-bed), two medical detachment intensive care units (32-bed), and one medical detachment intensive care ward (60-bed). Total medical personnel to support an Army field hospital is approximately five hundred." In any war, the field hospitals of most countries are configured in the same way." (100)

As there have been no exact figures of casualties since the Iraq occupation began, one can only wonder how many field hospitals would be needed based upon the estimate casualties over the years to now. "No one knows with certainty how many people have been killed and wounded in Iraq since the 2003 United States invasion. However, we know that between 186,694 to 210,038 Iraqi civilians have died and a total of 280,771 to 315,190 have died from direct war related violence caused by the U.S., its allies, the Iraqi military and police, and opposition forces from the time of the invasion through March 2023. The violent deaths of Iraqi civilians have occurred through aerial bombing, shelling, gunshots, suicide attacks, and fires started by bombing. Many civilians have also been injured." (101)

A commander of an army field hospital, a full bird colonel) told me about what she experienced when she was to move her hospital from the Kuwait staging area into Iraq. Under her command were approximately five hundred medical personnel. When she asked the staging people for their armed security escort, they informed her they had none available at the time. Looking intently at the staging people, she put them on notice. "I am not moving these people forward until everyone of my people are armed with an M16. Once the staging people complied with her request, she gave the order to move forward. The Colonel and her people would have been covered by Geneva Convention which states, "Medical personnel have the right to bear arms and may, in case of need, use them in their own defense or in that of the wounded and sick in their charge." (102)

As the field hospital moved forward towards Baghdad, the Colonel and her people experienced a lot of shock and awe, bombs exploding in a distance. Many Iraqi soldiers had surrendered their weapons and sat desponded along the road. She noted that the soldiers were not only an eerie site, but the distant bombs gave them much concern.

"The conflict in Iraq consisted of two phases. The first of these was a brief, conventionally fought war in March–April 2003, in which a combined force of troops from the United States and Great Britain (and smaller contingents from several other countries) invaded Iraq and rapidly defeated Iraqi military and paramilitary forces. It was followed by a longer second phase in which a U.S.-led occupation of Iraq was opposed by an insurgency. After violence began to decline in 2007, the United States gradually reduced its military presence in Iraq, formally completing its withdrawal in December 2011. American military casualties in the conflict included some 4,500 service members killed and some 32,000 wounded." (103)

Looking back, it was the second time that I came extremely close to being included as one of those casualties. We missed the explosion of a scud missile that hit the same marketplace where we ate lunch several days before, killing about fifty people. "Baghdad was rocked Friday by thunderous explosions in some of the most powerful bombardments of the Iraqi capital since the war began. An explosion at a Baghdad market killed about fifty people Friday, many of them women and children, according to medical officials in the city and news reports. Meanwhile, at about 1:30 Saturday morning, an enormous explosion rocked the Kuwaiti capital as a missile struck a popular shopping mall along the waterfront. There were conflicting reports as to whether it was an Iraqi or an American missile. The Associated Press reported that it was a Silkworm missile fired from southern Iraq, but Kuwaiti military officers said it was an American cruise missile that mistakenly struck (104)

Regardless of the risk that hung over our heads, we went about performing our duties. Besides reviewing emergency operational plans of the embassy, we wanted to make certain that the host country was prepared to respond to outside threats and could accommodate any medical or security needs of our people. This would include hospital and military support. To ascertain the medical capabilities of Kuwait, we met with administrators of hospitals.

When I asked the administrator of one hospital if he sent all his patient's home that were capable or close to being discharged. He replied that the Kuwait people like to stay in the hospital as long as possible. I then asked what he was going to do if Kuwait got hit with a chemical or biological weapon and hundreds showed up at the front door of his hospital. He immediately ordered his staff to make certain that my question was turned into a viable solution and ordered the discharge of as many patients as possible.

Although there were no pending threats against our embassy in Kuwait, there were numerous demonstrations across the globe against Kuwait's support of the United States' invasion of Iraq. As a result of the demonstrations, "Kuwait mounted a defense against signs of growing regional anger over the Gulf nation's unapologetic support for the U.S.-led war against Iraq. On Tuesday, the government was waiting for a response to a formal complaint filed a day earlier against Libya after protesters stormed the Kuwaiti embassy in Tripoli and raised the Iraqi flag on the roof. Elsewhere, the Kuwaiti embassy in Cairo received bomb threats on Monday and 12,000 Egyptian students mounted a protest outside the embassy against the war." (105

When this started happening, we received word that some of us were going to be deployed to another embassy. It was going to be one where there were many demonstrations in progress. Instead, we were sent to Bahrain in anticipation that a demonstration may occur. I thought they may have picked Bahrain because we had a large naval fleet in Bahrain and that may be where demonstrators may put our U.S. embassy at significant risk.

"U.S. Naval Forces Central Command (NAVCENT): NAVCENT has its headquarters in Manama, Bahrain, the home of the U.S. Fifth Fleet. U.S. Naval Forces Central Command is responsible for approximately 2.5 million square miles of area including the Arabian Gulf, Gulf of Oman, North Arabian Sea, Gulf of Aden, and the Red Sea. The U.S. Naval Forces Central Command's mission is to conduct maritime security operations, theater security cooperation efforts, and strengthen partner nations' maritime capabilities to promote security and stability in the U.S. 5th Fleet area of international waters, which encompass some of the world's most important shipping lanes." (106)

Like our embassy in Kuwait City, we were to interact with the Diplomatic Security Service section to make certain that their defense and contingency plans were sufficient and current. "Diplomatic Security Service (DSS) special agents and security professionals are assigned to regional security offices in every U.S. embassy and in most U.S. consulates around the world. The regional security office (RSO) manages a range of physical, technical, cyber, and personnel security programs to reduce threats to U.S. embassies and consulates.

RSOs lead and manage a worldwide force of tens of thousands of local guards — usually citizens of the host nation — who serve as the first line of defense against potential threats and secure the exterior of U.S. embassies and consulates. Under the direction of regional security officers, U.S. Marine Security Guards (MSGs), help secure U.S. embassies and consulates. MSGs protect classified information and equipment, secure diplomatic facilities overseas, and help evacuate U.S. citizens during times of crisis.

These guards patrol the grounds; inspect vehicles, visitors, and packages; and respond to alarms and requests for assistance. Their main mission is to reduce threats to U.S. embassies, consulates, and State Department personnel." (107)

CHAPTER 16

Hostages

We were housed at a local hotel during our stay in Bahrain. Every morning, we did the same drill of checking all areas of our vehicles for explosive devices before getting into them. Our security forces cautioned us not to go out at night and especially not go into the marketplace (known as the SHUK) at any time. To protect ourselves, we ate in the hotel restaurant. I made a mistake.

After a long day at the embassy, I returned too late to get anything to eat in the hotel. Hungry as I was, I made the mistake of driving late in the evening to a local restaurant. Being a hot and humid night, I ate my meal outside where I encountered a small sandstorm. This one, however, was more of a mist than a full sandstorm. After eating my meal, I started driving back to my hotel when I encountered a police barricade. A police officer insisted that I go down another road which would take me through what we were warned not to drive thru, the SHUK. To no avail, I tried to insist that I wanted to go towards my hotel.

Given no alternative by the police officer, I slowly drove thru the SHUK. Suddenly, a masked terrorist threw a Molotov cocktail (a hand-thrown incendiary weapon consisting of a glass bottle filled with flammable substances and equipped with a fuse) into the windshield of a nearby police car and burned two police officers. I quickly turned my vehicle around and started down another road that eventually led me back to my hotel. The next day, I read in the local newspaper that the two police officers perished. Again, I thought it could have been me that got taken out by terrorists. Another missed threat on my life.

The next mistake I made was to ask one of the local Bahamians for direction when driving thru the city. The person I asked said that he was going in that direction and would be more than willing to ride along to show you the way. Foolishly and without thinking, I agreed to let him into my vehicle. Luckily, nothing happened. If I had seen the entire story that was aired on Al Jazeera world news, I would have never offered to give him a ride. "When Al Jazeera launched from the Qatari capital, Doha, on Friday, November 1, 1996, it was the first independent news channel in the Arab world. Media in the Arab world, till then, was characterized by state-controlled narratives that denied audiences the right to know and the right to be heard." (108)

A young American who came to the Mid East was captured by terrorist. "A video running on an Islamist website has shown the apparent beheading of an American hostage in Iraq. The website said a top ally of al-Qaida leader Usama bin Ladin, was the man responsible for the beheading. The White House reacted angrily to the video of the killing, saying the killers would not be spared. "This shows the true nature of the enemies of freedom," White House spokesman Scott McClellan said. "We will pursue those responsible and bring them to justice." (109)

During one of my trips to a local restaurant with some of the embassy staff, we passed a large mosque. "The grand Al Fateh Mosque is both Bahrain's largest place of worship and among one of the largest mosques in the world. It was built under the patronage of the late Sheikh Isa bin Salman Al Khalifa in 1987 and was named after Ahmed Al Fateh. The mosque accommodates up to seven thousand worshippers and is crowned with the largest fiberglass dome in the world. The walls of the mosque are beautifully ornamented with Kufic calligraphy." (110)

Hearing about the significance and beauty of the mosque, I said we should stop by and look inside. The staff cautioned me, saying that there would be terrorists inside and I would not come out alive. I thanked them and agreed that we should return to the embassy.

On another occasion, I went to the hotel's gym for a workout. Some of the Bahrain people used the same gym. One of them approached me when he recognized by my clothing that I was an American. They can tell Americans by our western shoes and clothes. He asked me why are my people beating up on the Iraqi people? He was one of many people in the Middle East who saw us as aggressors. I thought it was best not to get into a conversation with him.

The ultimate danger was yet to come. We received word that there were a large group of demonstrators coming to surround our Bahrain embassy in protest to the Iraq war.

Photo 24-U.S. Embassy in Bahrain

Our security fortified the embassy, and our marines dawned their ballistic bullet proof vests and grabbed their fully automatic weapons. Within the hour, the demonstrators covered the outside walls of the embassy chanting slogans against our invasion of Iraq. The Ambassador and I sat on the porch at the roof top of the embassy watching the demonstration. I went inside the Embassy to check on our marines. Each of them had their weapons cocked and loaded, pointed at the suspicious demonstrators from various windows throughout the Embassy. The marines focused on those that had long robes and could hide weapons under them. Although tensions rose, the order was not given to fire upon the demonstrators. They were told to hold fast.

Some of us could remember back when Iranian demonstrators overran the Iranian Embassy and held the staff hostage for many days. The Iranians held the American diplomat's hostage for 444 days." (111) The thought crossed our minds that the same could happen to us.

The Ambassador and I vigilantly watched from a balcony at the top of the Embassy while large throngs of demonstrators surrounded us. I kept going inside to check on our marines who were in flak jackets and had their M-16's ready for an assault. The good thing is our embassy was heavily fortified. Whatever the case, you just did not have time to be concerned.

With Naval central command close by, we knew that they could respond if we were overrun. They were keeping an eye on the demonstrators from their headquarters on their naval base. Suddenly, the Bahrain army showed up to disperse the demonstrators. Shortly thereafter, we were able to resume normal embassy operations. Later, I received another Defense Meritorious Award which read as follows:

"Lieutenant Colonel Matthew J. Drozd distinguished himself while assigned to the Department of State Bureau of Political Military Affairs, Office of International Security Operations. Lt Col Drozd's outstanding show of initiative, dedication, and leadership contributed to successfully

fulfilling the mission of International Security Operations. While deployed to the Middle East during Operation Iraqi Freedom, Lt Col Drozd provided valuable input to regional governmental agencies and organizations of coalition partners in upgrading their mass casualty preparedness and response capabilities including defense against a potential release of a Weapon of Mass Destruction, including translation of a foreign message that averted the potential spread of a deadly virus. His team's valiant efforts not only enhanced the readiness response posture of foreign governments but also greatly increased the security of U.S. Embassies in the region."-Donald Rumsfeld, Secretary of Defense

CITATION

TO ACCOMPANY THE AWARD OF THE

DEFENSE MERITORIOUS SERVICE MEDAL

TO

LIEUTENANT COLONEL MATTHEW J. DROZD

UNITED STATES AIR FORCE

Lieutenant Colonel Matthew J. Drozd, U. S. Air Force, distinguished himself by exceptionally meritorious service as an Action Officer while assigned to the Department of State, Bureau of Political-Military Affairs, Office of International Security Operations from November 20, 2002 to May 20, 2004. During this period, Lt Col Drozd's outstanding show of initiative, dedication, and leadership contributed to successfully fulfilling the mission of International Security Operations. While deployed to the Middle East during Operation Iraqi Freedom, Lt Col Drozd provided valuable input to regional governmental agencies and organizations of coalition partners in upgrading their mass casualty preparedness and response capabilities including defense against a potential release of a Weapon of Mass Destruction. Lt Col Drozd further distinguished himself by keeping key decision makers abreast of critical events prior to launching Operation Iraqi Freedom and subsequent to the occupation of Iraq by coalition forces, including translation of a foreign message that averted the potential spread of a deadly virus. His team's valiant efforts not only enhanced the readiness response posture of foreign governments but also greatly increased the security of U.S. Embassies in the region. The distinctive accomplishments and exemplary performance of Lt Col Drozd reflect credit upon himself, the United States Air Force, and the Department of Defense.

9

CHAPTER 17

Like Father like Sons

A few days later, we learned that there was an offer for Asylum to Hussein and his two sons. "Bahrain's king has offered "safe exile" to Saddam Hussein, saying he hopes the Iraqi leader "would seriously consider this offer before the onset of war," the government-run Bahrain News Agency said Wednesday. Bahrain's palace, the seat of government, confirmed the offer, according to Bahrain TV.

King Hamad bin Isa Al Khalifa "announced that Bahrain is willing to accommodate Iraqi President Saddam Hussein, if he wishes to reside here, with dignity and without disgrace to Iraq." The king said that Bahrain's initiative "comes as part of its nationalistic responsibilities, towards ensuring security and stability in the region, in order to avoid war on Iraq and its people." The offer came during the Cabinet's "emergency session," when the king was asked "what would be a solution to avoid war and destruction."

The king said that "in order to avoid war and destruction, the Iraqi president must relinquish his authority to parties capable of finding a solution to the situation, and secure Iraq's honor and dignity." Bahrain did not initiate formal diplomatic contact to extend the offer." (112)

"As the invasion waged on, Hussein and his two sons refused the offer. "Saddam Hussein's sons, Qusay and Uday

Hussein, are killed after a three-hour firefight with U.S. forces in the northern Iraqi city of Mosul. It is widely believed that the two men were even more cruel and ruthless than their notorious father, and their death was celebrated among many Iraqis. Uday and Qusay were 39 and 37 years old, respectively, when they died. Both were said to have amassed considerable fortunes through their participation in illegal oil smuggling.

Uday Hussein, Saddam's first-born son, was the natural choice to succeed the feared despot. But even the amoral Saddam took issue with Uday's extravagant lifestyle, he is said to have personally owned hundreds of cars—and lacked personal discipline. As a result of Uday bludgeoning and stabbing one of Saddam's favorites, Saddam briefly had him imprisoned and beaten.

While Saddam began to favor his second son Qusay, Uday continued to make a name for himself among the Iraqi people for his sadism and cruelty. Prone to beating and torturing his servants and anyone else who displeased him, he was known to spend time studying new torture devices and methods to improve his technique. He even treated his so-called friends poorly—in one report, he forced some to drink dangerous amounts of alcohol purely for his amusement. Uday was also a man of unrestrained sexual appetites, sleeping with several women per night up to five nights a week. He was known for raping young women— some as young as 12—whom he found attractive, threatening them and their families' lives if they complained or spoke out against the crime. He would sometimes torture and kill his victims after sex.

The stories about Hussein's two sons collaborates what I heard when serving in Bahrain. Uday went to a racetrack and spotted a young girl who he wanted. She was with her parents. He directed his guards to bring her to him.

Having difficulty identifying which young girl he wanted, the guards asked which one of the many young girls he wanted. He ordered them to go and when they were near the young girl, he would flick his cigarette lighter. Later, the young girl's father went to the government to insist on having his daughter returned. The reply was "shut up or the next time it will be your wife!"

"Uday held several jobs during his father's regime, most notably publishing the most widely read newspaper in the country and heading Iraq's Olympic Committee. In that position, he is known to have beaten athletes whom he felt did not live up to expectations. He was also the head of the Fedayeen Saddam, one of his father's security groups. In 1996, Uday was shot while driving in his car. Though never proven, it has been speculated that his brother Qusay may have been behind the assassination attempt. The incident caused him to suffer a stroke and, despite surgery, left a bullet lodged in his spine. Although he recovered most functions, it is said that Uday lived with considerable pain for the rest of his life, which may have exacerbated his sadistic tendencies. The weakness he experienced after the shooting may also have contributed to his father's growing doubts about his suitability as a successor.

At the same time, Qusay was earning Saddam's trust. Married with four children, Qusay was said to be less sadistic than his brother but was still a cold and ruthless killer who was much feared throughout the country. While Uday often bragged about his excesses and violent exploits, Qusay was known to intentionally keep a much lower profile. He worshipped his father and worked hard to impress him. After he proved himself by brutally repressing the Shi'ite uprisings that occurred after the 1991 Gulf War—even doing some of the killing himself—Saddam rewarded Qusay with a series of more responsible posts, including command of Iraq's elite fighting force, the Republican Guard, and the Special Security Organization, Iraq's secret police. By that time, it had become clear that Qusay had replaced his brother as Saddam's heir.

Despite Qusay's superior reputation, observers noted with interest that Uday's Fedayeen outperformed the Qusay-led Republican Guard during the United States' 2003 invasion of Iraq. Qusay proved to be an ineffective leader, showing fear, and often second-guessing his own decisions. After the invasion, both brothers went into hiding and the U.S. government posted a $15 million reward for information leading to the discovery of either man's location. Though it was widely speculated that they would not be found together because of their mutual enmity, an informant's tip led U.S. Special Forces to a house in which they were both staying on July 22, 2003.

After drawing fire, the soldiers withdrew, until receiving backup of one hundred troops from the 101st Airborne division and armed Warrior helicopters.

Photo 25-101st Airborne battle Hussein's sons

Soldiers with the 101st Airborne Division (Air Assault) watch as a TOW missile strikes the side of a building that is suspected of harboring Uday and Qusay Hussein in Mosul, Iraq, July 22, 2003. Qusay and Uday were killed in a gun battle as they resisted efforts by coalition forces to apprehend and detain them. A battle ensued, after which Americans entered the house and found the bodies of the two brothers, as well as that of Qusay's 14-year-old son. They were buried in a cemetery near the city of Tikrit, their father's birthplace.

In the wake of their deaths, the American government drew criticism for releasing pictures of Uday's and Qusay's lifeless bodies, but insisted the move was necessary to convince the skeptical Iraqi people that the long-feared brothers were truly dead (We thought we saw newspaper photographs of only their faces with their bodies wrapped like mummies). About five months later, on December 13, 2003, their father, who also went into hiding after the U.S. invasion, was found and captured alive by American forces." (113)

CHAPTER 18

End of a Dictator

"His trial by special tribunal for multiple crimes committed during his reign began in October 2005. On November 5, 2006, he was found guilty of crimes against humanity and sentenced to death by hanging The final hour of Iraq's former ruler began about 5 a.m., when American troops escorted him from Camp Cropper, near the Baghdad airport, to Camp Justice, another American base at the heart of the city. There, he was handed over to a newly trained unit of the Iraqi National Police, with whom he would later exchange curses. Iraq took full custody of Mr. Hussein

Two American helicopters flew fourteen witnesses from the Green Zone to the execution site, a former headquarters of the Istikhbarat, the deposed government's much feared military intelligence outfit, now inside the American base. Mr. Hussein was escorted into the room where the gallows, with its red railing, stood, greeted at the door by three masked executioners known as ashmawi. Several of the witnesses described in detail how the execution unfolded and recounted what was said.

His executioners wore black ski masks, but Mr. Hussein could still see their deep brown skin and hear their dialects, distinct to the Shiite southern part of the country, where he had so brutally repressed two separate uprisings. The small room had a foul odor. It was cold, had bad lighting and a sad, melancholic atmosphere. It was cramped, with the witnesses and eleven other people, including guards and the video crew. Mr. Hussein's eyes darted about, trying to take in just who was going to put an end to him.

The executioners took his hat and his scarf. Mr. Hussein, whose hands were bound in front of him, was taken to the judge's room next door. He followed each order he was given. He sat down and the verdict, finding him guilty of crimes against humanity, was read aloud.

"Long live the nation!" Mr. Hussein shouted. "Long live the people! Long live the Palestinians!" He continued shouting until the verdict was read in full, and then he composed himself again.

When he rose to be led back to the execution room, he looked strong, confident, and calm. Whatever apprehension he may have had only minutes earlier had faded. The general prosecutor asked Mr. Hussein to whom he wanted to give his Koran. He said Bandar, the son of Awad al-Bandar, the former chief justice of the Revolutionary Court who was also to be executed soon.

The room was quiet as everyone began to pray, including Mr. Hussein. "Peace be upon Mohammed and his holy family." Two guards added, "Supporting his son Moktada, Moktada, Moktada." Mr. Hussein seemed a bit stunned, swinging his head in their direction. They were talking about Moktada al-Sadr, the firebrand cleric whose militia is now committing some of the worst violence in the sectarian fighting; he is the son of a revered Shiite cleric, Muhammad Sadiq al-Sadr, whom many believe Mr. Hussein ordered murdered. "Moktada?" he spat out, mixing sarcasm and disbelief.

Iraq's national security adviser asked Mr. Hussein if he had any remorse or fear. "No," he said bluntly. "I am a militant, and I have no fear for myself. I have spent my life in jihad and fighting aggression. Anyone who takes this route should not be afraid."

Mr. Rubaie, standing shoulder to shoulder with Mr. Hussein, asked him about the killing of the elder Mr. Sadr. They were standing so close to each other that others could not hear the exchange.

One of the guards, though, became angry. "You have destroyed us," the masked man yelled. "You have killed us. You have made us live in destitution." Mr. Hussein was scornful: "I have saved you from destitution and misery and destroyed your enemies, the Persians and Americans." The guard cursed him.

Two witnesses, uninvolved in selecting the guards, exchanged a quiet joke, saying they gathered that the goal of disbanding the militia had yet to be accomplished. The deputy prosecutor, Mr. Faroun, berated the guards, saying, "I will not accept any offense directed at him."

Mr. Hussein was led up to the gallows without a struggle. His hands were unbound, put behind his back, then fastened again. He showed no remorse. He held his head high. The executioners offered him a hood. He refused. They explained that the thick rope could cut through his neck and offered to use the scarf he had worn earlier to keep that from happening. Mr. Hussein accepted.

He stood on the high platform, with a deep hole beneath it. He said a last prayer. Then, with his eyes wide open, no stutter or choke in his throat, he said his final words cursing the Americans and the Persians.

The trapdoor swung open. He fell a good distance, but he died swiftly. After just a minute, his body was still. His eyes were still open, but he was dead. Despite the scarf, the rope cut a gash into his neck.

Saddam Hussein never bowed his head, until his neck snapped. His last words were equally defiant. "Down with the traitors, the Americans, the spies and the Persians." (114)

Upon the execution of Hussein and the killing of his two sons, United States President George W. Bush On May 1, 2003, gave a televised speech on the aircraft carrier USS *Abraham Lincoln*. Bush, who had launched the U.S.-led invasion of Iraq six weeks earlier, mounted a podium before a White House-produced banner that read "Mission Accomplished". Reading from a prepared text, he said, "Major combat operations in Iraq have ended. In the battle of Iraq, the United States and our allies have prevailed" because "the regime [the Iraqi dictatorship of Saddam Hussein] is no more". Although Bush went on to say that "Our mission continues" and "We have difficult work to do in Iraq," his words implied that the Iraq War was over and America had won. Bush's assertions—and the sign itself—became controversial as the Iraqi insurgency gained pace and developed into a full-on sectarian war. Most casualties, U.S. and Iraqi, military and civilian, occurred after the speech. U.S. troops fought in Iraq for eight more years before eventually withdrawing. In modern cultural relevance, the phrase "Mission Accomplished" is frequently used to refer to the perils of declaring victory too early in crises.

The ironic turn of events was that Hussein could have avoided the Executioner and lived out his life in luxury by accepting an offer of sanctuary from Bahrain and other countries. Arab officials say six non-Arab countries have also offered to take him in. "(115)

CHAPTER 19

Cost of Afghan and Iraq Wars

"The United States' war in Iraq, Operation Iraqi Freedom, undertaken to rid Iraq of its weapons of mass destruction, began with a phase of what television commentators called "shock and awe" bombing on March 19, 2003. Most U.S. and allied forces left Iraq in 2011, but the U.S. returned to significant military operations in Iraq and Syria in late 2014. The budgetary costs of United States wars consist of the "OCO" costs of direct military spending for operations by the Department of Defense and State Department, but they also comprise additional costs, including increases to the support or "base" Pentagon budget and funding for veterans' medical and disability care. The estimate provided here is for costs between 2003 and early 2023 and for the future costs in medical care of U.S. Iraq war veterans. Total U.S. costs to date are estimated at about $1.79 trillion, not including funds requested for FY2024. If the costs of future U.S. veterans medical and disability care are included, these costs will reach about $2.89 trillion by 2050.

Between 186,694 to 210,038 Iraqi civilians have died and a total of 280,771 to 315,190 have died from direct war related violence caused by the U.S., its allies, the Iraqi military and police, and opposition forces from the time of the invasion through March 2023. The violent deaths of Iraqi civilians have occurred through aerial bombing, shelling, gunshots, suicide attacks, and fires started by bombing. Many civilians have also been injured." (116)

The American war in Afghanistan incurred staggering costs — for the United States, Afghans and others — over two decades. The U.S. government spent $2.3 trillion, and the war led to the deaths of 2,324 U.S. military personnel, 3,917 U.S. contractors and 1,144 allied troops. For Afghans, the statistics are unimaginable: 70,000 Afghan military and police deaths, 46,319 Afghan civilians (although that is a significant underestimation) and some 53,000 opposition fighters killed. Almost 67,000 other people were killed in Pakistan in relation to the Afghan war. (117)

Looking at the staggering costs of the Iraq war, our leaders in Washington need to answer the question as to what Ukraine and Israel/Palestine wars are going to cost America. "To date, we have provided approximately $61.4 billion in military assistance since Russia launched its premeditated, unprovoked, and brutal full-scale invasion of Ukraine on February 24, 2022, and approximately $64.1 billion in military assistance since Russia's initial invasion of Ukraine in 2014." (118) "Conflicts in the Middle East have been very costly to the U.S., as well as to the rest of the world. An estimate of the total cost to the U.S. alone of instability and conflict in the region—which emanates from the core, Israeli Palestinian conflict—amounts to close to $3 trillion, measured in 2002 dollars." (119) This is an amount almost four times greater than the cost of the Vietnam war, also reckoned in 2002 dollars. With much of the weaponry used in these two wars supplied by America, one can only surmise that these countries are going to turn to us to rebuild that which was destroyed.

CHAPTER 20

Wrong Intel

As for Colin Powell's address to the United Nation asserting that Iraq was harboring weapons of mass destruction, I would wonder what he must have thought after it turned out that there were no such weapons found. "Powell used information that intelligence officials assured him was credible. There were reconnaissance photos, elaborate maps, and charts, and even taped phone conversations between senior members of Iraq's military. National security analyst Joseph Cirincione also criticized Powell's speech in comments to NPR. Particularly, Powell's assurances that there was solid evidence of sophisticated and illicit Iraqi weapons programs.

"Now we know that that just wasn't true," said Cirincione, then the director for non-proliferation at the Carnegie Endowment for International Peace. Journalists and members of Congress started digging into the rationale for war laid out in Powell's U.N. speech. They discovered faulty and exaggerated reports from an intelligence community under political pressure from top White House officials. There were also claims Bush took advantage of Powell's reputation by dispatching him to the U.N. To this day, the Iraq War is widely viewed as a foreign policy and humanitarian disaster." (120)

Serving at the State Department under Colin Powell as Secretary of State, I know and believe that he told the United Nations what he thought was true. He was a man of honor and if he chose to run for the Presidency, every person that I spoke to would have voted for him. He would have won in a landslide. I consider a great leader to be one who treats those who serve them with respect and compassionate care. I asked those who performed menial tasks and security for Colin Powell as to what they thought of him. All spoke extremely highly of him. One told me that when the copier gets broken, he is too humble to bother anyone. He gets down on all fours to fix it.

His son captured his resolve and character the best when he spoke at his father's funeral. "What type of man was my father. He had a classic Chevrolet Camaro that was worth quite a lot of money. The only mechanical issue that it had was that it could not go forward, only reverse. To help the local fire department, he asked if they would like to have it as a donation. Regardless of whether it could go in drive, they said they could auction it for quite a lot of money. He drove it three mile in reverse to get it to them."

I once stood close to him on the patio of the State Department when he was giving a news conference. My biggest regret is that I did not at least urge him to run for the Presidency.

CHAPTER 21

More Command Centers

Shortly after the capture of Hussein and the killing of his two sons, I returned to Washington and resumed my duties in the PEMAT of the Pol Mil Bureau. While there, the State Department was asked to send a representative to the U.S. Department of Health and Human Services (HHS) when Tommy Thompson oversaw it. Prior to his appointment as a cabinet member, he was the longest serving governor in Wisconsin history, January of 1987 to February of 2001. The reason for his request to the State Department was to fully man the new command center he proudly organized at approximately 3.5 million dollars. Along with other key agencies throughout Washington, we were tasked to man one of the desks of the command center and participate in a mock test where two American cities suffered a chemical, biological, radiological, nuclear, explosive (CBRNE) attack.

"Health and Human Services Secretary Tommy Thompson has wasted no time in constructing a state-of-the-art command center to manage any bioterrorism or public health emergency that might arise. In less than 60 days' time, Thompson finished the job, with the ribbon-cutting on the $3.5 million center occurring in December.

The center is just across from Thompson's office in the main HHS building at the foot of Capitol Hill, and it will not require plastic sheeting and duct tape to keep out germs and chemicals. The center has a self-contained ventilation system that allows government officials to take refuge there for an extended period, even if the rest of the building is crawling with anthrax or another harmful chemical or biological agent.

The center's purpose is to provide timely, accurate information and intelligence to the secretary so that he can make quick, well-informed decisions about a public health situation anywhere in the country. Special equipment can map and display the progression of illness outbreaks.

Tracking is key, Thompson said in an interview just after the center opened. If, for example, a chemical agent was released in a Minnesota town, officials at the command center could plug in the location and the weather forecast and then predict direction and travel time for the toxic plume. HHS could then advise people in Minnesota about which areas to evacuate and which hospitals to avoid.

Technology can also track non-terrorism events. It has already been used in tests to monitor the West Nile virus, the recent pharmaceutical plant fire in North Carolina, and the December typhoon in Guam. In the case of the West Nile, HHS was able to show, county by county, how and when the disease was spreading and how many people were dying.

The mapping also aids the monitoring of food poisoning cases, Thompson said. "We can have FDA saying we have this food poisoning in Milwaukee, and we have a map we can put up on that screen showing the quadrants in the city and see how it's spreading." He added, " We can have some of their experts here, and we can develop a plan right from here with the National Institutes of Health in Bethesda, Md. (NIH); the Centers for Disease Control (CDC) and Prevention in Atlanta; and the Food and Drug Administration (FDA), all working together with one map telling us how to do it."

It is also important for Thompson to be able to quickly locate his resources, including personnel. The command center tracks the fifty tons of medical supplies stashed in secret places throughout the country, and 8,000 medical responders who are ready to sprint to the site of an emergency.

Technology allows HHS to know the exact locations of its secret pharmaceutical stockpiles and medical supplies, which are split among twelve sites. "We can move 50 tons of supplies into any city in America, Alaska, or Hawaii within seven hours," Thompson said. In December, for example, Thompson sent a response team to Guam to manage the medical emergency from the typhoon. Other responders were put on alert. "If we have a crisis, we want to make damn sure we can call them up and they know what they're going to do-so we're putting more training in ... putting them on alert."

The command center combines various forms of communication-including ground-based and satellite systems-to ensure that if one fails, a backup is available. The computers, radios, and telephones in the network can also talk to one another. The idea is to be able to share information with state and local entities and with HHS's own relevant, but geographically dispersed, agencies, including the National Institutes of Health in Bethesda, Md.; the Centers for Disease Control and Prevention in Atlanta; and the Food and Drug Administration in Rockville, Md. In addition, the center has lines with other federal partners, such as the Federal Emergency Management Agency, the FBI, and the CIA.

The center houses twenty-six workstations for Thompson and other top HHS officials, including the surgeon general. It also has desks for representatives from the FBI, the CIA, and the Homeland Security Department. HHS says the center fills the gaps in communication that federal, state, and local agencies encountered during the 2001 terrorist attacks.

Video conferencing for up to ten participants is also possible. If a biological or chemical event occurs in Boston, for example, officials at the command center can watch the local news reports and use the video-conferencing tools to hook up the Massachusetts governor, the Boston police chief, the Homeland Security Department, and various federal agencies (the CDC, NIH, FDA, FBI, and CIA) and give the participants real-time, interactive communication. "We've got 10 screens here. We can interact," said Thompson." (121) After his tenure as Secretary of Health and Human Services, he later became interim President of the University of Wisconsin (UW) system. While there, he created a similar setup called a war room to track COVID-19 data on all the UW campuses." (122)

While manning one of the many desks in Secretary Thompson's HHS command center, he would give tours to governors, congressional leaders, and the news media. For some reason that I cannot explain, he always deferred to me and seemed to highlight me among the many agencies in attendance. He introduced me to some of the governors and congressional leaders. It was probably because State was one of the highest-ranking departments to man a desk. The exercise we performed was a mock CBRNE attack on two major US cities, one being Chicago. Our assignment was to monitor and respond accordingly.

Following my Stindt at the State Department, I volunteered for an assignment with the Joint Task Force-National Capital Region (JTF-NCR), "formerly known as Joint Force Headquarters-National Capital Region (JFHQ-NCR), is directly responsible for ceremonial missions and the homeland security and defense of what is called the National Capital Region, which includes the Washington D.C. area as well as surrounding counties in Virginia and Maryland. Primarily made up of joint military units within the National Capital Region, the JTF-NCR assists federal and local civilian agencies and disaster response teams in the event that the capital area's security is or possibly could be breached by acts of terrorism." (123)

In anticipation of major events in and around the capital, JTF-NCR would build operation plans for present and future events that are occurring or will occur in and around Washington DC. Such plans would include the funerals of presidents (present and future), other heads of state, inaugurations, major demonstrations, etc. The plans were constantly reviewed, updated, and then implemented when the event occurred.

I served under Major General Galen Bruce Jackman who escorted former First Lady Nancy Reagan, during the funeral of her husband. He was an outstanding officer to serve under. Under his leadership, we were finalizing plans for the protection of the President's inauguration. The task force has operations plans of ceremonial services such as a President's funeral, Inaugurations, and major events.

My assignment encompassed emergency medical services and medical readiness. We brought in IT planner specialists that would analyze what military forces and medical people we would need if the least cast catastrophe could occur and likewise do the same for the worst-case scenario. Worst case scenario would be the attack by a weapon of mass destruction, a nuclear, radiological, chemical, biological, or other device that is intended to harm many people.

Should a terrorist attack occur again in Washington or any other American city for that matter, the response needed was based upon the number of casualties. In times of unexpected terrorist attacks, it was critical to estimate as close as possible. Our technical capabilities to estimate what medical response we would require were very accurate.

During one of our group briefings, I presented one scenario that only a medical readiness CBRNE expert would have known. General Jackman commented that it was very thought provoking and took it very seriously. CBRNE weapons can be more devastating than an explosive weapon because in many cases, they may go undetected for a long period of time (covert weapon-, causing far more casualties eventually. "Chemical, biological, radiological, or nuclear (CBRN) weapons have been used since antiquity. Examples of their recent use include war fighting (World War One and the Iran-Iraq War), ethnic conflict (chemical weapon use against the Iraqi Kurds and in Syria), terrorism (release of sarin in the Tokyo underground, US anthrax letters) and assassination (ricin, polonium-210). In addition, CBRN incidents have also included accidental releases during peace time operations, and many of the principles for CBRN incident response can be applied to other hazardous material (HAZMAT) incidents. The impact of such weapons may have a range of implications for medical personnel, both military and civilian. The health consequences related to a real or perceived CBRN hazard are:

- The initial (immediate, acute, and delayed onset)
- The long-term (late onset or chronic) health effects
- The secondary exposure risk to medical personnel
- The requirement to conduct casualty hazard management that may include decontamination, isolation, and quarantine
- The implementation of wider public health reporting and travel restrictions for transmissible agents
- The potential impact on the health of individuals due to use of CBRN personal protective equipment, including heat illness and psychological stress

- The potential impact on the healthcare system to implement pre-exposure or postexposure prophylaxis
- The management of any casualty, including trauma, in a CBRN environment
- The presence of combined (CBRN and conventional) injury
- The traumatic effects due to a nuclear detonation

Each type of medical mission will have its own risk assessment with a spectrum of hazards including CBRN weapons, environmental hazards and endemic disease as well as conventional injuries due to trauma; this all-hazards approach is reflected by chemical, biological, radiological, environmental, endemic and traumatic hazards (CBRNEET). Some agents have no alternative uses other than as a weapon such as a nuclear weapon or Sulphur mustard gas." (124)

CHAPTER 22

Weapons of Mass Destruction

"The characteristics of a CBRN agent such as physical properties and stability as well as vulnerable routes of absorption will determine the delivery method used. The device or munitions used may also cause additional medical effects such as trauma (injuries) or psychological stress. The types of delivery are *overt* or *covert*. Overt releases are likely to follow a conventional major incident response, while a covert release may go unrecognized for a period." (125)

It is far more difficult for us to guard against and mitigate the attack of a biological weapon of mass destruction versus an explosive device. "Almost any disease-causing organism (such as bacteria, viruses, fungi, prions, or rickettsiae) or toxin (poisons derived from animals, plants or microorganisms, or similar substances produced synthetically) can be used in biological weapons. The agents can be enhanced from their natural state to make them more suitable for mass production, storage, and dissemination as weapons. Historical biological weapons programs have included efforts to produce aflatoxin; anthrax; botulinum toxin; foot-and-mouth disease; glanders; plague; Q fever; rice blast; ricin; Rocky Mountain spotted fever; smallpox; and tularemia, among others. Biological weapons delivery systems can take a variety of forms. Past programs have constructed missiles, bombs, hand grenades and rockets to deliver biological weapons. Several programs also designed spray-tanks to be fitted to aircraft, cars, trucks, and boats. There have also been documented efforts to develop delivery devices for assassinations or sabotage operations, including a variety of sprays, brushes and injection systems as well as means for contaminating food and clothing.

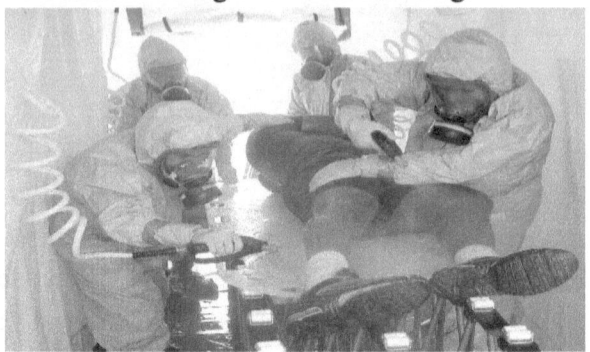

Photo 26-Military Decontamination Training

In practice, should a suspicious disease occur, it would be difficult to determine if it were caused by nature, an accident, sabotage, or an act of biological warfare or terrorism. Consequently, the response to a biological event, whether natural, accidental, or deliberate, would involve the coordination of actors from many sectors who together possess the capability to determine the cause and attribute it to a specific source. Likewise, the preparation for and prevention of such an event should also involve multi-sectoral coordination. The 20th century saw the use of biological weapons by individuals and groups committing criminal acts or targeted assassinations, biological warfare, and the accidental release of pathogens from laboratories (i.e., Covid released from Chinese Lab)." (126)

"Biological weapons can simply be delivered on products being delivered by shipping containers. Carrier conveyances, such as ocean containers, aircraft, rail cars, and commercial trucks, are pathways by which invasive plant and animal pests and diseases might be introduced into the

United States. The economic and environmental impact of such unintentional introductions can be significant. Invasive species are expensive to control and can reduce agricultural production, property values, and water availability. Although the numbers vary widely, some of the current research estimates that there are 50,000 (Pimentel, 2004) non-native species in the United States today. Of those 50,000 species, approximately 4,300 are considered invasive species.

Regarding terrorist chemical attacks, Explosive devices were used in 21% of attacks to deliver these chemical agents. Private citizens and educational facilities were targeted in 25% and 12% of attacks, respectively. The average number of attacks increased from six per year between 1970 and 2011 to 24.9 per year between 2011 and 2017 (coinciding with the start of the Syria conflict)." (127)

While trying to estimate casualties resulting from least case and most case terrorist attacks, I felt it would be almost impossible to ascertain the type of attack and how it would be delivered. It could be delivered in different forms, and the means of delivery could be undetectable. Case in point was the bombing in Oklahoma. "On the morning of April 19, 1995, an ex-Army soldier and security guard parked a rented truck in front of the Federal Building in downtown Oklahoma City. Inside the vehicle was a powerful bomb made of a deadly cocktail of agricultural fertilizer, diesel fuel, and other chemicals. The Bomber got out, locked the door, and headed towards his getaway car. He ignited one timed fuse, then another. Within moments, the surrounding area looked like a war zone. A third of the building had been reduced to rubble, with many floors flattened like pancakes. Dozens of cars were incinerated, and more than three hundred nearby buildings were damaged or destroyed. The human toll was devastating: 168 souls were lost, including nineteen children, with several hundred more injured. It was the worst act of homegrown terrorism in the nation's history."

To put it into perspective once again, the atomic bombings of Hiroshima, Japan, on August 6, 1945, was "Little Boy". The bomb was dropped by a USAAF B-29 bomber, Enola Gay. The bomb weighed 9,000 pounds and had a diameter of only twenty-eight inches. "In both cities the blast destroyed everything within a radius of one mile from the center of explosion, except for certain reinforced concrete frames as noted above. The atomic explosion almost destroyed Hiroshima's identity as a city. Over a fourth of the population was killed in one stroke and an additional fourth seriously injured, so that even if there had been no damage to structures and installations the normal city life would still have been completely shattered. Everything was heavily damaged up to three miles from the blast, and beyond this distance, although comparatively light, extended for several more miles. Glass was broken up to twelve miles." (128) The atomic bomb dropped on Japan brought a sudden end to World War II but also ushered in the nuclear age.

A similar bomb being the same size and weight could be transported to Washington by a small rental truck. The driver could detonate the bomb and leave the city in a car driven by a co-conspirator without anyone knowing he was here. With the effect of a three-mile radius, it would take out the Pentagon, the White House, the Capital, and surrounding administrative and historic museums. Besides the impact of the blast, the plume of the bomb would drop radioactive fallout for the surrounding residential communities.

Perhaps this is why unidentified drones were flying over the northeastern seaboard. Even though the Pentagon would not admit owning them, there was a good possibility that our military was flying them to detect a possible weapon of mass destruction located somewhere on the ground. To alert unsuspecting Americans on the ground, I wrote an OPED letter and sent it to hundreds of newspapers across the nation. It was titled: "A possible coverup of the mystery DRONES" and read "When trying to solve the mystery of the drones, I would like to remind everyone when our military covertly tested the Stealth Bomber. Even the families of the stealth pilots were not privy to the existence of these fighters nor to the fact that their loved ones were flying them. Flying only at night above western skies, the pilots fondly called themselves "Night Hawks." By not revealing their mission to anyone including their spouses, the pilots led double lives. The flying of these birds of war were among the most closely guarded weapons systems since the development of the atomic bomb. Another speculation we may entertain is that the Dones may be carrying specialized detection systems for uncovering what may be our next terrorist attack. If any of my two hypotheses are correct, Washington needs to do a better job of alleviating the concerns of those that have been helplessly watching these birds of prey flying above their homes without challenge or resolve from our military."

It would be extremely difficult for them to detect any weapon of mass destruction. Bottom line from all this is that it is extremely difficult to guard against, identify, and mitigate CBRNE weapons of mass destruction, especially biological viruses. Like how COVID crippled our nation for months, these types of weapons can be spread quickly, be far more devastating, and have lingering effects for extended periods of time. They are also extremely difficult to detect and once detected, there is no guarantee that we can find or develop vaccines to combat them.

CHAPTER 23

World's Reaction To 9-11

"Despite the horrific loss of life and destruction on September 11, 2001, the Nation drew strength and unity from its citizens as well as the world's citizens. What follows is a small sample of the thousands of condolence materials that poured into the United States' embassies located around the globe; from individuals, families, schools, businesses, organizations, and governments all representing over one hundred countries. In the days, weeks, months, and years following September 11th, condolences arrived on letters, postcards, sympathy journals, cards, newspapers, mass mailers, children's drawings, posters, flags, paper flowers and doves, ribbons, photographs, and bits of paper. These condolence materials are messages of hope, sympathy, and appeals for peace addressed to the President, the American people, the citizens of New York City, orphaned children, and all who lost someone in the tragedy. Upon review, it quickly becomes evident that although the terrorists had attacked the United States, the world remained interconnected by its common humanity.

Throughout Africa an outpouring of sympathy was received by United States' embassies. In this time of tragedy communities banded together and embraced their American brothers and sisters. Communities of farmers, church groups, Non-Governmental Organizations, entire villages, and cities, united to deliver messages and condolence books. Some communities held memorial gatherings, like Ridge Church in Accra, Republic of Ghana. Others presented artwork of collective expression such as the children of the Republic of South Africa and the farmers of the Republic of Zimbabwe. Community is a theme that appears repeatedly in these materials as Africans reached out to comfort not only the United States, but the broader world community.

Western Hemisphere

The countries located throughout the western hemisphere not only have a geographic connection to the United States, but the continents connect through a shared name, America. In solidarity many South American countries hosted official memorial gatherings in sympathy with the United States. Some nations, like the Republic of El Salvador, gathered as early as September 12th. People as varied as Presidents, bankers, school children, diplomats, teachers, and families signed condolence books. This section of condolence materials cannot be introduced without giving special mention to Canada. During the days following the terrorist attacks, the Nation's northern neighbor provided food and shelter to stranded passengers aboard grounded airplanes initially bound for the United States. The condolence materials from Canadians are varied and immense representing all the provinces, from Inuit school children writing from Nunavut to Québécois who wrote in French, to blood donors from Vancouver.

Asia and Oceania

When the news broke about the terrorist attacks occurring in the United States on September 11th, most of Asia was already experiencing Wednesday, September 12th. Many condolences express an undercurrent of people feeling ahead in minutes and hours by the clock, yet still powerless and unable to prevent the attacks. So far away in miles yet so close in heart, people expressed their support, love, unity, strength, and sympathy in letters and condolence books. Struggling to find the words many turned to their mother languages, whether Chinese, Kazakh, Japanese or Arabic. The condolences even included original artwork, such as colorful banners created by New Zealanders and origami paper cranes folded by Japanese school children. Despite the physical distance, the attacks on September 11th directly affected many Asians and Pacific Islanders, as evidenced by an Indonesian family who wrote in after losing their son in the World Trade Center.

Europe

Peace is the predominant theme of the condolence messages sent from Europe, a region that had worked hard for peace through a tumultuous 20th century which included two World Wars and the Cold War. Retirees from the North Atlantic Treaty Organization, an organization born from this history, sent in a message of peace. Irish school children authored poems about the September 11th attacks on paper cut-out in the shape of doves. Citizens of Russia, the former Cold War rival of the United States, sent in messages of support and freedom from terrorism. One that is particularly notable is from the Moscow Anti-fire Service to the firemen of New York and Washington illustrating the bridges that have been built over the decade between the end of the Cold War and September 11th as well as the solidarity between first responders throughout the world." (129)

"The scale and audacity of the terrorist attacks on September 11, 2001, spurred sweeping changes in the way the United States, its partners, and adversaries used the machinery of state and technology to respond to threats. In this Council of Councils global perspectives, five experts reflect on the legacy of the attacks and offer insights into the biggest changes in counterterrorism, human rights, surveillance, international law of war, and border security.

The Full Circle of Counterterrorism

The 9/11 attacks were a defining event for global extremists and terrorists. Widely considered the most egregious act of international terrorism, it killed almost three thousand people (2,977 victims plus the nineteen al-Qaeda terrorists), injured an estimated twenty-five thousand, and inspired attacks in Bali, Djerba, London, Madrid, and elsewhere. The horror of 9/11 galvanized the world to come together to try to defeat terrorism. To address the common threat, military forces, law enforcement authorities, and intelligence services built common databases, exchanged personnel, conducted joint training and operations, shared intelligence, technology, expertise, and experience. The driving force behind the effort—the United States—now faces a new set of daunting threats.

The scale and audacity of the terrorist attacks on September 11, 2001, spurred sweeping changes in the way the United States, its partners, and adversaries used the machinery of state and technology to respond to threats. In this Council of Councils global perspectives, five experts reflect on the legacy of the attacks and offer insights into the biggest changes in counterterrorism, human rights, surveillance, international law of war, and border security.

Rohan Gunaratna

Professor of Security Studies, S. Rajaratnam School of International Studies (Singapore)

The horror of 9/11 galvanized the world to come together to try to defeat terrorism. To address the common threat, military forces, law enforcement authorities, and intelligence services built common databases, exchanged personnel, conducted joint training and operations, shared intelligence, technology, expertise, and experience. The driving force behind the effort—the United States—now faces a new set of daunting threats.

The counterterrorism response to 9/11 evolved in four waves.

First, the U.S.-led coalition in Afghanistan dismantled the Taliban and al-Qaeda infrastructure in 2001 Dismantling the terrorist sanctuary in Afghanistan, where three dozen terror groups were training, prevented countless attacks worldwide. U.S. intelligence efforts targeted and eliminated terrorist leaders time after time.

Second, the United States invaded Iraq in March 2003—a fatal mistake. The hollowing out of the Iraqi military and the collapse of the administration led to a civil war, fostering an environment for the rise of al-Qaeda in Iraq. Although the Islamic State today is a shadow of what it was in 2015, its ideology and operational entities present a formidable threat to international security and stability.

Third, the United States established a dedicated Department of Homeland Security that brought its domestic intelligence and law enforcement entities under one umbrella. It also successfully prevented and preempted attacks against the U.S. homeland.

Fourth, the United States spearheaded global counterterrorism programs by offering training and supporting governments that needed capabilities to fight their domestic and regional threat groups, networks, and cells.

Now that Afghanistan has fallen again to the Taliban, which hosted al-Qaeda in an uneasy alliance, the revitalization of al-Qaeda is inevitable. Between the return of Taliban and the continued peril posed by the Islamic State, the global threat of terrorism is as bad as or worse than it was twenty years ago.

Now, though, United States is no longer the sole counterterrorism force in the world. China and Russia will need to protect their interests from terrorists at home and overseas.

Patrycja Sasnal

Head of Research, Polish Institute of International Affairs (Poland)

In the two decades since 9/11, the international human rights system has been abused and weakened. The global war on terror has blurred the lines of war, terror, and human rights. This new kind of armed conflict—geographically and temporally unlimited—is fought between terrorists and counter terrorists, both of which violated human rights, as is now known definitively from a vast literature on the topic

The United States not only co-opted allies in illegal actions such as using their territory for extraordinary rendition, but also further brutalized authoritarian regimes by pushing new counterterrorism legislation, handing over suspects caught in Afghanistan, Iraq, and Pakistan, and allowing arbitrary detentions and enforced disappearances. Such was the case of Egypt, Jordan, Morocco, and several Gulf states. In return for counterterrorism cooperation, the United States accepted violations of human rights in the form of prolonged states of emergency and hearing cases of ill-defined terrorism in special tribunals. events in 2011 known as the Arab Spring, causing some regimes to fall but leading in many to even greater violations of human rights today."

"A consequence of the post 9/11 war on terror is that counterterrorism has become an accepted pretext for other, unrelated policies globally. China and Russia often use it to justify actions against opposition, activists, minorities, or interventions in third countries.

The brutalization effect also harmed democracies. The example the United States set and complicity of its European allies in illegal practices eroded the standing and credibility of the West. The perceived hypocrisy of democracies—prime guarantors and advocates of international law—undermined the integrity of that law altogether.

The furthest-reaching societal effects of the war on terror are yet to be felt. A sense of permanent insecurity, widespread surveillance, Islamophobia, and other kinds of xenophobia have already resulted in the proliferation of conspiracy theories and general decay of trust in politics and experts. The war on terror has come home to roost."

Wesley Wark
Senior Fellow, Centre for International Governance Innovation (Canada)

The New World of Surveillance

The 9/11 attacks fundamentally reshaped the U.S. intelligence community and those of many of its close allies. In the words of a former CIA station chief, the CIA underwent a massive transformation—from gathering to hunting. This new mission supported an emphasis on kinetic counterterrorism, enshrined in the 2002 U.S. National Security Strategy, with its determination to "disrupt and destroy terrorist organizations of global reach."

The global war on terror required a shift in surveillance targets from traditional state threats and their militaries to much more amorphous terrorist networks. The nonstate actor threat required new tools and methods for surveillance. Led by the United States, the post-9/11 world of surveillance features an increasing reliance on a new tool of imagery intelligence—the drone—which rapidly became a dual-use weapon for both gathering and, in its armed form, hunting.

Drone use escalated during the Afghanistan conflict, as did attendant controversies about rules of engagement and civilian casualties. It spilled across borders, particularly into Pakistan, which harbored terrorist groups fighting in

Afghanistan, and into other theaters, such as Iraq, Somalia, and Syria. Although the United States led in drone innovation, it quickly entered the intelligence and military arsenals of many other states. As commercial and technical accessibility grew and costs fell, it even into the hands of terrorist groups such as the self-proclaimed Islamic State.

A second critical development was the rise of domestic and global internet monitoring, and with it the advent of mass data collection and analytics. Ingestion of vast quantities of what is technically described as unselected information required new data storage, management, and analysis tools. Mass data surveillance raised new global political tensions

Meanwhile, threats lost sight of in the years of preoccupation with terrorism have reemerged, conjuring new forms of state surveillance. The experience of COVID-19 has introduced the world to the need for systemic health surveillance within and beyond national borders.

John B. Bellinger III
Adjunct Senior Fellow for International and National
Security Law, Council on Foreign Relations (United States)
The Legal Legacy

The U.S. and global responses to the 9/11 attacks have resulted in significant changes in interpretation to international law rules and state practice governing the use of force against terrorists. Some of the George W. Bush administration's post-9/11 policies and legal interpretations were initially controversial, but many were later retained by the Barack Obama administration and adopted explicitly or tacitly by other governments.

Despite concerns expressed by human rights advocates, the Obama administration and many other governments accepted that governments may use military force against nonstate groups such as al-Qaeda and the self-proclaimed Islamic State and that the international laws of war, rather than simply domestic terrorism laws, may be the appropriate legal rules to apply. Many governments now also agree that threatened states may sometimes use military force against nonstate terrorist groups and terror suspects in unconsenting third countries if that country is "unwilling or unable" to mitigate the threat.

In its 2002 National Security Strategy, the Bush administration announced that the United States was prepared to act preemptively to counter threats from terrorists and rogue states even if the time and place of an attack remained uncertain.

One area in which international law rules have been hotly debated but remain unresolved two decades after the 9/11 attacks is the detention of terrorists captured by a state outside its territory. The Bush administration was criticized for placing hundreds of detained members of al-Qaeda and the Taliban in a "legal black hole" because it classified them neither as criminal suspects under U.S. law nor as prisoners of war under the Geneva Conventions. The Obama administration imposed stricter requirements for the humane treatment of detainees but continued to embrace the view that suspected terrorists could be detained under the laws of war until the end of the conflict. Legal experts (including the International Committee for the Red Cross) now acknowledge gaps and "legal haziness" in the international law governing detention of terrorists, but unfortunately no consensus on what rules should apply has emerged.

Presidents Bush, Obama, and Biden have all expressed concern about Guantanamo, and President Obama ordered the facility closed, but the U.S. Congress has passed legislation that has made closure difficult. Guantanamo could continue to be the most obvious legal legacy of the 9/11 attacks for several more decades.

Anne Koch
Associate, Global Issues Division, German Institute for International and Security Affairs (Germany)
The Mirage of Perfect Border Control

Among the immediate reactions in Western countries to the attacks of 9/11 was a rise in anti-Muslim sentiments and a reframing of migration control to counter the threat of further Islamist terrorist attacks. This led to a renewed emphasis on border security through the physical fortification of borders, a growing appetite for smart borders that rely on biometric data and increased intergovernmental data sharing. Authorities initially asserted that terror attacks came from foreign actors who slipped across the border. The data, however, does not support this idea: most jihadist attacks in the United States and the European Union (EU) have been conducted by citizens or legal residents of the country in question. Still, these efforts came with an illusion of the feasibility of near-perfect control. The effects reverberate today.

Twenty years on, European governments' reactions to the events currently unfolding in Afghanistan (that in and of themselves are a direct consequence of 9/11) bring the story full circle. Even days before the fall of the Afghan government, the European focus on migrant and refugee deportations to Afghanistan seemingly overrode concerns about the safety of local staff.

In this way, the mirage of—and subsequent fixation on—perfect border control continues to skew European governments' perspectives on current crises. It also deepens their dependency on authoritarian governments savvy at exploiting the EU's fear of uncontrolled immigration to their benefit." (130)

September 11 seemed fated to change radically and permanently the degree to which, and the way in which, the United States engaged with the rest of the world.

It is probably too soon to say for certain whether September 11 will prove to be such a "paradigm shift" along the lines of 1941 (when America abandoned isolationism), 1947 (when containment became the lens through which foreign policy was seen), or 1989 (when the "post-Cold War era" began). Much will depend on how the Administration responds, and whether it is able to maintain the level of focus and commitment on terrorism once the initial emotion and anger about the attack begins to subside. The political and psychological impact of the September 11 attacks will have long term implications for the ways in which the United States engages in the world. (131)

CHAPTER 24

Lessons learned from Afghanistan War

It was imperative for us to go after the Taliban and Bin Laden in Afghanistan and make them pay for all the innocent Americans they killed in the World Trade Centers and the Pentagon. In my opinion, however, it was not wise for us to occupy Afghanistan. Our losses and failure of what resulted speaks volumes in support of not sustaining a presence in Afghanistan. Once again, we did not take heed to what the Russians learned by their invasion of a forbidden landlocked multiethnic country covered with tall mountains and dry deserts.

"According to the Special Inspector General for Afghanistan Reconstruction (SIGAR), the U.S. government has now spent 20 years and $145 billion trying to rebuild Afghanistan, its security forces, civilian government institutions, economy, and civil society. The Department of Defense (DOD) has also spent $837 billion on warfighting, during which 2,443 American troops and 1,144 allied troops have been killed and 20,666 U.S. troops injured. Afghans, meanwhile, have faced an even greater toll. At least 66,000 Afghan troops have been killed. More than 48,000 Afghan civilians have been killed, and at least 75,000 have been injured since 2001—both significant underestimations.

At various points, the U.S. government hoped to eliminate al-Qaeda, decimate the Taliban movement that hosted it, deny all terrorist groups a safe haven in Afghanistan, build Afghan security forces so they could deny terrorists a safe haven in the future, and help the civilian government become legitimate and capable enough to win the trust of Afghans. Each goal, once accomplished, was thought to move the U.S. government one step closer to departing.

We should have learned from the Soviets that Afghanistan is a multi-cultured country that will fight against any foreign power that wishes to occupy it. "Islamic groups opposed the Soviet occupation. They were nationalists and against communism's suppression of religion. The Afghan army supported the Soviet Red Army, but the Soviets were not well trained and were poorly equipped. Islamic insurgent groups called the Mujahideen, were determined to fight against the Soviets. They were heavily armed as they were supplied by China and the USA, and they received training from the CIA. The Mujahideen employed guerrilla tactics against the Red Army. Using hit and run attacks they gained control of the rural and mountainous areas of Afghanistan."

The Soviet Union invaded Afghanistan for a different reason than that which provoked the United States invasion. The United States invaded to punish those responsible for 9/11 and to rid Afghanistan of bin Laden and the Taliban. In sharp contrast, "the Soviet Union invasion of Afghanistan was a Moscow-backed coup to install a new puppet leader, Babrak Karmal. The invasion triggered a brutal, nine-year-long Afghan civil war. Afghanistan's chaos alarmed Soviet leadership primarily because it increased the odds that Afghan leaders might turn to the United States for help. Top Politburo members warned Brezhnev in late October 1979 that Amin sought to pursue a more "balanced policy" and that the United States was detecting "the possibility of a change in the political line of Afghanistan. With 20/20 hindsight, it is easy to conclude that launching an invasion of Afghanistan to prop up an unpopular regime was a foolish, doomed venture. To Soviet leaders in Moscow during the short winter days of December 1979, however, the decision to do just that seemed logical—and inescapable.

The 1979 invasion triggered a brutal, nine-year civil war and contributed significantly to the USSR's later collapse in Afghanistan. By the time the last Soviet troops pulled out in early 1989, rumbling back across the ironically named "Friendship Bridge," the conflict had cost the lives of an estimated 1 million civilians and 125,000 Afghan, Soviet and other combatants. The war wreaked havoc not only on Afghanistan, but on the Soviet Union, whose economy and prestige took a severe drubbing. The military misadventure would contribute significantly to USSR's later collapse and breakup of the Soviet Union."

"While there have been several areas of improvement—most notably in the areas of health care, maternal health, and education—progress has been elusive and the prospects for sustaining this progress are dubious. The U.S. government has been often overwhelmed by the magnitude of rebuilding a country that, at the time of the U.S. invasion, had already seen two decades of Soviet occupation, civil war, and Taliban brutality.

In the report of the Special Inspector General for Afghanistan Reconstruction (SIGAR) was identified seven key lessons that span the entire 20-year campaign and can be used in other conflict zones around the globe.

1. **Strategy:** The U.S. government continuously struggled to develop and implement a coherent strategy for what it hoped to achieve. The challenges U.S. officials faced in creating long-term, sustainable improvements raise questions about the ability of U.S. government agencies to devise, implement, and

evaluate reconstruction strategies. The division of responsibilities among agencies did not always consider each agency's strengths and weaknesses.

2. **Timelines:** The U.S. government consistently underestimated the amount of time required to rebuild Afghanistan and created unrealistic timelines and expectations that prioritized spending quickly. These choices increased corruption and reduced the effectiveness of programs.

3. **Sustainability**: Many of the institutions and infrastructure projects the United States built were not sustainable. Reconstruction programs are not like humanitarian aid, which are not meant to provide temporary relief. Instead, they serve as a foundation for building the necessary institutions of government, civil society, and commerce to sustain the country indefinitely.

4. **Personnel:** Counterproductive civilian and military personnel pol icies and practices thwarted the effort. The U.S. government's inability to get the right people into the right jobs at the right times was one of the most significant failures of the mission. It is also one of the hardest to repair. U.S. personnel in Afghanistan were often unqualified and poorly trained.

5. **Insecurity:** Persistent insecurity severely undermined reconstruction efforts. The absence of violence was a critical precondition for everything U.S. officials tried to do in Afghanistan—yet the U.S. effort to rebuild the country took place while it was being torn apart.

6. **Context:** The U.S. government did not understand the Afghan context and therefore failed to tailor its efforts accordingly. Effectively rebuilding

Afghanistan required a detailed understanding of the country's social, economic, and political dynamics. However, U.S. officials were consistently operating in the dark, often because of the difficulty of collecting the necessary information. The U.S. government also clumsily forced Western technocratic models onto Afghan economic institutions; trained security forces in advanced weapon systems they could not understand, much less maintain; imposed formal rule of law on a country that addressed 80 to 90 percent of its disputes through informal means; and often struggled to understand or mitigate the cultural and social barriers to supporting women.

7. **Monitoring and Evaluation:** U.S. government agencies rarely conducted sufficient monitoring and evaluation to understand the impact of their efforts. Monitoring and evaluation (M&E) are the process of determining what works, what does not, and what needs to change as a result. Conceptually, M&E is straightforward, but in practice, it is extremely challenging. This is especially true in complex and unpredictable environments like Afghanistan, where staff turnover is rapid, multiple agencies must coordinate programs simultaneously, security and access restrictions make it hard to understand a program's challenges and impact, and a myriad of variables compete to influence outcomes."

SIGAR's extensive audit work on sectors spanning health, education, rule of law, women's rights, infrastructure, security assistance, and others collectively paints a picture of U.S. agencies struggling to effectively measure results while sometimes relying on shaky data to make claims of success. The U.S. government's M&E efforts in Afghanistan have been underemphasized and understaffed because the overall campaign focused on doing as much as possible as quickly as possible, rather than ensuring programs were designed well to begin with and could adapt as needed. As a result, the U.S. government missed many opportunities to identify critical flaws in its interventions or to act on those that were identified. These shortcomings endangered the lives of U.S., Afghan, and coalition government personnel and civilians, and undermined progress toward strategic goals.

In conclusion, this report raises critical questions about the U.S. government's ability to conduct reconstruction efforts on the scale seen in Afghanistan. As an inspector general's office charged with overseeing reconstruction spending in Afghanistan, SIGAR's approach has been technical; we identify specific problems and offer specific solutions. However, after 13 years of oversight, the cumulative list of systemic challenges SIGAR and other oversight bodies have identified is staggering. As former National Security Advisor Stephen Hadley told SIGAR, "We just do not have a post conflict stabilization model that works. Every time we have one of these things, it is a pick-up game. I do not have confidence that if we did it again, we would do any better."

This was equally apparent after the Vietnam War, when a war-weary and divided country had little appetite to engage in another similar conflict. After Vietnam, for example, the U.S. Army disbanded most active-duty civil affairs units and reduced the number of foreign area officers, the Army's "regionally focused experts in political-military operations." Special Forces moved away from counterinsurgency and instead focused on conducting small-scale operations in support of conventional forces. And USAID's global staff was gradually cut by 83 percent. In other words, according to former Vice Chief of Staff of the Army General Jack

Keane, "After the Vietnam War, we purged ourselves of everything that had to do with irregular warfare or insurgency, because it had to do with how we lost that war. In hindsight, which was a bad decision." After all, declining to prepare after Vietnam did not prevent the wars in Iraq and Afghanistan; instead, it ensured they would become quagmires.

Rather than motivating the U.S. government to improve, the difficulty of these missions may instead encourage U.S. officials to move on and prepare for something new. According to Robert Gates, former secretary of defense from 2006–2011:

I have noticed too much of a tendency towards what might be called 'Next-War-itis,' the propensity of much of the defense establishment to be in favor of what might be needed in a future conflict. Overall, the kinds of capabilities we will need in the years ahead will often resemble the kinds of capabilities we need today.

The post-Afghanistan experience may be no different. As this report shows, there are multiple reasons to develop these capabilities and prepare for reconstruction missions in conflict-affected countries:

- They usually go poorly.
- They were expensive. For example, all war-related costs for U.S. efforts in Afghanistan, Iraq, and Pakistan over the last two decades are estimated to be $6.4 trillion.
- Widespread recognition that they go poorly has not prevented U.S. officials from pursuing them.
- Rebuilding countries mired in conflict is a continuous U.S. government endeavor, reflected by efforts in the Balkans and Haiti and smaller efforts currently underway in Mali, Burkina Faso, Somalia, Yemen, Ukraine, and elsewhere.

- Large reconstruction campaigns usually start small, so it would not be hard for the U.S. government to slip down this slope again somewhere else and for the outcome to be like that of Afghanistan." (132)

The exodus of our troops from Afghanistan proved to be an embarrassment and a blemish on America. It was a shade of the exodus from Vietnam. Like Vietnam, the United States should never have escalated the war by having the boots of our soldiers on the ground of either country for such long periods of time.

A testimony of two former generals before Congress can provide some insight as to the withdrawal from Afghanistan.

Mark Milley, former Joint Chiefs of Staff chairman, and Kenneth McKenzie, who led US Central Command, testified for the first time since retiring. Republican lawmakers held President Joe Biden responsible for the disastrous exit, while Democrats blamed the Trump administration's deal with the Taliban. But the two generals seemed unwilling to back either party's argument.

Instead, they said that both the Biden and Trump administrations had had a role in the disastrous withdrawal, as had the administrations that preceded them.

The Doha agreement - a deal former President Donald Trump negotiated with the Taliban that set the terms for the US departure - "pulled the rug out, morale wise" of both the Afghan security forces and government, Mr. Milley said.

But he added later that the "fundamental flaw" of the US exit had been the timing of the Biden administration's decision to order a civilian evacuation in Afghanistan. He said it had come "too slow and too late".

He also emphasized that he had advised top American officials that the US "needed to maintain a minimum force of 2,500 troops on the ground" to prevent the Taliban from seizing control.

"Without this support, it was my view at the time, that it was a matter of 'when, not if' the Afghan government would collapse and the Taliban would take control," said Mr. Milley. Afghanistan President Ashraf Ghani's decision to flee the country as the Taliban marched toward Kabul was then "the straw that broke the camel's back", he said.

Still, both men maintained that no single factor alone had led to the US failure in Afghanistan, and they supported the idea that the US should review the entire 20-year history of the conflict, not just its conclusion - a point supported by Democrats. "We helped build an army, a state, but we could not build a nation," Mr. Milley said, calling the outcome a "strategic failure".

They also acknowledged that remaining in Afghanistan would have put American troops in harm's way, as the Taliban would have restarted its fight with the US for staying on beyond an agreed 31 August departure deadline, Mr. McKenzie said, citing intelligence reports he had reviewed.

Both men said the Taliban, which they characterized as a terrorist organization, harbored militants who wished to target the US.

"They themselves [the Taliban] don't have a desire to attack us and our homeland, but they do harbor entities and organizations that do have a desire to do that," Mr. McKenzie said.

Family members of American soldiers who died in the suicide blast at the Kabul airport and others who served in Afghanistan attended the hearing. They watched as the former military leaders gave their sober assessments about the US withdrawal.

As it was the two retired generals' first time testifying since leaving the service, both were able to be more candid in their criticisms of US civilian officials and policymakers.

Much of their criticism was directed at the US Department of State for not issuing the order to evacuate American civilian's months earlier.

Mr. McKenzie and Mr. Milley both testified that the US still did not know how many Americans were in Afghanistan, and it remains unclear how many were able to safely get out.

While much of the hearing rehashed old arguments made by Democrats and Republicans, there was some bipartisan news welcomed by lawmakers in the room.

Michael McCaul, the Republican chairman of the Foreign Affairs Committee, announced that the White House and Congressional leaders had agreed to grant 12,000 more special immigrant visas for Afghan nationals who assisted the US. He said it would be included in a budget deal that is expected to pass this week.

Veterans of the war in Afghanistan and lawmakers have been fighting to expand the number of visas for Afghanistan immigrants, as only about 7,000 remained. The US has issued about 1,000 per month recently, raising fears that they could run out.

US troops pulled out of Afghanistan after 20 years - the country's longest ever war - and it left many Afghans who supported American forces in danger, particularly as viable exits from the country closed.

The violent withdrawal dented perceptions of Mr. Biden's international competence. Republicans have since seized on the failed exit as key line of attack ahead of the November presidential election.

The Biden administration and Democrats have regularly blamed Donald Trump for negotiating the agreement with the Taliban that led to the withdrawal, arguing that his decisions "severely constrained" Mr. Biden's options.

A government watchdog found that both administrators were to blame for the disastrous withdrawal that saw Afghan forces overwhelmed." (132)

Lest we forget the billions in weapons and equipment that our government left behind. An NBC news article reported that "Weapons left behind by U.S. forces during the withdrawal from Afghanistan are surfacing in another conflict, further arming militants in the disputed South Asian region of Kashmir in what experts say could be just the start of the weapons' global journey. Like our military, the Soviet forces left equipment and weapons behind when they exited.

Authorities in Indian-controlled Kashmir tell NBC News that militants trying to annex the region for Pakistan are carrying M4s, M16s and other U.S.-made arms and ammunition

Photo-27-Abandoned Soviet Equipment

that have rarely been seen in the 30-year conflict. A major reason, they say, is a flood of U.S.-funded weapons that fell into the hands of the Taliban when U.S.-led NATO forces withdrew from Afghanistan in 2021.

Most of the weapons recovered so far, officials say, are from Jaish-e-Mohammad (JeM) or Lashkar-e-Taiba, both Pakistan-based militant groups that the U.S. designates as terrorist organizations. In a Twitter post last year, for example, police said they had seized an M4 carbine assault rifle after a gunfight that killed two militants from JeM.

Militants from both groups had been sent to Afghanistan to fight alongside or train the Taliban before the

U.S. withdrawal, said Lt. Col. Emron Musavi, an Indian army spokesperson in Srinagar, the capital of Kashmir.

"It can be safely assumed that they have access to the weapons left behind," he said in an email last year.

Government officials in Afghanistan and Pakistan did not respond to requests for comment.

Kashmir, a Himalayan region known for its beautiful landscapes, shares borders with India, Pakistan, Afghanistan, and China. A separatist insurgency in the part of Kashmir controlled by India has killed tens of thousands of people since the 1990s and been a constant source of tension between nuclear powers India and Pakistan.

The year opened in violence as Kashmir police blamed militants for a Jan. 1 gunfire attack that killed four people in the southern village of Dhangri, followed by an explosion in the same area the next day that killed a 5-year-old boy and a 12-year-old girl. At least six people were injured on Jan. 21 in two explosions in the city of Jammu.

While the U.S.-made weapons are unlikely to shift the balance of power in the Kashmir conflict, they give the Taliban a sizable reservoir of combat power potentially available to those willing and able to purchase it, said Jonathan Schroden, director of the Countering Threats and Challenges Program at the Center for Naval Analyses, a research group based outside Washington." When combined with the Taliban's need for money and extant smuggling networks, that reservoir poses a substantial threat to regional actors for years to come," he said.

More than $7.1 billion in U.S.-funded military equipment was in the possession of the Afghan government when it fell to the Taliban in August 2021 amid the withdrawal, according to a Defense Department report published last August. Though more than half of it was ground vehicles, it also included more than 316,000 weapons worth $512 million, plus ammunition and other accessories.

While large numbers of small arms that had been transferred to Afghan forces most likely ended up in the hands of the Taliban, "it's important to remember that nearly all weapons and equipment used by U.S. military forces in Afghanistan were either retrograded or destroyed prior to our withdrawal," Lt. Col. Rob Lodewick, said.

"The Defense Department report also pointed out that the operational condition of the Afghan army's equipment was unknown. Questions around the weapons being used in Kashmir were raised in January 2022, when a video of militants brandishing what may be American-made guns was shared widely on Indian social media. Though the origin of the weapons in such cases can be difficult to verify — some may be modified to look like U.S. weapons, while others may not have been manufactured in the U.S. — the Indian military says it has recovered at least seven that are authentic.

From the weapons and equipment that we recovered, we realized that there was a spillover of high-tech weapons, night-vision devices and equipment, which were left by the Americans in Afghanistan and were now finding their way toward this side," Maj. Gen. Ajay Chandpuria, an Indian army official, was quoted as saying by Indian media last year.

Kashmir Lt. Gov. Manoj Sinha said the government was aware of the issue and that measures were in place to combat the infiltration of U.S. weapons into Kashmir." (133)

"We are monitoring the situation closely and have taken steps accordingly. Our police and army are on the job," Sinha, the region's top official, said on the sidelines of a news conference last year at his official residence in Srinagar. Kashmir police official Vijay Kumar also said authorities were fully capable of countering the militant threat. "Our forces are tracking down militants on a daily basis," he said. "We are constantly upgrading our equipment and have the latest weaponry at our disposal."

The militant groups could be buying U.S. weapons from the Taliban in Afghanistan, where the United Nations says both groups have bases, or through smugglers in Pakistan, said Ajai Sahni, an author on counterterrorism who serves as executive director of the Institute for Conflict Management, a think tank in New Delhi.

Schroden said that although he had not seen substantial reports of U.S.-made weapons left behind in Afghanistan appearing outside of Kashmir, it would not be surprising if they eventually began turning up farther away in places such as Yemen, Syria, and parts of Africa.

"I suspect there hasn't yet been enough time for these weapons to percolate out that far," he said. "It's also possible that the Taliban have held tightly to most of them thus far as part of their efforts to consolidate power and seek legitimization from the international community."

Beyond the weapons, the Taliban's victory in Afghanistan gave an ideological boost to radical militants in Kashmir and elsewhere, said Ahmad Shuja Jamal, a former Afghan civil servant living in exile in Australia. Such militants, he said, "now see in clear terms the political dividends of long-term violence." (134)

"At various points, the U.S. government hoped to eliminate al-Qaeda, decimate the Taliban movement that hosted it, deny all terrorist groups a safe haven in Afghanistan, build Afghan security forces so they could deny terrorists a safe haven in the future, and help the civilian government become legitimate and capable enough to win the trust of Afghans. Each goal, once accomplished, was thought to move the U.S. one step closer to departing." (135)

CHAPTER 25

Lessons Learned from Iraq War

On May 1, 2003, President George W. Bush appeared in a nationally televised address aboard the aircraft carrier *USS Abraham Lincoln,* standing in front of a "Mission Accomplished" banner. The implication was that major combat operations in Iraq were over. But his team of top advisors said that was not the plan.

Photo 28-Aircraft Carrier Abraham Lincoln with Mission Accomplished Sign

Ari Fleischer, White House press secretary said that the banner read "Mission Accomplished." In the speech Bush gave, Bush said there were many parts of Iraq that were dangerous. Major combat operations were over, but it was going to take time and there was a lot of danger ahead. He gave a perfectly nuanced, qualified speech to end major combat operations, which were exactly chosen words for just that reason, because we knew there was still fighting in the Sunni triangle and especially in Fallujah.

The ship was steaming back from duty in and around the Gulf and was the longest-deployed ship in the history of the United States Navy. Our advanced people met the crew of the *Abraham Lincoln*. They flew to Hawaii and then boarded the ship as the ship was steaming back toward San Diego and the crew was excited: the Commander in Chief is coming out. He is going to declare combat is over from here. They asked if they could hang a sign in honor of them being the longest-deployed ship. They successfully, in their view, had completed their mission, which they did, and they wanted to have a sign that read "Mission Accomplished."

Our guys thought, *Great idea. It is a fitting tribute to you.* Certainly, it fit into the theme of what we were talking about. On May 2, it assuredly felt as if the mission had been accomplished: Saddam was out of power, Baghdad fell, hardly any lives had been lost. At that time, you could go to downtown Baghdad and eat at outdoor cafes. It was one of the safest places on earth, with no crime, no violence. People forget that we *were* greeted with flowers. That was the reality of May.

The banner was hung because our advance team thought it was a good idea, a tribute to the sailors and Marines aboard the ship. Bush landed in his flight suit, producing just tumultuous, fabulous pictures, but we started to hear a little "Is it over the top?" pushback from some people on TV.

White House deputy chief of staff for policy; director of the Office of Management and Budget; chief of staff said: "This is the episode that really resonates through time: the banner behind Bush on the aircraft carrier that said, "mission accomplished." Somebody allowed that to be put up. My understanding in retrospect was that the banner was intended for the sailors onboard that ship—they had accomplished their mission, and they were headed home. But somebody made a bad mistake allowing that to be in the photo.

Bush never said those words, and in fact if you go back and read his remarks, he is complimenting the troops on the great job they have done and preparing everybody for the important work that lies ahead. Yet that "mission accomplished" moment is an emblem. So, somebody did that." (136)

A good friend of mine, who served in World War II as a Tank Commander, said to me when he saw the banner, "They are wrong, it is not over. Its only just begun." It turned out that he was right.

While serving in the NMCC, I never saw on our Watch that there was clear and undeniable evidence that Iraq had a weapons cache of mass destruction. It seemed that instead of relying on sound intel, the powers to be were relying on hearsay.

An excellent article that can be found in the Council on foreign relations summarizes what we should have learned from the Iraq war and what I have always contended. We should have gone into Afghanistan and punished those that killed all the innocent Americans, but we should not have occupied.

"The decision to go to war was the initial and most grievous error, though a subsequent series of poor decisions compounded its effects. As was subsequently discovered, the justification for going to war was based on scanty and deeply flawed intelligence: Saddam Hussein did not have weapons of mass destruction, and the U.S. intelligence community knew that "Curveball," a principal source of that bad intelligence, was not dependable.

Senior regional experts warned of the perfect storm that could ensue if Saddam were toppled, and of the massive years-long reconstruction project that would be required to restore stability. Nevertheless, Secretary of State Colin Powell presented a stitched-together case for war before the United Nations, claiming that "what we're giving you are facts and conclusions based on solid intelligence."

Group think infected the U.S. government to an alarming degree. It is tempting to ask what if Colin Powell, the most likely candidate, had stepped down in protest? He voiced reservations but neither he nor any other principal explicitly argued against going to war. A former four-star general and chairman of the Joint Chiefs of Staff who presided over the earlier Desert Storm operation to evict Iraq from Kuwait, his resignation could have set off a chain reaction of resignations and congressional opposition sufficient to stop the invasion. He could have insisted on abiding by the Powell Doctrine, which was violated in every precept.

The Iraq War did not involve a clearly demonstrated vital interest; clear and obtainable goals and a withdrawal plan were not established; the risks and costs were not fully analyzed; and nonmilitary means were not exhausted. If the executive branch cannot apply these guidelines, Congress should.

Lesson learned: Adopt the Powell Doctrine and vigorously debate all your decisions. Listen to your experts and do not go to war when intelligence is weak.

The decision to stay: The error of the invasion was immediately compounded by the absence of an agreed withdrawal plan and the decision to embark on a massive, open-ended nation-building project. The occupation authority's first acts were to disband the Iraqi army and the Ba'athist governing party, igniting what would become a lethal, long-running insurgency and eventually a multinational terrorist organization that took over most of the country. A sectarian government stacked with elite politicians took root, along with a patronage system to divide the spoils of the hydrocarbon industry, further supercharging the insurgency.

Lesson: Do not engage in regime change. Again, Powell tartly summarized the consequences: "If you break it, you own it." The alternative was to engage in a surgical operation to seek and destroy identified weapons of mass destruction (WMD) facilities.

The decision to surge: By 2007 Iraq was on fire, and after numerous deliberations, the third major erroneous decision was reached, to double down on a military strategy with a "surge" of U.S. troops. This effort achieved a short-lived effect of dampening the violence but did not address the root causes of violence, which was the lack of a governance arrangement that Iraqis would accept. The overarching lesson is that foreign militaries are ill equipped to serve as social engineers, and societies only evolve at a generational pace.

The use of military force deserves to be carefully circumscribed and large-scale counterinsurgency eschewed. Foreign militaries may successfully eject invading forces, as occurred in Desert Storm, but an even more effective approach is to help the national forces defend their own country as currently in Ukraine. The military's record in intrastate counterinsurgency suggests that it often does more harm than good: Soldiers adopted the term "COIN math" to refer to the proliferation of enraged surviving family members who take up arms to avenge those who have been killed by foreign forces. **Lesson**: Do not use the U.S. military to conduct large-scale counterinsurgency or nation building.

The decision to stay: The decision to withdraw in 2011 was also beset by a series of errors. In 2008, the U.S. government negotiated a bilateral strategic framework agreement that was intended to pave the way for a more normal relationship with this significant Middle Eastern country via trade, cultural, and educational exchanges, with political and diplomatic ties taking precedence over military ones. This agreement has not been robustly implemented to this day.

Instead, the U.S. government decided to back sitting Prime Minister Nouri al-Maliki's bid for continued power, despite the fact that Iyad Allawi won a plurality in the 2010 election with broader support. Maliki's sectarian and personal ambitions were well known, and his subsequent actions in purging and politicizing the military and government set the stage for the advent of the Islamic State and the collapse of the Iraqi army, which had been built with billions of dollars of U.S. security assistance.

Lesson: Back democratic processes and leaders with broad-based support.

The Empowerment of Sectarians, Not Democracy

Iraq moved farther away from the goal of reforming the 2005 constitution, which did not address major issues of governance and resources that divided Iraq's Sunni, Shi'a and Kurdish population. Former U.S. Ambassador to Iraq Zalmay Khalilzad acknowledged its flaws by proclaiming its revision as his priority to persuade Iraqis to ratify the document. In the eighteen years since, the substantial human capital and immense oil resources of Iraq have been diverted into corruption and patronage politics rather than much needed electricity, water, health care, and education for the people. A vicious five-year battle commenced in 2014 to uproot the Islamic State from half of Iraq's territory, subjecting its people to yet more war. In this renewed spasm of violence, the United States felt compelled to intervene once more, although it had learned enough to back the Iraqi forces with advisors and material aid rather than attempting to lead the fight itself.

As of today, the political imperative of a functioning and responsive government remains unmet. In late 2019, the country's young population—most Iraqis are under age twenty-five—exploded in frustration. Months of protest were met by violence, mostly from Iranian-backed militias who have gained a strong foothold in the security service and in a segment of the Iraqi Shi'a political parties. High abstention rates in the last two elections indicate an alarming disillusionment with Iraq's democratic experiment. Modest electoral reform may be reversed by sectarians, and the government has yet to agree on a hydrocarbons law, resolution of disputed territories, and a truly democratic system.

Lesson: Make sure assistance supports democratic processes and needs of the population. Congress must be more aggressive in terminating programs that fail to achieve intended aims.

The Effects on U.S. Democracy

The costs of the Iraq War have been calculated at $8 trillion if the veterans' health-care costs are included; some 300,000 Iraqi civilians were killed, over 9 million displaced, and 4,598 U.S. troops and 3,650 contractors were killed.

The long shadow of Iraq extends beyond these quantifiable effects. The toll the war's decision-making has taken on U.S. democracy has been equally grievous. The absence of any formal reckoning eats at our soul. No leader has stepped forward with a full and honest mea culpa, as Robert McNamara did after the Vietnam War. Instead, a Vietnam era–like erosion of public confidence continues, stoking a current of isolationism that calls for no foreign involvement at all, and even more corrosive, a culture of brazen, arrogant mendacity that infects American politics.

Unlike in Britain, where the Chilcot inquiry forced all senior officials to testify in an exhaustive investigation and exposed the decision-making that led to the rush to war, the absence of sound rationale, and lack of preparation for the aftermath, there has been no effort in the United States to hold senior U.S. officials accountable for the failure to conduct a deliberate process. Sadly, none of the principal officials have publicly regretted the invasion and the enormous toll it took on both the United States and Iraq.

Lesson: Take measures to hold officials accountable and restore public confidence in government when you fail." (137)

CHAPTER 26

Never Ending Wars

The United States continually gets involved directly or indirectly wars across the world. One would wonder if we did not get involved in these wars, could we have paid off the national debt.

"The United States has been involved in many wars and minor conflicts since its birth, but the 12 major wars include the American Revolution, the War of 1812, the Indian Wars, the Mexican-American Wars, the Civil War, the Spanish-American War, World War I, World War II, the Korean War, the Vietnam War, the Persian Gulf War and the War on Terror (which encompasses the War in Afghanistan and Iraq War).

The United States has engaged in several wars that resulted in minimal gain or outright loss for the US. These include conflicts like the War of 1812, the Korean War, and the Vietnam War.

The Civil War was the deadliest war in American history. An estimated 360,000 Americans soldiers on both the sides of the Union and Confederacy met their end on the battlefield.

The periods of peacetime between wars has varied in the history of the United States. It can range anywhere as long as 45 years, like between the War of 1812 and the Mexican

American War, or as short as one year, like between the Korean and Vietnam War." (138)

The number of our soldiers killed in battle is mind bugling. What is more inexcusable is that many who paid the ultimate price could have been avoided if we had common sense leaders on both sides of the conflicts. These unsung heroes had a life, family, and future when they left to defend our freedoms. Other than a few wars like World War II, our leaders in Washington should never have taken their dreams and the dreams of their families away.

"American Revolution (1775-1783) Total U.S. Servicemembers 217,000 Battle Deaths 4,435 Non-mortal Woundings 6,188

War of 1812 (1812-1815) Total U.S. Servicemembers 286,730 Battle Deaths 2,260 Non-mortal Woundings 4,505

Indian Wars (approx. 1817-1898) Total U.S. Servicemembers (VA estimate) 106,000 Battle Deaths (VA estimate) 1,00

Mexican War (1846-1848) Total U.S. Servicemembers 78,718 Battle Deaths 1,733 Other Deaths (In Theater) 11,550 Non-mortal Woundings 4,152

Civil War (1861-1865) Total U.S. Servicemembers (Union) 2,213,363 Battle Deaths (Union) 140,414 Other Deaths (In Theater) (Union) 224,097 Non-mortal Woundings (Union) 281,881 Total Servicemembers (Conf.) 2 1,050,000 Battle Deaths (Confederate) 3 74,524 Other Deaths (In Theater) (Confederate) 3, 4 59,297 Non-mortal Woundings (Confederate) Unknown

Spanish-American War (1898-1902) Total U.S. Servicemembers (Worldwide) 306,760 Battle Deaths 385 Other Deaths in Service (Non-Theater) 2,061 Non-mortal Woundings 1,662

World War I (1917-1918) Total U.S. Servicemembers (Worldwide) 4,734,991 Battle Deaths 53,402 Other Deaths in Service (Non-Theater) 63,114 Non-mortal Woundings 204,002

World War II (1941 –1945) Total U.S. Servicemembers (Worldwide) 16,112,566 Battle Deaths 291,557 Other Deaths in Service (Non-Theater) 113,842 Non-mortal woundings 670,846 Living Veterans 5 389,000

Korean War (1950-1953) Total U.S. Servicemembers (Worldwide) 5,720,000 Total Serving (In Theater) 1,789,000 Battle Deaths 33,739 Other Deaths (In Theater) 2,835 Other Deaths in Service (Non-Theater) 17,672 Non-mortal Woundings 103,284 Living Veterans 1,165,000

Vietnam War (1964-1975) Total U.S. Servicemembers (Worldwide) 6 8,744,000 Deployed to Southeast Asia 7 3,403,000 Battle Deaths 8 47,434 Other Deaths (In Theater) 8 10,786 Other Deaths in Service (Non-Theater) 8 32,000 Non-mortal Woundings 9 153,303 Living Veterans 5, 10 6,262,000

Desert Shield/Desert Storm (1990-1991) Total U.S. Servicemembers (Worldwide) 2,225,000 Deployed to Gulf 694,550 Battle Deaths 148 Other Deaths (In Theater) 235 Other Deaths in Service (Non-Theater) 1,565 Non-mortal Woundings 467 Living Veterans 5, 10 1,680,000

America's Wars Total (1775 -1991) U.S. Military Service during Wartime 41,892,128 Battle Deaths 651,031 Other Deaths (In Theater) 308,800 Other Deaths in Service (Non-Theater) 230,254 Non-mortal woundings 1,430,290 Living War Veterans11 14,918,000 Living Veterans (Periods of War & Peace) 19,210,000 Global War on Terror (Oct 2001 – Sept 2021)

The Global War on Terror (GWOT), including Operation Enduring Freedom (OEF) and Operation Iraqi Freedom (OIF), were ongoing conflicts. The GWPT ended September 11, 2021, the twentieth anniversary of the attacks.

For the most current GWOT statistics visit the Department of Defense website." (139)

Vietnam War

The Vietnam War is just one of those many wars that should never have taken innocent lives.

Before the Afghanistan war, "the Vietnam War was the longest and most unpopular foreign war in U.S. history and cost 58,000 American lives. As many as two million Vietnamese soldiers and civilians were killed. When U.S. troops left Afghanistan, the war will have lasted two decades and spanned four presidencies. The longest war in U.S. history has come at the financial cost of close to $1 trillion. It has killed more than 2,000 American soldiers and, according to some estimates, hundreds of thousands of Afghans."

To boot, the administration left behind large caches of weapons and material, many of which are turning up in other insurgent conflicts. "More than $7.1 billion in U.S.-funded military equipment was in the possession of the Afghan government when it fell to the Taliban in August 2021 amid the withdrawal, according to a Defense Department report published last August. Though more than half of it was ground vehicles, it also included more than 316,000 weapons worth almost $512 million, plus ammunition and other accessories. Beyond weapons, the Taliban's victory in Afghanistan gave an ideological boost to radical militants in Kashmir and elsewhere, said Ahmad Shuja Jamal, a former Afghan civil servant living in exile in Australia. Such militants, he said, "now see in clear terms the political dividends of long-term violence. Authorities in Indian-controlled Kashmir tell NBC News that militants trying to annex the region for Pakistan are carrying M4s, M16s and other U.S.-made arms and ammunition that have rarely been seen in the 30-year conflict. A major reason, they say, is a regional flood of U.S.-funded weapons that fell into the hands of the Taliban when U.S.-led NATO forces withdrew from Afghanistan in 2021." (140)

You would think that our government would have learned from the loses of equipment and weapons when we pulled out of Vietnam.

An article in the New York time date 1975 reported The South Vietnamese have lost more than $1 billion in American military weapons and other equipment over the last two weeks, according to qualified Vietnamese sources. The abandonment of hundreds of artillery pieces, trucks, planes, mortars, tanks, armored personnel carriers, rifles, and ammunition—coupled with the rapid retreat of army units— is viewed by Vietnamese and Western sources as a stunning and quite possibly irreversible military and psychological blow for South Vietnam.

A senior Western official, who has spent more than a decade in South Vietnam, said today: "These losses are very, very, very considerable. It is a catastrophic loss." Another informed Western source said: "We've made no attempt to quantify the loss, but it is staggering. The equipment has not been saved at all and we are facing a devastating failure."

"An informed Vietnamese said that the armed forces logistics command, which controls the inventory of all military equipment, had made a tentative estimate of at least $1 billion in equipment losses—virtually all of it left over by the Americans — because of the Government's abrupt decision to abandon two-thirds of the nation and the hasty, panicky exodus of civilians and troops that followed. Lack of coordination: As the scale of the military retreat becomes apparent, Western military analysts and Vietnamese sources express dismay and alarm at the lack of armed-forces coordination, "the failure of leadership up and down the line" in the chaos that has engulfed army units beset with mass defections and the huge loss of equipment to the advancing North Vietnamese. One intelligence source said: "There's been a complete loss of control by most of the army, by civilians. Self-preservation is everything, there's total panic at Da Nang airport, the army has left an extraordinary amount of equipment behind in the north and Central Highlands. It has become a tragedy that I just cannot grasp." (141)

"There are many lessons of Vietnam, but three stand out in explaining why the United States lost the war—ignorance, arrogance, and the absence of a viable local ally. All three continue to characterize American policy today and help to explain why wars in Iraq and Afghanistan also have failed to achieve success.

MISGUIDED INTERVENTIONS

The United States entered Vietnam without an understanding of the country's history and culture. We did not speak the language or know the people. We viewed Vietnam through the lens of a Cold War struggle against communism rather than as a national independence struggle against colonialism and foreign domination. We did not realize the extent of the social revolution in Vietnam led by the National Liberation Front (NLF), which gave land to the tillers and solidified support for the liberation struggle. We did not understand that the war was lost politically before it ever began militarily.

U.S. interventions in Iraq and Afghanistan were equally ill-informed. We entered without the ability to speak Arabic, Pashto or other local languages and had little or no understanding of tribal and ethnic dynamics. We were unprepared for the armed resistance and terrorist insurgencies that arose against us and the regimes we created. We did not realize in Iraq that removing Saddam Hussein would benefit Iran and Shia militias, or that a war against the Taliban in Afghanistan would intensify violence and instability in Pakistan.

Closely allied with ignorance is arrogance, the tendency to exaggerate our own power and underestimate that of our foes. In Vietnam we believed that American military superiority would guarantee success, that military firepower and technology could overpower our adversaries and force them to capitulate. We did not realize that an overreliance on military means can create new enemies and strengthen the very forces we seek to overcome. We watched helplessly as Saigon's repression and our own military attacks drove people into the arms of the NLF. We miscalculated the strength of the resistance forces and their tenacity and determination to fight despite heavy losses.

Today we continue to believe in the myth of American exceptionalism if military superiority gives us the right to function as the world's policeman. We do not understand the limits of military power or realize the negative consequences of our interventions. We believe as before that our advanced technology, now including drones, can defeat our enemies. During the Cold War we viewed local conflicts as part of a global struggle against communism. Today we misjudge diverse crises from Libya to Yemen through the singular lens of countering global terrorism. We are engaged militarily in a growing number of countries, yet insurgent forces remain strong, and we face a new and even greater threat now with the emergence of ISIS.

LOCAL GOVERNANCE MISSING

The third factor that has undermined American policy from Vietnam to the present is the absence of credible political partners. Without a local governance system that can win the trust and loyalty of local populations, external military intervention cannot succeed. Accountable governments capable of delivering public goods are essential for generating political stability, economic opportunity, and peace. These have been missing in American interventions from Vietnam to Afghanistan.

The Saigon regime was a foreign creation and depended entirely on external assistance for its political, economic, and military survival. The Diem regime that emerged with American support after the Geneva accords lacked political legitimacy and had little support outside the Catholic community, which was less than 10 percent of the population. Diem's repression and corruption led to his assassination in the CIA-backed coup of 1963, followed by years of revolving door military dictatorships and then the autocratic Thieu regime. Despite massive levels of American economic and military sustenance, Thieu's government never attracted substantial political support. The American-created Saigon army looked impressive on paper when U.S. American troops left, but it collapsed rapidly in the face of the final assault from Hanoi's forces in 1975.

Similar problems have plagued American interventions in Afghanistan and Iraq. The Kabul regime is rated among the world's most corrupt and has been unable to command much popular support or gain control over the country's restive regions. It could not function without massive external financial and political support. In Baghdad sectarian violence has been rampant, and Shia militias have suppressed Sunni communities, prompting some to turn to ISIS for protection.

The American-created Iraqi army has proved powerless against ISIS. It has been easy for the United States to overthrow dictatorships but exceedingly difficult to replace them with legitimate governments.

The lessons of Vietnam remain as relevant now as they were decades ago. Military intervention is more often the problem than the solution in American foreign policy." (142)

"The frustrating experience of Vietnam is indelibly etched in the minds of America's senior military officers, and from it they seem to have taken three general lessons. First, the military has drawn from Vietnam a reminder of the infinite limits of American public support for US involvement in a protracted conflict.

Second, the military has taken from Vietnam (and the concomitant repercussions in the Pentagon) a heightened awareness that civilian officials are responsive to influences other than the objective conditions on the battlefield. A consequence has been an increase in traditional military suspicions about politicians and political appointees.

Finally, the military took from Vietnam a new recognition of the limits of military power in solving certain types of problems in world affairs. Vietnam planted doubts in many military minds about the ability of US forces to conduct successful large-scale counterinsurgencies. These misgivings do not in all cases spring from doubts about the capabilities of American troops and units per se; even in Vietnam, military leaders recall, US units never lost a battle. Rather, the doubts that are part of the Vietnam legacy spring from a number of interrelated factors: worries about a lack of popular support for what the public might perceive as ambiguous conflicts; the previously mentioned suspicions about the willingness of politicians—not just those in the executive branch—to stay the course; lurking fears that the respective services have yet to come to grips with the difficult tasks of developing the doctrine, equipment, and forces suitable for nasty little wars. These lessons have had a chastening effect on military thinking." (143)

Brookings Edu posted another hindsight on the Vietnam War, why it was the wrong war, and lessons learned from the war.

"Twenty-five years after the ignominious American withdrawal from what was then South Vietnam, this much is clear: the United States lost the war but won the peace. Indeed, it is difficult to imagine how things could have turned out much better if we had won the war. The United States remains the dominant power in the Asia-Pacific region. U.S. alliances with such critical states as Japan, South Korea and Australia are robust; U.S. relations with China are extensive if not always warm. Even U.S. relations with Vietnam are now proper and improving. The region is mostly democratic, wealthy and at peace. And despite gloomy predictions to the contrary, "dominos" did not fall to Communism after we lost in Vietnam.

Also worth noting is that some 15 years after the flag came down over the American Embassy in Saigon and the helicopters flew away from its roof, the Cold War ended. In this case, though, the United States and the West won the war. This outcome resulted not just from Soviet shortcomings—exacerbated by the Soviet "Vietnam" in Afghanistan—but from American perseverance. The U.S. failure in Vietnam did not trigger the wholesale retreat from responsibility into isolationism that many feared would result.

Still, the wrong war

None of these changes the reality that the Vietnam War was the wrong war—an unnecessary war. This in no way cheapens or in any way detracts from the sacrifice by so many Americans. Rather, the judgment is a strategic one:

The American commitment to Vietnam exaggerated its importance. What happened on the ground in that country could not alter the basic shape of the strategic competition between the United States and the Soviet Union. It was a distraction, one that wasted resources of every kind. The notion that the war fundamentally affected U.S. interests everywhere proved mistaken.

Moreover, the United States misread the threat. Washington was slow to see the growing divide between Moscow and Beijing. Communism was not monolithic. Nationalism counted for more. This was true as well in Vietnam, where the Communists in both the North and the South were more nationalists than instruments of the Soviet Union or anyone else.

Why did we get so involved then? More than anything else, it was domestic politics, and the concern of John F. Kennedy—and to an even greater extent Lyndon Johnson—that the American people would not forgive the politicians or the party that "lost" Vietnam. Both remembered the price paid by Democrats charged by Sen. Joe McCarthy (R-WI) and others with "losing" China.

The irony, of course, is that Johnson paid an enormous price for prosecuting the war as he did. His attempt to build the Great Society went unfinished. He himself did not stand for re-election. And Richard Nixon was elected, ushering in more than two decades of Republican domination of the White House interrupted only by the fallout of Watergate.

Lessons Learned

The lessons from that war are still applicable today: not permitting domestic politics to determine foreign policy; asking hard questions about history and culture before the United States commits its prestige and its men and women in uniform; not underestimating the power of local forces in global politics.

The Vietnam War was not simply the wrong war; it was also fought in the wrong way. Military force should only be used decisively, not gradually. Civilian officials should set basic policies but allow the professional military to run wars without micromanagement. Quantitative measures—how many bombs are dropped, how many enemy troops killed—may be irrelevant to the course of the battle and should not be taken as proof of progress. Airpower alone wins few campaigns. High technology is no panacea and cannot in and of itself defeat a committed adversary. What is worrisome about this cataloguing of lessons is how many of them have been violated in such faraway places as Somalia and Kosovo.

The good news, though, is that the American people seem ahead of their leaders in not forgetting Vietnam's lessons or repeating its mistakes. It remains possible for the United States to commit itself and to fight high-cost military interventions so long as American people believe the stakes justify them. It is also possible to sustain commitments where the stakes are low so long as the costs of intervening are kept modest. What the American people will not stand for, however, are interventions where U.S. interests are modest, but the costs in human and financial terms are high. This principle, as much as anything else, is what Vietnam must teach us—and what we would only forget at great peril to ourselves." (144)

Korean War

Korea would be another long and costly war. Five lessons from the Korean war would be appropriate to what we should have learned from another long and drawn-out war in a distant land and at that time a foreboding frontier.

"The Korean War broke out in an era of great-power competition. Today's great-power competition is quite different, but many of the dynamics that turned the Land of the Morning Calm into a battlefield 70 years ago are present now. Thus, the Korean conflict offers important lessons for maintaining stability in today's world.

Do not Prioritize Yourself Out of Conventional Deterrence: As the former World War II allies began facing off in a new Cold War, the Pentagon well understood it would be a global struggle. Yet even as the Cold War was heating up, U.S. military budgets were being squeezed to accommodate demands for a domestic "peace dividend." The Pentagon's answer was to prioritize American global commitments. Europe, of course, was the main concern, so cuts were made everywhere else. This left the U.S. with a weak post-war occupation force in South Korea. The military chiefs decided that, if war broke out there, we would not fight. As a result, they made no contingency plans for fighting on the peninsula.

When President Truman awoke to news of the North Korea invasion South Korea, he immediately understood the danger of allowing Communist aggression, sanctioned, and supported by Moscow, going unchallenged. A U.S. presence in Asia was crucial to global stability. America was on its way to turning Japan, a former enemy, it into a key free world ally—a crucial geostrategic objective. The war in Korea threatened the peace and security of all Northeast Asia. America had to respond.

Of course, strategists should prioritize and devote most resources to countering the greatest threat. On the other hand, a good strategy cannot compromise on any meeting any danger that threatens core vital interests. Those risks are not worth taking.

As a global power with global interests and responsibilities, America needs sufficient military power to respond to all of them. During World War II, for example, the allies focused first on the greatest threat—Nazi Germany—but they did not stop fighting the war in the Pacific. They balanced commitments. They did not neglect them.

This lesson is particularly crucial for facing off in today's great-power competition. Though China may be the greatest concern, America cannot focus solely on Asia. For one thing, China's influence and destabilizing activities are global. U.S. counteractions must be global as well. Further, the U.S. cannot neglect other critical theaters, including Europe and the Greater Middle East; we have critical interests and peace-keeping responsibilities there as well.

No More Task Force Smith: When President Truman ordered the American military to help defend South Korea, the Pentagon sent in the closest troops available: occupation forces from Japan. The brigade-size force, called Task Force Smith, lacked the training, readiness, and equipment to function as a credible combat unit. They were not even a speed bump.

Many folks take the wrong lesson from Task Force Smith. This was not just about being unprepared. Even if Task Force Smith had been the best-trained brigade in the world, they still would have been crushed by an invading army of overwhelming size.

Quantity has a quality all its own. It is not just being present that matters. The U.S. must have forces that represent a credible deterrent in all the key places around the world. That means forces that can be protected and reinforced. Potential enemies must know at the front end of a conflict there are no cheap, easy wins when the Americans are around.

Do not Rob Peter to Pay Paul: Eventually the U.S. deployed sufficient forces to blunt the North Korean invasion. However, they lacked the additional power needed to go on the offensive and liberate the occupied parts of the country. They needed two divisions. At the time, the entire U.S. strategic reserve of active divisions was... two. If the Pentagon sent them to Korea, there would be nothing available to reinforce Europe. At great strategic risk, Korea got the extra divisions. Meanwhile, the Pentagon scrambled to build up additional forces to meet global commitments.

Since the end of the Cold War, the U.S. has practiced global sourcing for operations. In other words, they have pulled troops from all around the world to meet contingencies. But that model is not sustainable In today's great-power competition. Today, the U.S. must focus on peace and stability in Europe, the Greater Middle East, and the Indo-Pacific all at the same time, as well as do other necessary operations around the world and at home (like helping respond to COVID). Nor can the U.S. depend on penny-packets of forces stationed in the U.S. to be deployed like fireman rushed to the scene of the blaze anywhere in the world.

The U.S. must be concerned that events in one theater will consume so much attention it opens up opportunities for competitors to make mischief elsewhere. Working in concert with friends and allies, the U.S. must be able to deliver credible conventional deterrence in Europe, the Middle East, and the Indo-Pacific simultaneously. If moving stuff around jeopardizes deterrence in any of these areas, then we have a problem.

Always Be Prepared to Play Great-Power Politics: North Korea would have never marched South without a greenlight from Stalin. And it would not have able to survive the war without the armed intervention of China.

Now, there might not be a hidden hand behind every ill will aimed at America today. And, certainly, not all threats are equal. Nevertheless, Washington must ably recognize and respond appropriately to great power threats, in their many shapes and guises. Can we be sure, for example, that out of frustration China might not resort to state-sponsored terrorism and armed surrogates? Who knows? The lesson here is: Do not be surprised like we were in Korea.

In Great Power Politics, Form Follows Function: In Korea, when the two sides fought to a standstill, the U.S. did not sign a peace treaty. That was for a simple reason. There was no peace. There still is not. Those who argue we should go ahead and do a peace treaty now—to build trust and confidence—get it backwards. If we had trust and confidence, signing the treaty would be an afterthought.

There are no prospects for enduring peace in Korea unless North Korea agrees to stop threatening others. And, unlike 70 years ago, today that means denuclearizing. If North Korea agrees to denuclearize, heck yes, sign that piece of paper.

In great-power competition, do not mistake the process for progress. Whether it is arms control treaties or any other measures, first you need to protect and safeguard your interests. Then statecraft can play an important role: working to reach deals of mutual interest that satisfy both sides.

"Smart" diplomacy on its own is no more able to make America safe today than it was during the Cold War. Safety rests in strength. First, demonstrate the capacity to protect your interests. Refuse to compromise on that. Then talk. And, if there is progress, seals the deal. (145)

Persian Gulf War

One of the most recent wars, The Persian Gulf War, offers other lessons and cautionary tales that still resonate today. One is that the U.S. military is capable of waging and winning a big, complicated intervention half a world away. In that sense, the gulf war ended the Vietnam syndrome, a belief held by many U.S. citizens and leaders that the United States couldn't successfully wield military power around the globe and that, as with Vietnam, the results of such an operation would be disastrous. They were not.

As the date for launching the Persian Gulf War approached 25 years ago, President George H.W. Bush was resolute in public, but privately he was filled with sadness and concern. He knew what war was like, having served as a young Navy lieutenant whose torpedo bomber was shot down by the Japanese in the South Pacific during World War II. As commander in chief, he understood that many soldiers might lose their lives or suffer grievous injuries, and that he was responsible for what happened to them.

Bush sat down on Dec. 31, 1990, New Year's Eve, and wrote an emotional letter to his five children reflecting a father's desire to reassure his children about the rightness of what he was about to do, and a commander in chief's worries about those he was about to send into battle.

Addressing the letter to "Dear George, Jeb, Neil, Marvin and Doro," he wrote (with his customary disregard to spelling and grammar), "When I came into this job I vowed that I would never ring my hands and talk about 'the loneliest job in the world' or ring my hands about the 'pressures or the trials.'

"Having said that I have been concerned about what lies ahead. There is no 'loneliness' though because I am backed by a first-rate team of knowledgeable and committed people. No president has been more blessed in this regard."

President Bush added: "We have waited to give sanctions a chance, we have moved a tremendous force so as to reduce the risk to every American soldier if force has to be used; but the question of loss of life still lingers and plagues the heart.

"My mind goes back to history: How many lives might have been saved if appeasement had given way to force earlier on in the late '30s or earliest '40s? How many Jews might have been spared the gas chambers, or how many Polish patriots might be alive today? I look at today's crisis as 'good' vs. 'evil'–yes, it is that clear."

Bush overcame his trepidation and began the conflict less than three weeks later. And Bush's intervention is still widely considered a prime example of how war can be waged effectively in the modern era and how a commander in chief should behave at a time of crisis.

Bush succeeded in many ways. He proved that he had the temperament and leadership skills to forge a massive international coalition to get the job done. He showed how to delegate responsibility where appropriate and declined to micro-manage the day-to-day operations as President Lyndon Johnson had done, wrong-headedly, in Vietnam. And as the letter to his children indicated, he demonstrated the ability to understand that he was risking people's lives and needed to do everything possible to minimize casualties and still achieve victory.

Military historian and journalist Rick Atkinson said in a 1996 PBS interview, "He was a warrior himself and this very much shaped George Bush's view of the world. His approach to foreign affairs was shaped by 30 years in government....He did not have to be told that the strangulation of up to 40 percent of the world's oil was a direct and immediate threat to American interests and those of all the Western democracies....Bush was very much a man for whom World War II had been a defining experience of his youth....He was a man for whom shades of gray and nuances were annoying. He was fundamentally a man who viewed life in black and white terms. That's why it was much more comfortable for Bush to talk about this as a moral crusade."

The Persian Gulf War offers other lessons and cautionary tales that still resonate today. One is that the U.S. military is capable of waging and winning a big, complicated intervention half a world away. In that sense, the gulf war ended the Vietnam syndrome, a belief held by many U.S. citizens and leaders that the United States couldn't successfully wield military power around the globe and that, as with Vietnam, the results of such an operation would be disastrous. They were not.

Bush also showed that a president could rally the country and the world behind his leadership. He won Congress's endorsement for the military operation and also got the United Nations Security Council to sign on after strenuous efforts to gain support. (146)

My concerns about our country becoming embroiled in another world war can best be summarized in an OPED letter that I sent to major newspapers throughout the United States. My letter was titled "Nuclear saber rattling could lead to mass destruction."

"The recent speech by Russia's President Vladmir Putin referencing new nuclear threats is best rebuked by comments from a former leader of the Soviet Union, Mikhail Gorbachev in 2017. "Politicians and military leaders sound increasingly belligerent and defense doctrines more dangerous…it all looks as if the world is preparing for war." Mr. Gorbachev also said "While state budgets are struggling to fund people's essential social needs, military spending is growing. Money is easily found for sophisticated weapons whose destructive power is comparable to that of weapons of mass destruction."

Nine countries possess more than 15,000 nuclear weapons and the U.S. and Russia possess approximately 93 percent which could be quickly launched. Each is far more powerful than the bomb dropped on Japan, which killed approximately 140,000 innocent people. Our country alone has spent more than $20 billion per year on nuclear weapons. If only 1 percent of the nuclear arsenals were launched, over twenty-one million people would perish as well as the environment of any survivors.

As one who served at the highest level of the military at the Pentagon during 911, I know all too well what the result can be if world leaders continue to rattle their sabers. Such irresponsible rhetoric could lead to boots on the ground. We need to ask ourselves if we are prepared to put our loved ones in those boots and to continue this frivolous spending on weapons of mass destruction, ignoring so many other pressing needs of our people.

A quote by former President Harry Truman could best sum up what the result could be if we continue down this path of nuclear proliferation and the unnecessary build up of the world's military. "If we do not abolish war on this earth, then surely one day, war will abolish us from the earth."

CHAPTER 27

Money Pits

"Half a billion dollars of aircraft that flew for about a year. A huge $85 million hotel that never opened and sits in disrepair. Camouflage uniforms for the Afghan army whose fancy pattern would cost an extra $28 million. A healthcare facility listed as located in the Mediterranean Sea.

These are part of a catalog of "waste, fraud and abuse" complaints made against the United States' reconstruction efforts in Afghanistan– an effort totaling $145 billion over 20 years – made by the United States' own inspector general into the war. But the in-depth audits detailing these findings have, for the most part, been taken offline at the request of the State Department, citing security concerns." (147)

"The total cost of the war, according to the Pentagon, was $825 billion, a low-end estimate: even President Joe Biden has cited an estimate that put the amount at over double that – more than $2 trillion, a figure that factors in long-term costs such as veterans' care. The interest on the debt runs into hundreds of billions already.

The $145 billion reconstruction effort lacked oversight, leading to Congress to set up the Special Inspector General for Afghan Reconstruction (SIGAR) in 2008. SIGAR published quarterly reports that gained less attention at the time than was commensurate with the expenditure they addressed, critics said, and were sometimes denied the information they needed by the Pentagon – especially when it came to assessing security in the country.

A State Department spokesperson told CNN they had asked SIGAR to "temporarily" remove the reports, owing "to safety and security concerns regarding our ongoing evacuation efforts." They added SIGAR had the authority to restore them "when it deems appropriate." (148)

What follows are ten notable cases, stripped of identifying details, collated by CNN over the years. (149)

1) Kabul's winter blanket

The Tarakhil power plant was commissioned in 2007 as a backup generator for the capital in case electricity supply from Uzbekistan was compromised. A vast, modern structure, it ran on diesel-fueled turbines, supplied by a brand-name engineering giant. There was one catch: Afghanistan had scant diesel supply of its own and had to ship the fuel in by truck – making the plant too expensive to run.

The facility itself cost $335 million to build and had an estimated annual fuel cost of $245 million. The most recent SIGAR assessment said at best it was used at just 2.2% capacity, as the Afghan government could not afford the fuel. USAID declined to comment.

A half-billion-dollar fleet of cargo planes that flew for a year

Afghanistan's fledgling air force needed cargo planes. In 2008, the Pentagon chose the G222 – an Italian-designed aircraft designed to take off and land on rough runways. That first year, according to a speech made by SIGAR's chief John Sopko, citing a USAF officer, the planes were busy.

But they would not be sustainable. The aircraft were only noticed by SIGAR when Sopko noticed them parked at Kabul airport and asked what they were doing there. Six years after the procurement was launched, the sixteen aircraft delivered to Afghanistan were sold for scrap for $40,257. The cost of the project: $549 million.

The $36 million Marines HQ in the desert, neither wanted nor used

Sopko said in a speech this 64,000-square foot control center in Helmand epitomized how when a project starts, it often cannot be stopped.

In 2010, the Marines were surging troop numbers in Helmand, the deadliest part of Afghanistan. A command-and-control center on the main base of Camp Leatherneck was ordained as part of the effort, although Sopko recalled the base commander, and two other marine generals said it was not needed as it would not be completed fast enough.

Sopko said the thought of returning the funds allocated to Congress was "was so abhorrent to the contracting command, it was built anyway. The facility was never occupied, Camp Leatherneck was turned over to the Afghans, who abandoned it." It cost $36 million, was never used, and seems to have been later stripped by the Afghans, who also never appeared to use it.

Major Robert Lodewick, a DoD spokesman, said in a statement the SIGAR report contained "factual errors," objected to how it implied "malfeasance" by some officers, and said the $36 million figure included ancillary costs like roads to the HQ.

$28 million on an inappropriate camouflage pattern

In 2007, new uniforms were being ordered for the Afghan army. The Afghan defense minister Wardak said he wanted a rare camouflage pattern, "Spec4ce Forest," from Canadian company Hyper Stealth.

A total of 1.3 million sets were ordered, costing $43-80 each, as opposed to $25-30 originally estimated for replacement uniforms. The uniforms were never tested or evaluated in the field, and there is just 2.1% forest cover across Afghanistan.

In testimony, Sopko said it cost taxpayers an extra $28 million to buy the uniforms with a patented pattern, and SIGAR projected in 2017 a different choice of pattern could have saved a potential $72 million over the next decade.

DoD spokesman Lodewick said the report "overestimated" the cost, and "incorrectly discredited the value of the type of pattern selected," adding a lot of the fighting in Afghanistan occurred in verdant areas.

$1.5 million daily on fighting opium production

The US spent $1.5 million a day on counternarcotics programs (from 2002 to 2018). Opium production was, according to the last SIGAR report, up in 2020 by 37% compared to the year before. This was the third-highest yield since records began in 1994.

In 2017, production was four times what it was in 2002. A State department spokesperson noted "the Taliban have been the primary factor contributing to poppy's persistence in recent years" and "that the Taliban have committed to banning narcotics."

$249 million on an incomplete road

An extensive ring road around Afghanistan was funded by multiple grants and donors, totaling billions during the war. Towards the end of the project, a 233-kilometer section in the North, between the towns of Qeysar and Laman, led to $249 million being handed out to contractors, but only 15% of the road being built, a SIGAR audit reported.

Between March 2014 and September 2017, there was no construction on this section, and what had been built deteriorated, the report concluded. USAID declined to comment.

$85 million hotel that never opened

An extensive hotel and apartment complex was commissioned next to the US Embassy in Kabul, for which the US government provided $85 million in loans.

In 2016, SIGAR concluded "the $85 million in loans is gone, the buildings were never completed and are uninhabitable, and the U.S. Embassy is now forced to provide security for the site at additional cost to U.S. taxpayers."

The audit concluded that the contractor made unrealistic promises to secure the loans, and that the branch of the US government who oversaw the project never visited the site, and neither did the company they later hired to oversee the project. A State department spokesperson said they did not manage the construction, and it was "a private endeavor."

The fund that spent more on itself than Afghanistan

The Pentagon created the Task Force for Business and Stability Operations (TFBSO) expanded from Iraq to include Afghanistan in 2009, for whose operations in Afghanistan Congress set aside $823 million.

Over half the money spent by TFBSO – $359 million of $675 million – was "spent on indirect and support costs, not directly on projects in Afghanistan," SIGAR concluded in an audit.

They reviewed eighty-nine of the contracts TFBSO made, and found "7 contracts worth $35.1 million were awarded to firms employing former TFBSO staff as senior executives."
An audit also concluded that the fund spent about $6 million on supporting the cashmere industry, $43 million on a compressed natural gas station, and $150 million on high-end villas for its staff.

DoD spokesman Lodewick said SIGAR did not accuse anyone of fraud or the misuse of funds, took issue with "weaknesses and shortcomings" in the audit, and said "28 of TFBSO's 35 projects met or partially met their intended objectives."

The healthcare facility in the sea

A 2015 report into USAID's funding of healthcare facilities in Afghanistan said that over a third of the 510 projects they had been given coordinates for, did not exist in those locations. Thirteen were "not located in Afghanistan, with one located in the Mediterranean Sea." Thirty "were located in a province different from the one USAID reported."

And "189 showed no physical structure within four hundred feet of the reported coordinates. Just under half of these locations showed no physical structure within a half mile of the reported coordinates." The audit said that USAID and the Afghan ministry of Public Health could only provide "oversight of these facilities [if they] know where they are." USAID declined to comment.

At least $19 billion lost to "waste, fraud, abuse"

An October 2020 report presented a startling total for the war. Congress at the time had appropriated $134 billion since 2002 for reconstruction in Afghanistan.
SIGAR was able to review $63 billion of it – nearly half. They concluded $19 billion of that – almost a third – was "lost to waste, fraud, and abuse."

DoD spokesman Lodewick said they and "several other U.S. Government departments and agencies are already on record as having challenged some of these reports as inaccurate and misleading" and that their conclusions "appeared to overlook the difference between reconstruction efforts that may have been mismanaged willfully/negligently and those efforts that, at the time of the report, simply had fallen short of strategic goals." (148)

Since the start of the Iraq War, the United States has sent tens of billions of dollars in assistance to Iraq, a large portion of which has been squandered or simply disappeared. Government auditors say some $61 billion was spent on reconstruction projects in Iraq from 2003 to 2012. At least 10 percent of the money cannot be accounted for. Some 15 percent of the money spent, or $8 billion, was wasted.

The Misuse of monies spent by the United States in Iraq was no different than that of monies misused in Afghanistan.

The audit also found that much of the money spent in Iraq was ineffective. Many development projects are still unfinished, and the futility of the money spent on training Iraqi troops has been on full display during the recent ISIS advance.

American money began to disappear as soon as the Iraq War began. In 2004, $19 billion in reconstruction assistance was provided to Iraq. From 2005 to 2009, $26 billion was sent to Iraq for the same purpose.

A Congressional Research Service (CRS) report published in 2009 said much of this money was lost to waste, fraud, and abuse. Stuart W. Bowen, Jr., then Special Inspector General for Iraq Reconstruction (SIGIR), testified to Congress in 2009 that 15 to 20 percent of this money was wasted.

Lost IRS E-mails Point to an Abuse of Power and Cover-Up. "The overuse of cost-plus contracts, high contractor overhead expenses, excessive contractor award fees, and unacceptable program and project delays all contributed to a significant waste of taxpayer dollars," Bowen told Congress back in 2009.

The CRS report outlined many of the poor accounting practices that have led to widespread waste in Iraq. "A January 2005 SIGIR audit found that the CPA [Coalition Provisional Authority, the American governing body that controlled Iraq at the time] 'provided less than adequate controls' for $8.8 billion of [reconstruction] resources it moved through Iraqi ministries. An April 2005 audit concluded that CPA managers of [reconstruction] funds distributed in the South-Central region of Iraq could not account for more than $96.6 million in cash and receipts. An October 2005 audit found that South-Central personnel could not account for more than $20.5 million in Rapid Regional

Response Program funds and made $2.6 million in excessive payments."

Waste was not limited to mismanagement, however. Sometimes it was criminal, the report found. "In late 2005, several U.S. citizens were criminally charged with respect to the handling of these funds—and have since pled guilty. In February 2007, five more were indicted, of whom four were convicted and one pled guilty," CRS reported.

Does not End with the End of War

The U.S. began disengagement with Iraq two years before the official withdrawal in 2011. However, money has not stopped flowing to the country. $3.1 billion in foreign assistance has gone to Iraq since 2009. The peak year was 2011, when the U.S. sent $1.2 billion; the lowest year was 2014, when $48 million was sent.

SIGIR closed shop in 2013, but not before conducting one final audit of Iraq reconstruction spending. The audit found that $220.2 billion had been provided to Iraq for reconstruction and development projects and the Iraqi military – with the United States providing $61 billion (the rest came from international assistance and $146 billion through the Iraqi capital budget).

The final review of how this money was spent is damning. The findings show that the United States was unable to adequately track where and how money was spent because of gaps in reporting. This led to numerous instances of money missing.

For instance, SIGIR simply could not find $3.2 billion meant for development projects. The military was only able to track" $7.1 billion of the $19.6 billion obligated by DoD," SIGIR found.

The money DOD managed to track went to an array of different programs, including police stations, training, ammunition, and weapons. The collapse of the Iraqi military seems to indicate that this money was misspent.

Overall, SIGIR found that "about 10 percent of the $60.6 billion spent on U.S. funded Iraq reconstruction" cannot be accounted for. It is estimated that at least an additional 15 percent of that - $8 billion - was wasted.

"We found that incomplete and unstandardized databases left us unable to identify the specific use of billions of dollars spent on projects, because the U.S. government agencies involved were not required to manage project data in a uniform and comprehensive manner," the report concluded." (150)

CHAPTER 28

Afghanistan and Iraq Today

With the sacrifice of life and money, we need to look if all the efforts of the United States was worth it.

AFGHANISTAN TODAY according to an article by the Pew Research Center. (151)

"In August 2021, the United States withdrew the last of its troops from Afghanistan, ending its military presence there after nearly 20 years. The U.S. exit from Afghanistan resulted in the Taliban regaining control of the country and created a refugee crisis as many Afghans fled. It also raised fears that terrorists might use Afghanistan as a safe haven, as was the case with Ayman al-Zawahiri, the al-Qaida leader who was discovered in the nation's capital, Kabul, and killed in a U.S. drone strike late last month.

A year after the U.S. military exit from Afghanistan, here is a look back at how people in the United States and other countries have viewed the troop evacuation and its aftermath, as well as their broader attitudes about the war. All findings are based on previously published Pew Research Center surveys.

At the time of the military evacuation, 54% of Americans said the decision to withdraw U.S. troops from Afghanistan was the right one, according to a survey conducted in August 2021. Around four-in-ten Americans

(42%) said the decision was the wrong one. There was a sharp partisan divide on this topic. While 70% of Democrats and Democratic-leaning independents said the decision to withdraw troops was the right decision, about half as many Republicans and GOP leaners (34%) shared this view. Most Republicans (64%) instead said the decision was wrong.

In the same survey, 69% of U.S. adults said the United States mostly failed in achieving its goals in Afghanistan. About a quarter (27%) said the U.S. succeeded. There was partisan agreement on this question: About seven-in-ten in both parties said the U.S. mostly failed to achieve its goals.

Americans harbored doubts about the war in Afghanistan even before the withdrawal of U.S. troops. In a spring 2019 survey, 59% of U.S. adults said that considering the costs versus the benefits to the United States, the war in Afghanistan was not worth fighting, while 36% said it was. The balance of opinion was about the same among U.S. military veterans.

Both during and after the troop withdrawal, large majorities of Americans expressed negative views of the Biden administration's handling of the situation in Afghanistan. In both August and September 2021, about seven-in-ten or more said that the administration had done an only fair or poor job dealing with the situation there, with around four-in-ten or more saying it had done poorly. In both surveys, fewer Americans said the administration had done an excellent or good job. In the September survey, for instance, only 24% said this.

A large majority of Republicans (82%) said in September 2021 that the administration had done a poor job managing the situation in Afghanistan. Conservative Republicans were twenty-one percentage points more likely than moderate and liberal Republicans to say this (89% vs. 68%).

One-in-five Democrats also said the Biden administration had done a poor job dealing with the Afghanistan situation. About twice as many said the administration had done only a fair job (38%) or an excellent or good job (40%).

Veterans and non-veterans were also divided on this question. While similar shares of veterans (76%) and non-veterans (74%) said in September 2021 that the Biden administration had done an only fair or poor job dealing with the situation in Afghanistan, veterans were more likely than non-veterans to say the administration managed it poorly (60% vs. 47%). Only about a quarter or fewer in either group said the administration had done an excellent or good job, with very few giving it an excellent rating (4% of veterans and 5% of non-veterans). As is the case with the public, veterans' views on these issues are deeply divided along party lines.

Last September, a majority of Americans (56%) said they favored admitting thousands of Afghan refugees into the U.S., according to the same survey, which was conducted after the U.S. evacuated thousands of Afghans from the country. About four-in-ten (42%) opposed this move.

These views were deeply divided by partisanship. At the time, 63% of Republicans either strongly (29%) or (34%) opposed the U.S. admitting thousands of refugees from Afghanistan into the country. About a third (35%) said they favored admitting these refugees.

By contrast, three-quarters of Democrats were in favor of admitting refugees, including a third who strongly favored it. Liberal Democrats (87%) were more likely than conservative and moderate Democrats (66%) to support this.

About half of liberal Democrats (49%) said they strongly favored admitting refugees from Afghanistan.

Despite majority support for admitting refugees, Americans were divided on whether the government was conducting adequate security screenings for those arriving in the U.S. from Afghanistan. About four-in-ten Americans (43%) said they were very or confident that the government was conducting adequate security screenings, while 55% were not too confident or not at all confident. Democrats were more likely than Republicans to express confidence in the government's security screenings.

In a spring 2022 survey of 18 countries, people viewed the U.S. decision to withdraw all troops from Afghanistan as the right one, but many said the withdrawal itself was not handled well. A median of 52% across the surveyed countries said the troop pullout was the right choice, compared with a median of 39% who said it was the wrong choice.

Public opinion in these countries was more negative when it came to how the U.S. exit from Afghanistan was handled. A median of 56% said it was not handled well, while a median of 33% said it was. In only two surveyed countries, Poland and Malaysia, did half or more of adults approve of the way the situation in Afghanistan was handled.

Most Americans said in August 2021 that Taliban control of Afghanistan is a threat to the security of the United States. Half (46%) said Taliban control represented a major threat to the U.S., and another 44% saw it as a minor threat. Republicans (61%) were far more likely than Democrats (33%) to view a Taliban-controlled Afghanistan as a major security threat.

In a January 2022 survey, 55% of Americans said that defending against terrorism should be a top priority for the president and Congress to address this year. Of the eighteen issues asked about, defending against terrorism was among the top priorities identified. The survey preceded the U.S. military's drone strike on al-Qaida leader Ayman al-Zawahiri in Kabul in July.

Americans tend to prioritize the terrorism issue differently based on factors including age and partisanship. About three-quarters of adults ages sixty-five and older (76%) said that defending against terrorism should be a top priority for the president and Congress, compared with 32% of those under thirty. And two-thirds of Republicans (65%) said it should be a top priority, compared with 48% of Democrats.

IRAQ TODAY According to Council on Foreign Relations (152)

"Six years after the war against the Islamic State, Iraq still faces significant challenges to its recovery. Over one million people remain internally displaced while three million people need humanitarian assistance as Iraq continues its reconstruction. In addition to reintegrating liberated Sunni communities into the political system, the government has struggled to achieve the demobilization and integration of powerful Shiite militias, which formed during the fight against the Islamic State, into the Iraqi security forces. The government also faces ongoing tensions with Kurdish groups pressing for greater autonomy in the north following a failed independence referendum in October 2017. Since the start of the Israel-Hamas War, Iraq's stability has deteriorated significantly, with Iran-backed militias targeting U.S. forces in the west and north of the country.

Background

Since the U.S.-led invasion in 2003, Iraq has undergone a long period of instability, with armed groups like the self-proclaimed Islamic State taking advantage of the power vacuum left by the disbandment of the military and the ban on Saddam Hussein's Baath party. In 2014, the Islamic State advanced into Iraq from Syria and took over parts of Anbar province, eventually expanding into the northern part of the country and capturing Mosul in June 2014.

Former President Barack Obama authorized targeted air strikes against Islamic State militants in Iraq and Syria, and the United States formed an international coalition of nearly eighty countries to counter the terrorist group. Regional forces—including as many as thirty thousand Iranian troops—joined the Iraqi army, local tribes, and the Kurdish Peshmerga in operations to retake territory from the Islamic State, recapturing Tikrit in April 2015, Ramadi in December 2015, Fallujah in June 2016, and Mosul in July 2017.

The Trump administration sharply escalated the U.S. presence in Iraq in early 2017 to bring a swift end to the Islamic State, and the Iraqi government declared victory over the group in December 2017. Since then, most foreign troops have withdrawn from Iraq, except for a small U.S. contingent.

In late April 2018, the U.S. military officially disbanded the command overseeing the fight against the Islamic State in Iraq, declaring an end to major combat operations against the group. Roughly 2,500 U.S. troops remain in Iraq at the invitation of the Iraqi government as part of a mission to train, advise, and assist the Iraqi military in fighting domestic terrorism.

Underlying sectarian tensions in Iraq among Sunni and Shiite groups, as well as tensions between Kurdish groups in the north and the government in Baghdad, exacerbated the fight to dislodge the Islamic State. These tensions intensified after the U.S. invasion in 2003 and the fall of Saddam Hussein, now threatening the stability of the new Iraqi government as it looks to rebuild the country and prevent a resurgence of the Islamic State. There also remains a larger concern that the aftermath of the conflict and challenges of reconstruction and reintegration will lead to the breakup of Iraq and that sectarian tension will plague the region for years to come, possibly expanding into a proxy conflict among various international groups.

A coalition of parties won a surprise victory in Iraq's May 2018 parliamentary election. Their victory raised questions about continued Iranian influence in Baghdad, as al-Sadr's Shiite bloc has historically remained at odds with Iranian-backed groups in Iraq. Following the 2021 election, which saw increased representation for minority groups, the newly elected parliament could not form a coalition government, precipitating a political crisis.

The assassination attempt on Prime Minister Mustafa al-Kadhimi in November 2021 led to armed clashes between the Iraqi government and the Iran-backed militias accused of orchestrating the attack. Amid the political crisis, the entirety of al-Sadr's political bloc resigned from parliament in a gamble aimed at pressuring the government to elect a president. The move backfired as al-Sadr's bloc was quickly replaced, allowing the Shiite groups backed by Iran to assume a majority in the parliament. Al-Sadr retired from politics in August 2022, leaving control of the Iraqi government to his Iranian-backed rivals.

In October 2022, Abdul Latif Rashid was elected president, promising to return the country to normalcy. The premiership was ultimately handed to Mohammad Shia al-Sudani, a long-time ally of Iran. His pro-Iran government includes ministers with ties to several U.S.-designated terrorist organizations, including Kataib Hezbollah. However, al-Sudani has taken a measured approach by expressing a desire to keep U.S. forces in Iraq while continuing his predecessor's "balance and openness" policy. The United States remains concerned about Iran's increasing involvement in Iraq and its government, which has disrupted Iraqi relations with the United States and reintegration with other Arab countries, particularly the wealthy Gulf Cooperation Council (GCC) states.

Meanwhile, the Islamic State continues to plague Iraq, despite its diminished presence. The Islamic State has reverted to its insurgency roots and refocused to orchestrating a hit-and-run campaign. For example, it planted a bomb near the city of Kirkuk in December 2022 that targeted and killed nine federal police officers. In response, the United States announced that it would keep its troops in Iraq to fight the Islamic State.

Recent Developments

Since late 2022, Iraq has faced economic and infrastructural issues. In November, a gas cylinder explosion killed fifteen people in the northern city of Sulaimaniyah, and in October, a gas tanker explosion in Baghdad killed at least nine people. In January, al-Sudani replaced the Central Bank governor after the value of the Iraqi dinar hit new lows, and the previous governor essentially quit. To solve these critical issues, al-Sudani has implemented several measures, including approving a $152 billion budget meant to add public sector jobs and increase public salaries.

However, Iraq's political instability persists. In late March 2023, the Iraqi government passed amendments that would increase the size of electoral districts, reducing opportunities for smaller parties and independent candidates to win seats in future elections. These amendments were supported by the Iran-backed Coordination Framework but proved to be controversial, sparking demonstrations and prompting several MPs to leave and postpone the session. Similarly, in late June, over fifty MPs resigned from the local parliament in Iraq's Kurdish region. They protested a court ruling by the Iraqi Federal Supreme Court that rejected their decision to delay regional elections. The ruling is another sign that Baghdad has largely reigned in the Kurdish region's autonomy, having asserted its control over oil revenue and key infrastructure.

Days later, thousands of Iraqi followers of a Shiite cleric protested in major Iraqi cities, criticizing the burning of a Quran during a demonstration in Sweden, demanding the Swedish ambassador's expulsion from Iraq, and storming the Swedish embassy in Baghdad.

In August 2023, Iran-aligned groups killed Kurdish protestors in the disputed northern city of Kirkuk over the handover of a building to the Kurdish Democratic Party (KDP). Following days of deadly ethnic clashes, the Supreme Court in Baghdad halted Al-Sudani's order to return the building to the KDP on September 1. The oil-rich province lies along the fault line between the Kurdish autonomous region and areas controlled by Iraq's government. It has been the center of some of Iraq's worst violence since the Islamic State. Meanwhile, Turkey has escalated its military attacks against the Kurdistan Workers Party (PPK) in northern Iraq, including a drone strike that killed seven members on August 24. In late August, Turkey called on Iraq to designate the PKK as a terrorist organization, citing the group's threat to both Iraqi and Turkish security.

At the end of August 2023, the Iranian government announced that the central Iraqi government had pledged to disarm and relocate militant groups from the Kurdish region of northern Iraq by September 19. Despite the joint success of the Iraqi government and the Kurdish Regional Government in Erbil, tensions between Turkey and the Kurds increased following a PKK suicide bombing outside of a government building in the Turkish capital Ankara in October. Although no casualties besides the two PKK-linked attackers were reported, the attack was the first in the Turkish capital since 2016. In response, Turkish forces conducted air strikes in northern Iraq, destroying sixteen targets of the PKK. The situation continued to escalate with further Turkish strikes in northern Iraq in 2024 following a PKK December 22 attack on a Turkish base that killed twelve soldiers, and a similar attack on January 12 that killed nine more.

Over the course of the Israel-Hamas War, Iran-backed militia groups in Iraq and Syria have targeted U.S. troops in the region over 165 times in opposition to Israel's campaign in Gaza. The remaining 2,500 U.S. troops in Iraq have been subject to consistent attacks on their bases, such as the Al-Asad Airbase in western Iraq, where an attack on October 17 resulted in the death of an American civilian contractor. In February 2024, the United States conducted a series of retaliatory strikes in response to an attack in Jordan on a U.S. military outpost near the Syrian border that killed three American soldiers. The strikes included more than eighty-five targets throughout Iraq and Syria and were the first in a multi-tiered response by the Biden administration. According to the Iraqi government, sixteen people, including civilians, were among those killed in the first round of U.S. strike s, while twenty-five were injured. On February 5, 2024, Russia called a UN Security Council meeting, where the Russian Ambassador to the United Nations accused the United States of violating international law by striking Iraq and Syria." (152)

CHAPTER 29

Assignment Korea

The fallout from 911 did not stop with the attacks in New York and the Pentagon. Our military was in dire need of backup support and people to fill in for critical assignments. Besides serving for the Joint Chiefs of Staff and the State Department, I volunteered to fill-in for numerous military members who were being deployed to other critical areas supporting the global war on terrorism.

A short period of time had passed since my last assignment when I volunteered for a six-month tour of duty in South Korea. Two of my brothers, Tom, and John, served in South Korea before me. Tom was there in the 1960's, John was there in the 1980s and I served there approximately seventeen years ago. My assignment was based in Daegu, South Korea's fourth largest city and the self-proclaimed fashion capital of the country. Daegu has a population of approximately 2.4 million people and is known for its hot summers and trendy markets.

The South Korean tour of duty was to last six months. The unit needed someone to replace one of their people who was deployed to the Middle East. Two of my brothers, Tom, and John, served in South Korea before me. Tom was there in the 1960's, John was there in the 1980s and I served there approximately seventeen years ago. My assignment had me based in Daegu, South Korea's fourth largest city and the self-proclaimed fashion capital of the country. Daegu has a population of approximately 2.4 million people and is known for its hot summers and trendy shopping markets.

My assignment was to move critical medical assets so our troops will have immediate access to them if North Korea launches an all-out attack against South Korea. The goal was to save the lives of our troops. Members of my Squadron met me upon my arrival. After having dinner with them, they took me to my quarters. It was a warm summer night in Korea. As we walked up to the door to my lodging, I almost walked into the largest spider web I have ever seen. It spanned about seven foot in circumference. Luckily, I stopped in my tracks before being intertwined in its web.

I was told the spider was the Sorcerer or Shaman, the most prolific spider in South Korea. "The spiders on these webs were neither as large nor colorful, possibly as it is right at the end of their mating season and the end of autumn. Their webs, however, were not just large, three meters across, but densely intertwined. The genes of the mu-dang have been used in genetically cloning silkworms to produce stronger silk. Only the female carries the red marking and apart from being larger than the male, she has cannibalistic tendencies after mating." (153) To add to my nightmares about spiders, the base played the spider movie Arachnophobia on my first night in South Korea.

My quarters were on a Republic of South Korea air base. It was once an American base but was turned over to the South Korean military. "The base encompasses the Daegu International airport which serves the city of Daegu and the surrounding area in southeastern South Korea. The airport is also a military base for the ROKAF's 11th Fighter Wing, South Korea. The squadrons fly the F-15K. I would watch the planes take off during the night. I was told that they fly parallel to the Demilitarized zone that separates North and South Korea."

I was awoken early by what sounded like the beating of bongs on a large symbol. At night, I heard a drum. (Photo 28) "When you first hear about "the morning gong and evening drum", this phrase may be mistaken as: "the gong is sounded in the morning and the drum is hit in the evening." In Buddhism, the correct way to explain is: "In the

Photo 29-Monk beating drum bell

morning, the gong is sounded first then the drum is hit; in the evening, the drum is hit first and then the gong is sounded." Both the gong and the drum are one of the most important Dharma instruments to the temple. In Buddha's time, the gong and drum were used to gather everyone to announce the precepts, mealtimes, Dharma talks etc. Up until now, they announce the times to wake up and go to bed. The Korean temple bell is not only beautiful in its form, but also well known for its magnificent and peaceful sound across all Buddhist countries. The bell shape looks like an upside-down urn. The most celebrated and the biggest temple bell in Korea is the Emille Bell weighing about twenty-five tons." (154)

My fate during my stay in Korea was to hear the bongs every day. After a while, the sound became enchanting to me. When I later returned to the states, I missed the sound of the bongs and to this day, the bongs and classical music of South Korea still resonates in my mind.

Next to my squadron was an Army battalion. Many of their people volunteered for a tour in Korea after spending an extended period in the Middle East. When you are assigned to a tour in Korea, some have the option to bring your family. If you choose to do so, however, you must commit to two years in the country rather than just one. Combat zones provide military people with different options. The army has no limits on the amount of time you may have to spend in a combat zone (i.e., Iraq). In sharp contrast, the Air Force deploys people under a concept which is termed Air Expeditionary Force (AEF).

The USAF Air Expeditionary Force AEF is designed to provide CINCs with RAPID, RESPONSIVE, and RELIABLE airpower options that meet specific theater needs by providing a wide range of capabilities. These forces are used to augment existing land-based forces when necessary. In turn, the AEF was developed to allow the National Command Authorities NCA access to a rapid response air force from CONUS without having to maintain an immediate readiness force in-theater. The savings over an in-theater air force is substantial and provides the NCAs with the flexibility to wait until the last minute to commit air forces. The Air Expeditionary Force is a specifically tailored package of fighter-bombers, associated personnel, and support equipment possessing the characteristics of rapid deployment employment of a light and lethal design. The primary role of the AEF is to maintain a level of force presence in the Area of Responsibility AOR, provide deterrence during periods of heightened tensions, and to augment the existing ground forces. This force would provide precision air-to-ground, air-to-air, and suppression of enemy air defenses SEAD capabilities. Since the Air Expeditionary Force is in its infancy, the Air Force is just beginning to develop the AEFs capabilities, feasibility, and functionality. The Concept of Operation has been developed and validated by Central Command, CENTCOM, but has not been organized or tested in any other Commands Areas of

Responsibility AOR. The Secretary of the Air Force and the Air Force Chief of Staff developed a strategy for the 21st Century that encourages the AEF concept and provides the framework for future expeditionary exploration. (155)

"The Korean Demilitarized Zone (DMZ) is a strip of land running across the Korean Peninsula that serves as a buffer zone between North Korea and South Korea. It divides the Korean Peninsula in half. The Demilitarized Zone incorporates territory on both sides of the cease-fire line as it existed at the end of the Korean War (1950-1953) and was created by pulling back the respective forces 1.2 miles along each side of the line. The DMZ became a de facto international border and one of the tensest fronts in the Cold War. The DMZ is about 160 miles long and approximately 2.5 miles

The border between North and South Korea is one of the most heavily guarded stretches of land in the world. The DMZ, littered with scores of mines and barbed-wire fences, is nightmarishly difficult to cross, except the . DMZ is a special buffer zone inside what is known as the "truce village" of Panmunjom, about thirty-five miles north of Seoul

Photo 30-North and South Korean guards at DMZ

Every year, hundreds of thousands of people usually visit the JSA for a chance to see North Korean soldiers just dozens of feet away and to officially step into North Korean territory inside a United Nations administered conference room that straddles the military border. A visit there feels like a military theater, with the stern warnings from the South Korean soldiers under United Nations (UN) command not to make gestures at their counterparts. Since demarcation, the DMZ has had numerous cases of incidents and incursions by both sides, although the North Korean government typically never acknowledges direct responsibility for any of these incidents. This can be a highly risky place if mutual respect is not maintained on both sides.

North Korea is one of the world's most repressive states. The government restricts all civil and political liberties for its citizens, including freedom of expression, assembly, association, and religion. It prohibits all organized political opposition, independent media, civil society, and trade unions. The arbitrary arrest and punishment of crimes, torture in custody, forced labor, and executions to maintain fear and control across the country. Besides the DMZ, North Korea is a highly controlled country where human rights are ignored." (156)

Upon reaching the first day of my duty, I met with my squadron to define our mission. Copying what was done in the NMCC, I pointed the finger at every member of my squadron to ask if they had any input and then said. "If we find that any of you are better equipped to lead on anything, we are going to follow. If any of you have any input of importance, you need to say it now! If not, you need to point the thumb and not the finger because you have the ability here and now or any time of my stay to lay it on the table.

One day while eating in the base dining hall, a South Korean air force Major struck up a conversation with me. Although he had a long Korean name, he identified himself as "Jason." Following a lengthy discussion, he invited me to join him and his wife at a summer condominium that he owned. I checked with our security guards to make certain that it was okay.

After spending an interesting and fun-filled weekend with Jason and his wife, we became close friends. Through his eyes, I started seeing the soul of Korea. Our first adventure was to visit the beach of Haeundae in the seaside town of Busan. The city was amazing. Haeundae Beach is Korea's most representative beach! Haeundae Beach is unlike other beaches in Korea in that the sandy shore stretches between the sea and tons of tall buildings, creating a beautiful view that is even more stunning when the sun sets!

I had an older friend back in the states that once told me that her brother was killed in the Korean war. There was a war memorial in Soul that was dedicated to American and other country warriors that paid the ultimate price to keep South Korea free from being taken over by North Korea. The memorial was like the Vietnam Wall. I told my friend that I would go to the memorial and find her brother's name. When I decided to go, I invited my friend Jason to go along.

Photo 31-War memorial in South Korea for all countries

The memorial was like our Vietnam Wall memorial. It had the names of fallen soldiers etched on stone tabloids and etched into books. When we found the name of my friend's brother on each of them, I had Jason place his finger next to them and took a photo of them. Jason was a recent graduate of the South Korean's Air Force Academy and far too young to serve in the Korean war. He was born long after it.

As we were walking away to leave, Jason grabbed my arm and kept calling my name. Not knowing what he wanted, I responded "what do you want Jason?" Looking intently at me, he retorted. "When you go back, thank them for me and my family for what they did. If it were not for what they did, my family and I would not be free today!

To this very day, I thank not only Korean vets but all vets on his behalf. When I meet up with a Korean vet, I thank every one of them and tell them the story conveyed to me by Jason. I was befriended by other Koreans. They invited me to attend their churches. South Korea is one of the few countries in the world where both Christmas and Buddha's birthdays are observed as public holidays." It is a multi-religious society, with Christianity, Buddhism, and various other religions coexisting alongside shamanism. Over the past century, Christianity has experienced substantial growth in South Korea, with approximately 20 percent of the population identifying as Christian. Buddhism closely follows, representing around 16 percent of the country's population. The rapid expansion of Christianity in South Korea is particularly noteworthy given the country's deep historical ties to Confucianism. Nevertheless, there has been a noticeable shift in the religious landscape in recent years, especially among the younger generation, who are gradually turning away from religious affiliations." (157)

The South Korean soldiers are some of the fiercest fighters in the world. Some ate dog meat because they thought it would give them strength. Like parts of Vietnam and southern China, South Korea has a history of consuming dog meat. It was traditionally viewed in South Korea as a food that could help people beat the heat during the summer and was also a cheap and readily available source of protein at a time when poverty rates were far higher.

There are about 1,100 dog farms operating for food purposes in South Korea, and about half a million dogs being raised on these farms, according to the Ministry of Agriculture, Food and Rural Affairs.

But the practice has also come under criticism in recent decades, with animal rights activists at the forefront; international rights groups such as Humane Society International (HSI) have worked to rescue dogs from South Korean farms and relocate them overseas.

I heard several stories about U.S. military members who first came to Korea with their families and unknowingly ate dog meat at a restaurant. One story was where an officer and his family left it up to a server to serve whatever she thought would be tasty. After the meal, the family raved about how tasty the meal was. When asked what they ate, the server told them it was dog. At first, they thought she was kidding only to find out that it was a dog. The kids immediately got pale and sick to their stomachs.

Another officer was walking down the street when she saw cute puppies in a store window. Thinking she would like to take home a pet; she picked one out and said she would be back to pick the puppy up in an hour or two. When she returned, the clerk handed her a bag with a butchered puppy.

When South Korea hosted the Olympics, the government told the shop owners not to hang butchered dogs in their windows.

"CNN reported that South Korea's parliament passed a bill Tuesday banning the breeding and slaughter of dogs for consumption, ending the traditional yet controversial practice of eating dog meat after years of nationwide debate. The bill received rare bipartisan support across South Korea's divided political landscape, highlighting how attitudes toward eating dog have transformed over the past few decades during the country's rapid industrialization.

The law will ban the distribution and sale of food products made or processed with dog ingredients, according to the corresponding committee of the National Assembly. However, customers who consume dog meat or related products will not be subject to punishment – meaning the law would target those working in the industry such as dog farmers or sellers.

Under the bill, anybody slaughtering a dog for food can be punished for up to three years in prison or fined up to thirty million Korean won (about $23,000). Anyone who breeds dogs for eating, or who knowingly acquires, transports, stores, or sells food made from dogs, also faces a lower fine and prison time. (158)

The next time Jason and I met up over lunch, he suggested that we visit the Buddha and the Buddhist monks on the southern peak of Mount Palgong of the Taebaek Mountains, one of the most heavily visited attractions. "At least early in Buddhism in Korea, many temples were in the mountains, because of a practical mixture of Buddhism with Shamanism that was present in Korea before 372. Shamanism taught that the mountains were home to the spirits, so it was natural to combine Buddhist and Shaman thought in the placement of Buddhist temples." (159)

"Throughout the year, rain or shine, day and night, the steep, rugged mountain path is always teeming with people. They want to offer a prayer to the Buddha on the mountaintop at an elevation of 830 meters. They are mostly women, carrying on their shoulders a little backpack or a cloth-bag containing candles or rice for offerings.

Quietly, immersed in their thoughts, they plod slowly up the rocky trails, some murmuring sutras and some running their fingers along prayer-beads. Their social backgrounds may be as diverse as their looks and appearances, but their minds are equally preoccupied with one thing: the success in the college entrance examination of their children or grandchildren about this time of the year, preferably into prestigious universities.

The Buddha statue is on the southern peak of Mount Palgong of the magnificent Taebaek Mountains. It is a little less than an hour's bus ride from downtown Daegu, where the bus leaves every five minutes and gets to the foot of the mountain by way of the picturesque suburbs.

Photo 32-Buddha statue on Mount Palgong Korea

The sculpture of the Buddha statue looks a bit clumsy and rough compared to images of the Buddha elsewhere. Neither does it have the kindly, compassionate smile which is the universal symbol of Buddhas. However, the large, thick trunk, the long, thoughtful ears and the firmly closed lips together make him look impressive and dignified. He is believed to be Yaksa-yeorae-bul, the Healing Buddha or the Buddha of Medicine, who is in this world to help the sick and relieve their pain. Another intriguing feature of the seated Buddha statue is a hat-like piece of stone on his head, which is very unusual and strange. In addition, the hat-stone is

264

determined to be different from the stone of his main body and unavailable in the region, adding more mystery as to why and how it got there and by whom. Though the specific year is unknown, it is assumed that the Buddha statue was erected during the Unified Silla Kingdom period of the eighth century.

The statue was designated later as National Treasure No. 431. Whatever secret the Buddha might have about his hat, those who come to visit the Buddha seem to simply admire the odd-looking but charming headgear and the romantic nickname, the Hatted Buddha or "Gat Bawi. "Furthermore, an astounding fact about the Buddha is that rumors have long been circulating among worshippers across the country that "the Buddha does listen to the wishes of prayers, if their wishes are genuinely sincere and honest, fulfilling their desires eventually." Hence the number of visitors doubles around the early part of each lunar month which is believed to be spiritually sacred. Also, when the college entrance scholastic ability tests begin nationwide in December, many earnest worshippers climb the precipitous peak before daybreak.

There is a little, old shrine perched on the hill beneath the statue. The large stone altar in the shrine is crowded with people bustling about to offer rice or to light their wishing candles. Some drop a generous wad of money in their alms chest. Every five minutes or so, the two huge brass bowls on each corner of the altar brim over with rice and two female attendants are busy emptying them into an underground storage room below.

The open ground opposite the altar is packed with dozens of worshippers, sitting cross-legged on the cold concrete floor, some without a cushion, to say prayers to the Buddha. Some of them are offering deep bows by bending their knees countless times. Some sit in the posture of meditation and others sit quietly with their palms joined together to make a wish. They are all here to win the heart of the merciful Buddha for their loved ones." (160)

Jason and I reached the mountain before noon, and it was a warm sunny day. There was a trail to the mountain, which was not very steep, more like a swish back trail. When we were about a hundred yards up the mountain, I noticed stacks of rocks which people obviously placed on top of one another. Jason told me that it was a custom to place a rock on top and make a wish, which people hoped would come true. Later I researched the meaning of Korean's placing one stone upon the other, especially the mountain of the Buddha with the hat. I found an article written by someone who simply identified themselves as *Stonewalker*.

"You can see unique but not special structures in Korean mountain. These are piles of stones. Nobody knows where these stone piles came from and when these began. Only what I am remembering is my grandma had put one stone on the pile of stones when she had visited the Buddhist Temple. Time is changing. Religion in Korea has also changed a lot. Even though Korea was a Confucian country, Christianity have prevailed over Korean society for one hundred years since the door had been open to the religion from outside.

Some scholars had guessed that the purpose of the piling stones had a defensive and secure meaning. In the past, I could have seen the piles of stones in the entrance of the village. I heard the reason they had piled stones in the entrance of the village when I was an elementary school pupil. In peace time people gathered the stone when they passed the entrance of the village. They said that piling stones were combat readiness when enemy invaded.

But the stone piling in the mountain is supposed to be quite different from the combat readiness at the entrance of the village. The stone piling in the mountain seemed to express people's sincere hope and wish. There is religious meaning in stone piling.

Whenever I have visited the mountain, I find, and 1 look around the stone piles with caution. There were so many stone piles in Gyeryong mountain (the one we climbed) than another mountain. The shapes were various than other mountains. There were many more wishes and hopes. Usually, people put only one stone over the other stones. You can estimate how many people have prayed for their wishes. People's wishes are simple, healthy and kids' success entering college. One thing we should remind is that people's wishes are all connected.

As I wrote, people placed stones on other stones what someone had already put on. It means that our wishes could be attained with relations with people. I heard so many times from my grandma that if you want to be treated well and receive fortune, you should do good things for others. When you did good behavior, then your children or grandchildren will receive the paybacks from heaven. Strangely enough Christianity and my grandma's traditional religious teaching was all but similar.

In Korean culture, the custom of stacking rocks on top of one another is called "doldap" (돌탑), which translates to "stone tower," and is often seen as a practice associated with wish-making, prayer, and a connection to the mountain spirits, with people building small stone stacks in nature, particularly near temples or hiking trails, to express their hopes and desires; this act is considered a form of reverence for the natural world and a way to achieve balance and harmony."

An older gentleman summed it up quite nicely. "The more you pile up the stones, the more you serve the people.

You can get a safe place in heaven. You have built a home for the poor" (161)

Once we reached the top of the mountain, we walked around and climbed a bit further up to the very top of the mountain where the Buddha stature overlooked the valley floor. Hung below the Buddha were prayer flags. Prayer flags are part of Tibetan Buddhist religious practices. They are used to spread goodwill and compassion throughout the universe. These flags are sacred and should be treated with respect. Prayer flags are hung on poles or strung on lines. They are typically located along mountain peaks or ridges or flying above monasteries, temples, and private homes. (162)

Being as adventurous as I am, I asked Jason to see if we could meet the head monk. Jason looked at me with question in his eyes, repeatedly saying. "Monk, monk, I never met a Buddhist monk. The monks on this mountain lived in a monastery which was about a hundred feet below the Buddha temple but still quite high on the mountain top." Monks may live austere lives, but they do have some creature comforts. They have a housekeeper, and some have cell phones. I pointed to a lady who was a staff member of the temple.

After conversing with the lady, Jason said that the monk will meet us for a brief while because he is not feeling well. I told Jason that it is an excuse not to spend much time with us. I was surprised to see that the monk was quite young and outgoing. Most Buddhist monks are small and seem distant. This monk was good looking and had features different than most monks. Later I found out he was an accountant that decided to become a Buddhist monk.

When he found out that I was an American, he invited us to join him below the temple for drinks and refreshments. After conversing for three hours cross legged on the floor stretched out under a table, I told him that we did not want to keep him back from his monk duties. As he was now into conversing with us, he said he had plenty of time.

After getting up to leave, he invited us back to join him for an evening dinner. We said we would very much like to join him and would get back to him soon.

While I was serving in Korea, I would phone friends and family back home. I decided to call my friend Chuck. Chuck believed in angels. He even rode around with an angel plate on the front of his vehicle. He lost his wife to an unexpected illness and only had one daughter. He set up a nursing scholarship in her memory because she was a nurse. When I phoned Chuck, his daughter answered his phone and told me that they received sad news. Chuck came down with a terminal and very threatening illness. When Chuck got on the phone, he seemed confident that he would overcome it.

After a couple of weeks went by, I phoned Chuck again. Once again, his daughter answered. She sadly told me that Chuck went into a comma and the doctor told her emphatically that she would not see her father conscious again and the end was near. She told me that it was sad because he wanted to go home one more time and I would not see her father alive again.

I called Jason and asked him to tell the monk that we were coming to take him up on his dinner invitation.

This time when we returned to climb the mountain, it was nightfall. The trail up the mountain was lined with burning torches. You could see the stars and the moon through the trees and hear the growls and howls of animals. As we started to climb, I told Jason that I was going to enact the ancient tradition of laying a stone and making a wish for my friend Chuck. I was going to wish that he would come out of the coma so he could go home one more time. The other was that he would not suffer a terrible end which was common for the type of illness that had befallen him. I gently laid two stones on top of others that were forming a tower and made my wishes.

As we climbed, I could hear the chants and bongs of a Buddhist service underway on top of the mountain. The entire atmosphere and site was like what one might see in an Indiana Jones movie. One thing the monks were emphatic about is that no one is allowed to take photos of their services.

Upon our reaching the lower monastery, I told the monk that I was going to climb to the Buddha and make a wish and say some prayers for my friend Chuck. Upon ascending to the Buddha, an eerie feeling overcame me. It was only me and the Buddha with lit candles on top of that mountain. I could hear wild animals all around me. Whatever might befall me, I was determined to make my wish again, say prayers, and lit a candle for my friend Chuck. I returned to join the monk and Jason after completing my mission.

Sitting crossed legs under the temple, we ate the tradition monk food. "Korean temple food does not use any animal products except dairy products. Korean Buddhism forbids meat. The Buddha said in the Nirvana Sutra, "Eating meat extinguishes the seeds of compassion." Buddhism teaches that compassion means to embrace all living beings as oneself.

Korean temple food has also traditionally meant that monks and nuns do not use five pungent vegetables (onions, garlic, chives, green onions, and leeks), these are called the "o-shin-chae", because they hinder spiritual practice. The prohibition of the five pungent vegetables is a preventive measure to guard Buddhist practitioners from distractions during meditation. In addition, the prohibition is also meant to prevent any attachment to the flavor of strong spices, which may also disturb practice. These characteristics of temple food show how monastic meals are a means through which Buddhist monks and nuns realize the interdependence of all lives and that they must strive to establish a world in which all live together in harmony." (163)

Photo 33-Service of Buddhist monks

After enjoying the meal, I pulled out my cell phone and asked the monk if I could take photos of their service. As he was now my friend, he gave me his permission despite their temple's no photo policy. Upon leaving, we exchanged information, and I invited the monk to visit me in the United States.

It was now one week left before I was scheduled to leave for home and thought I would call Chuck's daughter. Upon reaching her, she excitedly told me that her and her father experienced a miracle. Despite the doctor saying that we would never see her father alive again, he came out of the coma and is going home one more time. She put Chuck on the phone. Chuck told me that he knew he was not out of the woods, but he was feeling fine.

Before leaving Korea, I toured around the country using their rail system which is far more advanced than ours and traveled at lightening high speeds of 190 miles per hour.

"South Korean railroad system covers the whole country and allows tourists to enjoy the view at high speed.

The most popular routes in Korea are Seoul-Busan, Daegu-Seoul, , Seoul-Gwangju, Daejeon-Seoul. Around 2.5 million people visit Korea annually, uncovering its beauty and traditions, learning culture and rituals. The availability of detailed railway routes, schedules, and a comprehensive train map online is invaluable for anyone planning to explore South Korea. It allows travelers to effortlessly plan their journeys, ensuring they can make the most of their time in this vibrant country. From historical sites in Gwangju to the technological marvels of Seoul, the train system connects you to a multitude of experiences filled with discovery, culture, and unforgettable memories. The South Korea train is the fastest and most convenient way to travel through South Korea. Take a ride anywhere in country in less than 3 hours and enjoy a state-of-the-art transport." (164)

One of the sights that I wanted to see was the President's house of South Korea's which would be comparable to our White House, only they call it their Blue House.

Photo 34-South Korea presidential house-the Blue House

"The signature markings of the Presidential Residence of Cheong Wa Dae are its blue tiles on the Main Office; it is the first thing to catch one's attention upon viewing the premises. Approximately 150 thousand tiles compose the roof of the Main Office. Each tile was baked individually to make them strong enough to last for hundreds of years. The blue tiles and the smoothly curving roofline blend beautifully with Bugaksan Mountain in the backdrop. "(165)

When I landed in Pittsburgh, I went to see Chuck in the hospital. He was sitting in bed watching the Steeler game. The next day his daughter asked Chuck what he would like to eat. He said that he would like a breakfast from his favorite breakfast place. That night, his daughter received a call that Chuck passed away peacefully in his sleep.

Believe what you may but there must have been something in the prayer and wish that I made high on top of the South Korean mountain.

CHAPTER 30

Space and Beyond

I came across a request for support at Space and Missiles System Center in El Segundo California.

'The Space and Missile Systems Center, a subordinate unit of U.S. Space Force, is the center of technical excellence for developing, acquiring, fielding, and sustaining military space systems. SMC's mission is to deliver resilient and affordable space capabilities. The center is responsible for on-orbit check-out, testing, sustainment and maintenance of military satellite constellations and other Department of Defense space systems' is headquartered at Los Angeles AFB in El Segundo, Calif. The center employs an estimated 6,300 people including military, civilians, and contractors at LAAFB and other locations worldwide. Its vision is to forge an agile team that delivers innovation, war-winning capabilities and deliver resilient, affordable, and sustainable space capabilities for the nation. The Space Systems Command facility is used for developing, maintaining, and deploying satellite constellations for the Department of Defense space systems.

Los Angeles Air Force Base is the home of U.S. Space Force's Space and Missile Systems Center -- the "birthplace" of U.S. Air Force's ballistic missile and military space program. Headquartered in El Segundo, Calif., SMC is the U.S. Space Force's center of acquisition excellence for acquiring and developing military space systems. Its portfolio includes the Global Positioning System, military satellite communications, defense meteorological satellites, space launch and range systems, satellite control networks, space based infrared systems and space situational awareness capabilities. LAAFB is also the home of the 61st Air Base Group and is the only active-duty military installation located within the greater Los Angeles metropolitan area. Its historical lineage can be traced back to WWII.

The mission of the Advanced Systems and Development Directorate is to drive future Space capabilities through collaborative innovation, development planning and demonstrations. Headquartered at Kirtland AFB, New Mexico with operating locations at Los Angeles AFB, Calif., Hill AFB, Utah and NASA/Johnson Space Center, Texas, SMC/AD is composed of four mission divisions and four support divisions.

The Global Positioning Systems Directorate is a joint-service, multinational, civil/military systems directorate with more than 700 DoD/contractor personnel responsible for development, launch and sustainment of the Global Positioning System, the world's premier navigation and timing standard. The directorate is responsible for the development and procurement of over 250,000 receiver systems and the United States' nuclear detonation detection system.

The Range and Network Division is responsible for modernizing and sustaining the world-wide Air Force Satellite Control Network as well as the nation's Launch and Test Range Systems located at Vandenberg AFB, Calif., and Cape Canaveral AFS, Fla.

The Remote Sensing Systems Directorate's mission is to develop, deploy, and sustain surveillance capabilities in support of missile warning, missile defense, battlespace awareness, technical intelligence, and environmental monitoring mission areas." (166)

My duties were to help protect the security and integrity of our satellites and the base. The threat of interfering with our satellites and compromising their operation is ongoing and increasing every year.

"The Number of satellites that are circling our earth every day, the importance on securing our satellites, and the potential for satellites colliding with one another may best be depicted in an *IFL Science article*.

Photo 35-Earth Science and Remote Sensing Unit

"Satellites whizzing about over our heads provide us with telecommunications and precise positioning, as well as keeping us safe with weather forecasting and many other analyses, like keeping an eye on wildfires, floods, ice, and pollutants released into the atmosphere.

But the population of satellites has skyrocketed (pardon the pun) in the last several years, and this has changed the landscape (skyscape?) of what is going in orbit. As of today, June 11, there are 11,780 satellites orbiting our planet according to the United Nations

Office for Outer Space Affairs (UNOOSA). Most of them are functioning and in low-Earth orbit.

Geostationary orbit (GEO) is also known as geosynchronous orbit, and it is located 35,786 kilometers (22,236 miles) in altitude above Earth's equator. A satellite placed there will follow the same spot on the Earth's surface as it moves around the planet with the same period it takes the Earth to spin. There are currently 552 satellites there. Communications and weather forecasting satellites are often placed in GEO.

Then there is medium-Earth orbit (MEO), a vast region from 2,000 kilometers (1,243 miles) up all the way to GEO. This is a prime location for navigation satellite constellations such as the Global Positioning System, Galileo, GLONASS, and BeiDou. There are 199 satellites currently in this orbit, but some space internet providers are considering moving here.

And the reason for that is that low-Earth orbit (LEO) is getting crowded. There are currently 8,110 satellites in LEO and 6,050 of them are from SpaceX's megaconstellation Starlink. The project from Elon Musk's company aims to double its current number to reach 12,000 satellites. And it could be expanded even more, to 34,400 satellites.

There are many concerns about the deployment of so many satellites, especially in LEO. One major concern is how it is changing the night sky both for advanced astronomy but also just in terms of light pollution, even in areas that do not have artificial lights.

The other concern is the massive increase in space junk. Space is big for sure, but interesting and valuable orbits are a small subset of that. Satellites need to have their orbits readjusted often, and all these movements lead to some of them crossing paths. But what happens when the satellites are no longer working? There are almost 3,000 objects like that! Their orbits will continue to change but with no ability for us to control them (there are some proposed <u>countermeasures</u> though).

A collision in space could herald worse to come. Collisions beget collisions simply because a piece of space junk breaking apart becomes a swarm of space junk. Scientists are concerned that we could end up in a Kessler Syndrome situation, where the number of collisions and amount of space debris grow exponentially. This scenario could render entire regions of near-Earth space a danger to pass through." (167)

"The Aerospace Industries Association released a new infographic, "Secure Our Satellites," highlighting the importance of satellites on our modern way of life, the threats they face, and why we need to protect them. To protect and defend our satellites, we must build resilient space architectures and strengthen partnerships between industry and government. With the global space economy valued at $469 billion and 152,000 Americans directly employed in the space industry, threats to United States assets in orbit cannot be ignored.

Space provides essential capabilities in supporting national security, the economy, and the environment. Satellites provide communications services, remote sensing and intelligence collection, positioning, navigation, and timing services, weather and climate information, and warning against hostile missile threats. Modern financial institutions could not function without accurate timing services provided by satellites. The goods Americans buy and sell every day get to their destinations utilizing satellite navigation that enables trade in a globalized world market.

However, our adversaries recognize our dependence on satellites and are actively working to threaten American access to the benefits of space. As a result, they have developed dangerous threats to our assets in space. Satellites can be destroyed or crippled by direct attacks using ground-launched missiles, high-energy lasers, or other satellites also in orbit. In addition to directed threats, environmental factors like space debris can threaten satellite operations, which in turn can have effects on our ability to use satellites on the ground.

This infographic emphasizes the importance of the space domain on what we do on Earth, and highlights threats that can hold satellites at risk. As industry continues to innovate new ways to utilize satellites for our benefit, it is essential to strengthen partnerships between commercial companies and the government to protect space systems. The Aerospace Industries Association stands ready to help bridge that gap between industry and government and foster collaboration to secure our satellites." (168)

We must be constantly on guard for rogue countries and terrorists using space to harbor weapons of mass destruction. Most notably, Russia has reportedly launched a satellite that may have the capability to attack and destroy our satellites now circling the earth.

"The US says Russia launched a satellite last week which it believes may be capable of attacking other such probes. "Russia launched a satellite into low Earth orbit that we assess is likely a counter space weapon," said Pentagon spokesman Brig Gen Pat Ryder on Tuesday evening.

It was on the "same orbit" as a US government satellite, he said, adding that Washington would continue to monitor the situation and had to be ready to protect its interests. Russia has not publicly commented on the issue.

Moscow and Washington - two global rivals - have repeatedly clashed over space weapons issue at the UN in recent weeks, with both sides accusing each other of seeking to militarize space.

Earlier on Tuesday Russia's foreign ministry spokeswoman Maria Zakharova claimed the US was seeking to turn space into an "arena for military confrontation".

Several military experts have long warned that space is likely to be the next frontier of warfare in an increasingly technology-dependent world.

On Tuesday, Gen Ryder said the Pentagon believed the Russian satellite was "presumably capable of attacking other satellites in low Earth orbit". "Russia deployed this new counter space weapon into the same orbit as a US government satellite. "And so, assessments further indicate characteristics resembling previously deployed counter space payloads, from 2019 and 2022.

"We have a responsibility to be ready to protect and defend, the domain, the space domain, and ensure continuous and uninterrupted support to the Joint and Combined Force," the Pentagon spokesman added.

Separately, a spokesperson for the US Space Command told Reuters news agency that the satellite was "likely a counter space weapon presumably capable of attacking other satellites in low Earth orbit".

The spokesperson said the satellite - Cosmos 2576 - was launched on 16 May from Russia's Plesetsk cosmodrome, about 800km (497 miles) north of Moscow.

In its statement, Russia's Roskosmos state space agency said the launch on 17 May was "in the interests of the defense ministry of the Russian Federation". It said its launch vehicle Soyuz-2.1b was used.

The different reported launch dates might be explained by the fact that the Moscow time zone is three hours ahead of GMT.

Neither Moscow nor Washington provided any further details. But space analysts say that Cosmos 2576 appears to be on the same orbit as America's USA 314 satellite. Since launching a full-scale invasion of Ukraine in February 2022, Russia has warned that US satellites aiding the Ukrainian military could become legitimate targets. In February, the White House admitted Russia was developing a "troubling" new space weapon but insisted that it had yet to deploy it.

It came after a senior Republican congressman issued a cryptic warning about a serious national security threat, sparking intense rumors around the Washington DC.

A report released by the Washington DC-based Center for Strategic and International Studies last year suggested that Russia is developing a range of anti-satellite (ASAT) weapons, including a missile that was successfully tested against a defunct Soviet-era satellite in November 2021." (169)

The Pentagon recently reported that Russia is developing a nuclear weapon to go into space. "A senior Pentagon official warned lawmakers that Russia is developing an "indiscriminate" nuclear weapon to go in space, confirming reports from several months ago and describing potentially devastating effects in orbit.

"The concept that we are concerned about is Russia developing, if we are unable to convince them otherwise, to ultimately fly a nuclear weapon in space, which would be an indiscriminate weapon," said Assistant Secretary of Defense for Space Policy John F. Plumb at a House Armed Services Committee hearing.

In February, Rep. Mike Turner (R-Ohio), the chair of the House Intelligence Committee, issued a statement warning of a "serious national security threat." White House

National Security Council spokesman John Kirby then confirmed media reports that the danger involved an anti-satellite weapon the Russians have been developing, which would violate an international treaty that bans the deployment of nuclear weapons in space.

Various Pentagon officials subsequently warned of the widespread destruction a nuke could wreak in space, without outright saying that the Russians were developing such a weapon. Space Development Agency director Derek M. Tournear, for example, noted that detonating a nuclear weapon in space would destroy commercial, civil, and military satellites and constitute an "attack on the world."
Plumb offered even more detail, saying in his written testimony that such a weapon "could pose a threat to all satellites operated by countries and companies around the globe, as well as to the vital communications, scientific, meteorological, agricultural, commercial, and national security services."

In low-Earth orbit (LEO) in particular, Plumb cautioned most satellites aren't hardened against a nuclear detonation, making them especially vulnerable to damage. The outcome could vary based on factors like the detonation type and location, but satellites in the blast zone would likely be destroyed. He also suggested a sufficiently powerful nuclear detonation in the right location could render LEO unusable for up to a year.

"It is not imminent in the way that we should have to worry about it right now, but we are concerned about it," said Plumb. "The department and the entire administration, and I know this Congress is taking this deadly seriously."

The U.S. has a significant number of satellites in LEO, both civil and military, like the Space Development Agency's Proliferated Warfighting Space Architecture and SpaceX's Starlink constellation.

"And those could be what a Russian weapon system might be trying to counter, is that proliferated, architecture that we're seeing used so well in Ukraine and as part of our overall architecture moving forward for the United States," Charles Galbreath, senior fellow at the Mitchell Institute for Aerospace Studies, told Air & Space Forces Magazine in February.

In addition to military and commercial satellite damage, Galbreath cautioned of potential indirect effects from the detonation, referencing the Cold War-era "Starfish Prime" test. In 1962, the U.S. detonated a nuclear weapon in low-Earth orbit, disabling eight out of twenty-four satellites and causing a power blackout in Hawaii.

Russian President Vladimir Putin has denied any intention to deploy nuclear weapons in space. However, Russia recently vetoed a U.N. Security Council resolution, co-proposed by the U.S. and Japan, urging Member States not to develop such weapons. Russia's U.N. Ambassador cited the resolution's inadequacy in banning all space weapons as the reason for the veto.

Moscow is now considering proposing a resolution calling on all nations to urgently prevent the placement of any weapons in outer space "for all time," according to the Associated Press.

Earlier this week, Secretary of Defense Lloyd J. Austin III said if a nuclear device were detonated today in outer space, it would have "devastating consequences," and that it is "irresponsible for anybody to even consider deploying or employing a nuclear device in space." Austin was addressing a lawmaker's question regarding Russia's veto and China's abstention of the U.N. proposal by the U.S. and Japan, at a separate House Armed Services Committee hearing. Plumb also criticized Moscow and Beijing's stance at the U.N., calling it "hypocritical and unbelievable," given the nations' continued development and fielding of counterspace weapons." (170)

"Most recently, Moscow used their launch rocket Soyuz, to launch two Iranian satellites into space. As Iran is considered a Rogue state (axis of evil connotation) and not a trusted ally of ours, one can only wonder what the mission of the two Iranian satellites was. Iran's two satellites, named Kowsar and Hodhod, were the first launched on behalf of

Photo 36-Russian Soyuz 18 Booster Rocket

the country's private sector. In 2022, a Russian rocket launched an Iranian Earth observation satellite called Khayyam that was built in Russia on Tehran's order, and in February Russia put another Iranian satellite named Pars-1 into orbit." (171) Future launches of Rogue nation satellites could prove devastating for America and its satellites.

Tuesday's launch comes as Russia and Iran have expanded ties in various spheres. Ukraine and the West have accused Tehran of providing Moscow with hundreds of exploding drones for use on the battlefield in Ukraine and helped launch their production in Russia. The Iranian drone deliveries, which Moscow and Tehran have denied, have allowed for a constant barrage of long-range drone strikes at Ukraine's infrastructure.

My tour of duty at Space and Systems Center and a robotic space project at one of the major universities whet my appetite for becoming more involved in space exploration. Google offered a thirty-million-dollar prize to any university that could land a robotic probe on the moon. I joined the university's team but soon left after becoming disenchanted with the direction of the project. One of the key members, however, had a fascinating way to profit from the venture by harvesting oxygen on the moon for future space explorations. The key issue was the cost of a launch. Back then, Elon Musk's Space X was not existence. The lowest cost of a missile launch was offered by the Russians at a cost of twenty million dollars. To afford such a launch, the university would have to solicit contributions.

Watching the presidential debates, I was astonished that none of the moderators posed a question about space exploration. The only candidate that did touch upon it during the campaign was Donald Trump. Concerned that we need to place more emphasis on space exploration, I decided to write a letter about space exploration,

Money is easily found for sophisticated weapons whose destructive power is comparable to that of the weapons of mass destruction. We need to ask ourselves if we are prepared to continue this frivolous spending on weapons of mass destruction while ignoring other pressing needs of our people.

The renowned physicist Stephen Hawkins has confirmed what I have been saying to friends, family, and students for years and that is we must look to the universe for ways to preserve our heritage and the human race. Mr. Hawkins estimates that we have approximately 1,000 years to migrate to another planet in our solar system before the Earth is no longer habitable.

It is sad that since John F. Kennedy, no president or presidential candidate for that matter, has placed a high priority on space exploration. Not once did panelists put forth questions to candidates in recent debates about space exploration and specifically whether they had a plan to save our civilization when our Earth spins out of existence.

We are so intent on protecting that which we have built and those who will continue our heritage, yet we are so very shortsighted by not placing more emphasis on space exploration, the only gateway to the survival of life as now exists on Earth. If we continue to ignore the inevitable destruction of the Earth, those whom we love and all that we love and all that we have built will perish, and there will be no trace that we ever existed.

Hopefully, space visionaries like Elon Musk may help pave the way for humankind to migrate to another planet safely if Stephen Hawkins prediction comes true.

"Musk founded Space X. "whose mission of Space X includes building on the achievements of Falcon 9, Space X is working on a next generation of fully reusable launch vehicles that will be the most powerful ever built, capable of carrying humans to Mars and other destinations in the solar system.

Space X has gained worldwide attention for a series of

Photo 37-Starship Rocket

historic milestones. It is the only private company capable of returning a spacecraft from low Earth orbit, and in 2012 their Dragon spacecraft became the first commercial spacecraft to deliver cargo to and from the International Space Station. And in 2020, Space X became the first private company to take humans there as well.

While most rockets are designed to burn up on reentry, Space X rockets can not only withstand reentry but can also successfully land back on Earth and re-fly again. SpaceX's Starship represent a fully reusable transportation system, designed to carry both crew and cargo to Earth orbit, the

Moon, Mars and beyond. Starship is the world's most powerful launch vehicle ever developed, capable of carrying up to 150 metric tons fully reusable and 250 metric tons expendable.

To quote Elon Musk, "You want to wake up in the morning and think the future is going to be great…and that is what being a spacefaring civilization is all about. It is about believing in the future and thinking that the future will be better than the past. And I cannot think of anything more exciting than going out there and being among the stars." - Elon Musk." (Space X website)

Elon Musk is so dedicated to SpaceX's mission and to Mars exploration that he put the two in that order with reference to his own mortality: "I will go if I can be assured that SpaceX would go on without me. I have said I want to die on Mars, just not on impact." (172)

A quote on Space X by Elon Musk

CHAPTER 31

Return to the Pentagon

After serving for several months at Space and Missile Systems, a critical assignment came up serving on the Joint Staff at the Pentagon.

Prior to leaving Space and Missile Systems Center for an assignment at the Pentagon, I inadvertently received an email from an administrator at my place of employment to another administrator at my university that was intimidating and threatening. Because I was one of the top fund raisers for the university, they wanted me back to raise more money. To further intimidate me, they evaluated me in a performance report when I was not working at the university for the past years. In all my years at the university, I always received the highest performance rating. I was especially surprised in view of the fact that I was one of the few administrators that endowed an award at the University, the *Matt Drozd Family Humanitarian Assistance and Community Service Award*. "The award was to honor and recognize students who have unselfishly given of themselves by performing community service and/or providing humanitarian assistance to their community, state, country, or have assisted the people of other nations in recovering from such catastrophic losses caused by famine, pestilence, and natural disasters." Despite my service to the University and my not even being present long enough at the University to warrant a review, they rated me at the lower rating level when they should have never rated me in the first place. I informed them that my country came first before my well-being. To protect my retirement, I gave a year notice that I was retiring. I investigated the possibility of legal action but did not pursue it at the time for fear of further repercussions.

A military legal officer (JAG) informed me that they were in violation of the "Soldiers and Sailors Relief Act. "In 1940, Congress passed the Soldiers' and Sailors' Civil Relief Act (SSCRA) to provide protection to those called to military service in the armed forces. The SSCRA was updated after the Gulf War in 1991 but remained unchanged as of 2003. In December 2003, President Bush signed into law the Servicemembers Civil Relief Act (SCRA). The SCRA was written to clarify the language of the SSCRA and to update the SSCRA to reflect new developments in American life since 1940. This law is a complete revision and provides significant protection to service members. It also provides protection to Reservists and members of the National Guard (when activated under Title 10 orders)." (173)

To add insult to injury, I applied for a similar position at another campus a couple of years later and was further discriminated against. I did not even get an interview.

Upon arriving at the Pentagon, I was assigned to J2 of the Joint Chiefs of Staff. They needed people to serve on a special briefing unit of the Joint Staff. I was to fill in for those on the Joint Staff that were being deployed overseas or called for another assignment.

"The Directorate for Intelligence, J-2, supports the Chairman of the Joint Chiefs of Staff, the Secretary of Defense, Joint Staff and Unified Commands. It is the national level focal point for crisis intelligence support to military operations, indications and warning intelligence in DoD, and Unified Command intelligence requirements.

The J-2 coordinates joint intelligence doctrine and architecture, and managed intelligence for joint warfighting assessments. J-2 serves as the Intelligence Community manager for Support to Military operations, and is the Director of the Joint Warfighting Capabilities Assessments for Intelligence, Surveillance, and Reconnaissance under the Joint (174)

I was assigned to a team of four officers that were to collect information globally and input into a Top-Secret PowerPoint brief that was forwarded on to the Chairman, the Secretary of Defense, and the President and his staff. The briefs were updated seven days a week, twenty-four hours a day. Based upon the briefs, the powers to be could make credible decisions on events that could impact our national security. Our teams manned the command center around the clock, giving us little time for social life and sleep. Like before, all I had time to do was go to duty, go back to my quarters to eat, sleep, exercise and do it repeatedly.

We served in teams of four high ranking military officers. My team included two navy fighter pilots, myself, and an Army ranger. The army ranger, Steve, and I kidded one another constantly. One night, we asked one another what we had done to support the global war on terrorism. Upon his urging, we went to pull ourselves up on the unclassified computer. My son, Matthew, who bore the same name as me came up when I googled my name. Matthw almost made the Olympic swimming team. Although you could clearly see it was not me, I kiddingly took credit as it being me. Steve's image came up with him being interviewed by CNN. He commanded the battalion that captured Sadam Hussein.

In December 2003, Operation Red Dawn came to its planned conclusion: with deposed Iraqi dictator Saddam Hussein pulled from a "spider hole" near a farmhouse in Ad

Dawr, Iraq, south of his hometown of Tikrit. His capture was a story nine months in the making after the American-led coalition launched its invasion of Iraq in March of that year. Hussein, of course, would spend the next three years incarcerated, awaiting his eventual execution.

Alaa Namiq -- the farmer who hid the dictator for those 235 days of 2003, dug the spider hole in which Hussein was captured and even served as the former president's personal hairdresser -- was also captured. He spent at least six months in the Army's notorious Abu Ghraib prison for aiding Hussein.

Halkawt Mustafa, a Norwegian-Kurdish journalist and filmmaker, read the Post's article about Namiq. He then spent the next decade telling the story of how an Iraqi farmer who knew little about Saddam Hussein came to hide him from 150,000 U.S. troops for the better part of a year. That story is now the documentary film "Hiding Saddam Hussein," which premiered Dec. 1, 2023, at the Red Sea International Film Festival in Jeddah, Saudi Arabia.

The last time Hussein appeared in public as president of Iraq was on April 9, 2003, the same day Baghdad fell to American forces. He was seen standing on top of a car hood, mobbed by loyal Iraqis for the last time since forcing his predecessor out of power in 1979.

In all that time, Namiq only ever saw the president on his one-channel television or heard his voice on state radio. The next thing he knew, Hussein was knocking on his door, asking for help. In all that time, Namiq only ever saw the president on his one-channel television or heard his voice on state radio. The next thing he knew, Hussein was knocking on his door, asking for help.

"He came here, and he asked us for help, and I said yes," Namiq, now in his fifties, told The Washington Post. "He said, 'You might be captured and tortured.' But in our

Arab tribal tradition and by Islamic law, when someone needs help, we help him." "At that moment, the thought didn't cross my mind that 150,000 soldiers were looking for him," Namiq says in the trailer for the documentary film.

Though Namiq's farm was near Hussein's hometown and U.S. troops would be looking for him in the area, the erstwhile president knew he would be caught if he fled to family or friends. This farmer's home was just far enough away from Tikrit (and any Hussein family and friends) to give Hussein the chance to get away clean or start an insurgency to help him regain power. As time goes on, however, the likelihood of a pro-Saddam resurgence grows less likely." (175)

After we got over the kidding of one another, I asked Steve for his accounting as to how the capture of Hussein transpired. Normally it is a Lt Colonel who commands a battalion. Steve explained to me the reason for him being in command that day was because his Lt Colonel was told to take leave because he was worn out from serving such long and tedious duty days. That left Steve to take over command of the battalion.

Steve gave me the details of how they located him. "They received a lead that Hussein was holed up in this little village. Steve's battalion went into search for him. After searching through most of the houses, one of his men called to him about something he found. While walking down one of the dirt roads one of Steve's soldiers tripped over a prayer rug. Looking down, he saw a wooden corner of a trap door. Upon opening it, they saw a man lying face down. Pulling the man up, they repeatedly asked him if he was Saddam Hussein. The man was so out of it, he could not answer. Steve's orders were to load the man into a helicopter for transport to compare his DNA to those of his ancestors. Once doing so, they confirmed it was Hussein.

Another instance that really made us want to do more was when the terrorists sent us photos of a slain American soldier. They were carrying his body while cooking food and playing strange music. We were told that terrorists shot him with automatic weapons hidden under their robes. I became anxious when I noticed that the man wore his dog tags like me. He had a gold chain with one dog tag and a St Christophers metal.

After completing my tour on the J-2, I received another medal for my service.

"Lieutenant Colonel Matthew J. Drozd, distinguished himself by meritorious achievement while serving as Liaison Officer to the National Military Command Center's Critical Action Team, Joint Operations Division, Command, Control, Communications, and Computer Systems Directorate, The Joint Staff. Colonel Drozd diligently tracked significant staff actions for OPERATION IRAQI FREEDOM and ENDURING FREEDOM, and expertly presented this data in daily briefings to the Secretary of Defense and the Chairman of the Joint Chiefs of Staff. As the key advisor to the Deputy Director for Operations for all operational matters within the US Central Command area of responsibility, he superbly analyzed three months of Multi-National Force-Iraq's significant events data to clearly and succinctly present to the Secretary of Defense a case for United States troop levels in Iraq."

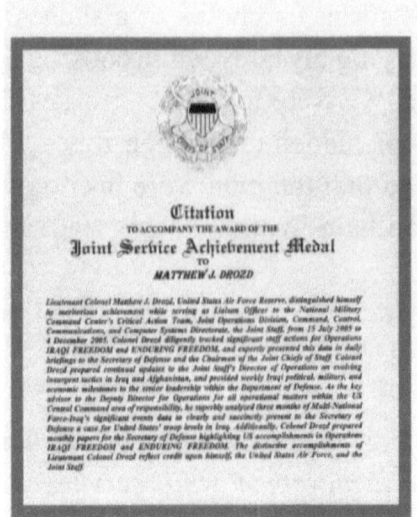

CHAPTER 32

New Ways to Protect America

The September 11 commission and its findings

"In 2002 President Bush had appointed a commission to investigate the September 11 attacks, and two years later it issued its final report. The commission found that the key pre-September 11 failure at the CIA was its not adding to the State Department's "watch list" two of the "muscle" hijackers (who were trained to restrain the passengers on the plane), the suspected al-Qaeda militants Nawaf al-Hazmi and Khalid al-Mihdhar. The CIA had been tracking Hazmi and Mihdhar since they attended a terrorist summit meeting in Kuala Lumpur, Malaysia, on January 5, 2000. The failure to watch-list the two al-Qaeda suspects with the Department of State meant that they entered the United State under their real names with ease. On January 15, 2000, 10 days after the Malaysian meeting, Hazmi and Mihdhar flew into Los Angeles. The CIA also did not alert the FBI about the identities of the suspected terrorists, which could have helped the bureau locate them once they were inside the United States. According to the commission, this was the failure of not just a few employees at the CIA but many CIA officers and analysts. Some 50 to 60 CIA employees read cables about the two al-Qaeda suspects without taking any action. Some of those officers knew that one of the al-Qaeda suspects had a visa for the United States, and by May 2001 some knew that the other suspect had flown to Los Angeles.

The soon-to-be hijackers would not have been difficult to find in California if their names had been known to law enforcement. Under their real names they rented an apartment, obtained driver's licenses, opened bank accounts, purchased a car, and took flight lessons at a local school; Mihdhar even listed his name in the local phone directory.

It was only as a result of questions raised by a CIA officer on assignment at the FBI, that the two al-Qaeda suspects were watch-listed and their names communicated to the FBI. Even then the FBI sent out only a "Routine" notice requesting an investigation of Mihdhar. A few weeks later Hazmi and Mihdhar were two of the hijackers on the American Airlines flight that plunged into the Pentagon.

The CIA inspector general concluded that "informing the FBI and good operational follow-through by CIA and FBI might have resulted in surveillance of both al-Mihdhar and al-Hazmi. Surveillance, in turn, would have had the potential to yield information on flight training, financing, and links to others who were complicit in the 9/11 attacks."

The key failure at the FBI was the handling of the Zacarias Moussaoui case. Moussaoui, a French citizen of Moroccan descent, was attending flight school in the summer of 2001 in Minnesota, where he attracted attention from instructors because he had little knowledge of flying and did not behave like a typical aviation student. The flight school contacted the FBI, and on August 16 Moussaoui was arrested on a visa overstay charge. Although Moussaoui was not the "20th hijacker," as was widely reported later, he had received money from one of the September 11 coordinators, Ramzi Binalshibh, and by his own account was going to take part in a second wave of al-Qaeda attacks following the assaults on New York and Washington.

The FBI agent in Minneapolis who handled Moussaoui's case believed that he might have been planning to hijack a plane, and the agent was also concerned that Moussaoui had traveled to Pakistan, which was a red flag as militants often used the country as a transit point to travel to terrorist training camps in Afghanistan. On August 23 (or 24, according to some reports) CIA director George Tenet was told about the case in a briefing titled "Islamic Extremist Learns to Fly." But FBI headquarters determined that there was not sufficient "probable cause" of a crime for the Minneapolis office to conduct a search of Moussaoui's computer hard drive and belongings. Such a search would have turned up his connection to Binalshibh, according to Republican Sen. Charles Grassley, a leading member of the Senate Judiciary Committee, which has oversight of the FBI. The 9-11 Commission also concluded that "a maximum U.S. effort to investigate Moussaoui conceivably could have unearthed his connection to Binalshibh." (176)

The United States has made significant progress in securing the nation from terrorism since the September 11, 2001, attacks. Nevertheless, work remains as the terrorist threats facing the country have evolved in the last ten years and continue to change. Following 9/11, the federal government moved quickly to develop a security framework to protect our country from large-scale attacks directed from abroad, while enhancing federal, state, and local capabilities to prepare for, respond to, and recover from threats and disasters at home. A key element of this framework included the creation of the Department of Homeland Security (DHS) in March 2003, bringing together twenty-two separate agencies and offices into a single, Cabinet-level department.

Created with the founding principle of protecting the American people from terrorist and other threats, DHS and its many partners across the federal government, public and private sectors, and communities throughout the country have strengthened the homeland security enterprise to better mitigate and defend against dynamic threats. Many of the features of this new, more robust enterprise align with – and respond to – recommendations contained in the 9/11 Commission Report, released in July 2004 to assess the circumstances surrounding 9/11 and to identify ways to guard against future terrorist attacks.

In April 2011, the Department of Homeland Security (DHS) announced the implementation of the new National Terrorism Advisory System (NTAS), replacing the former color-coded alert system, which had become obsolete. NTAS is designed to communicate information more effectively about terrorist threats by providing timely, detailed information and recommended security measures to the public, government agencies, first responders, airports and other transportation hubs, and the private sector.

Under NTAS, DHS will coordinate with other federal entities to issue detailed alerts to the public when the federal government receives information about a specific, credible terrorist threat. NTAS alerts provide a concise summary of the potential threat, which may include a geographic region, mode of transportation, or critical infrastructure potentially affected by the threat; actions being taken to ensure public safety; and recommended steps that individuals, communities, businesses and governments can take to help prevent, mitigate or respond to a threat. NTAS Alerts contain a provision indicating a specific date when the alert expires.

Information sharing: In the ten years since 9/11, the federal government has strengthened the connection between collection and analysis on transnational organizations and threats. Terrorism-related information sharing across the intelligence community has greatly improved, and through the establishment of the DHS Office of Intelligence & Analysis (I&A), we have strengthened the ability to convey intelligence on threats to the homeland in a context that is useful and relevant to law enforcement and homeland security officials at the state and local level.

One example of the Department 's efforts to work with state and local officials, as well as community groups, is focused on Countering Violent Extremism (CVE). Over the past year, DHS has collaborated with its partners to develop a training curriculum for state and local law enforcement that is focused on community-oriented policing to help frontline personnel identify activities that are indicators of potential terrorist activity and violence. In conjunction with local communities and DOJ, DHS has published guidance on best practices for community partnerships to prevent and mitigate homegrown threats. DHS has also participated in dozens of community roundtable discussions and trained more than 2,300 state and local personnel on CVE related topics.

DHS also supports state and major urban area fusion centers, which interact regularly with JTTFs and serve as focal points within the state and local environment for the receipt, analysis, gathering, and sharing of threat-related information including classified intelligence. Fusion centers are uniquely situated to empower front-line law enforcement, public safety, fire service, emergency response, public health, critical infrastructure protection, and private sector security personnel to understand local implications of national intelligence, thus enabling local officials to better protect their communities.

Federal Partners: Initiatives to support law enforcement operations and protect the country from terrorists and other threats. A critical partner for DHS, JTTFs are led by the FBI and coordinate resources and expertise from across the federal government to investigate terrorism cases. DHS has provided hundreds of personnel, including U.S. Immigration and Custom Enforcement (ICE) special agents, U.S. Secret Service (USSS) agents, Federal Air Marshals, U.S. Customs and Border Protection (CBP) officers, U.S. Citizenship and Immigration Services (USCIS) officers and representatives from the Federal Emergency Management Agency (FEMA) and the U.S. Coast Guard (USCG), to support the 104 JTTFs across the country. Tribal Partners: The Obama Administration has focused on building strong relationships with Tribal governments and law enforcement across the nation.

The private sector is an integral component of the homeland security enterprise, and through the Department's private sector office, DHS has worked to improve coordination of private sector engagement across the Department, facilitating more effective and rapid communication with key organizations and bolstering regionally focused information sharing efforts.

The Administration has also expanded information sharing with its international partners. DHS, in collaboration with DOJ and the Department of State (DOS), has signed Preventing and Combating Serious Crime (PCSC) Agreements with 17 Visa Waiver Program (VWP) countries and one non VWP country to share information about terrorists and criminals.

DHS has worked with its federal, state, local and private sector partners, to expand the Nationwide Suspicious Activity Reporting Initiative (NSI), an administration effort to train state and local law enforcement to recognize behaviors and indicators related to terrorism, crime and other threats; standardize how those observations are documented and analyzed; and enhance the sharing of those reports with law enforcement and communities." (177)

CHAPTER 33

War takes its Toll

My other assignments included serving on the African desk under the Secretary of the Air Force. Much of my duty required working requests from foreign countries that wanted to purchase aircraft such as Fl-16's. High Tech and equipment classified as top secret were not included in the sale and stripped of the aircraft before delivery.

While serving in the Air Force International Affairs Mideast/Africa Division, our team supplied munitions to Israel for their defense during the 2006 Lebanon war, a conflict fought between Hezbollah and Israel. Two Israeli generals came in to thank us for our support. The African Division wanted me to extend my tour on active duty. As I never refused when duty called, I tried to obtain a waiver to extend my military service but because I was previously granted an age waiver to stay beyond retirement, the military personnel could not grant it.

Upon receiving notification that I reached the age limit for retirement, I received several more decorations including one for performing humanitarian missions while serving in the Medical Operations Division, Office of the Surgeon General at the Pentagon. The decoration recognized me for:

"Coordinating approval for the Secretary of the Air Force directed Humanitarian Response Capability Package,

which provided the Service's first consolidated humanitarian relief capability. It further read that my efforts were key to implementing Air Force engagement strategy with five African nations. Colonel Drozd built unmatched rapport with African countries and interagency counterparts. He tirelessly worked on the baseline for Africa's country plan to implement Department of Defense Security Cooperation Guidance."

THE UNITED STATES OF AMERICA

TO ALL WHO SHALL SEE THESE PRESENTS, GREETING:
THIS IS TO CERTIFY THAT THE PRESIDENT OF THE UNITED STATES OF AMERICA AUTHORIZED BY EXECUTIVE ORDER, 16 JANUARY 1969 HAS AWARDED

THE MERITORIOUS SERVICE MEDAL

TO

LIEUTENANT COLONEL MATTHEW J. DROZD

FOR

MERITORIOUS SERVICE
22 DECEMBER 2005 TO 30 SEPTEMBER 2006

ACCOMPLISHMENTS

Lieutenant Colonel Matthew J. Drozd distinguished himself in the performance of outstanding service to the United States as Operational Plans Officer, Current Medical Operations Division, Air Force Medical Operations Agency, Office of the Surgeon General, Pentagon, Virginia. During this period, Colonel Drozd demonstrated great professional skill as Air Force medical operations center on-call duty officer, allowing timely situational awareness of worldwide medical operations for senior Air Force leadership. He coordinated approval for the Secretary of the Air Force-directed Humanitarian Response Capability Package, which provided the Service's first consolidated humanitarian relief capability. While working in the Office of the Deputy Under Secretary of the Air Force International Affairs MidEast/Africa Division, his efforts were key to implementing Air Force engagement strategy with five African nations. Colonel Drozd built unmatched rapport with African countries and interagency counterparts. He tirelessly worked on the baseline for Africa's country plan to implement Department of Defense Security Cooperation Guidance. The singularly distinctive accomplishments of Colonel Drozd culminate a distinguished career in the service of his country and reflect great credit upon himself and the United States Air Force.

GIVEN UNDER MY HAND
6 JULY 2007

LAWRENCE M. RIDDLES, Col, USAF, MC, CFS
Commander, Air Force Medical Operations Agency
Office of the Surgeon General

Before leaving home, I learned that the Pentagon referred me to the White House as a possible appointee to be Secretary of the Army. After returning home, I received a letter from the White House stating they would like to schedule a meeting to talk to me about the appointment. It may have been my broad background of service. I believe that I may have a record in the military. I may be the only military member that served on the Joint Staff, Office of the Secretary of Defense, and the State Department. Plus, I did these simultaneously. When I called, they said that they would like to see me as soon as possible and there was no travel expenses.

I scheduled the meeting. Upon arriving at their offices, they asked me to fill out some paperwork and answer some questions. Two of the questions asked if I worked to elect the President and did, I make any contributions to his campaign. After I filled out the paperwork, I was ushered in to see one of their top people. He told me that the President preferred to appoint one of his friends, but I was more qualified, and he did not possess the same to-secret clearances as me. If he did not pass the clearances, then I would be next up. They must have come through because I was asked next if I would like to be considered Director of FEMA. Knowing that I would have to report to the Secretary of Homeland Security and the problems in FEMA, I declined.

Looking back on my military duties, I may have several records. I may have the longest break in service for someone who returned voluntarily a second time after being out of the military for over twenty years. At the time, I was over the age for receiving a commission but because of my previous military time and background, I received a waiver to commission in the medical service corps of the Air Force. I served for three different chairman of the Joint Chiefs of

Staff, the Secretary of Defense, the State Department, the Cabinet Secretary of Health and Human Services, the Air Force Surgeon General, the Joint Task Force for the National Capital Region, both the Army and the Air Force, at Space and Missile Systems Center, and one of three brothers who served to protect our troops and the people of South Korea.

Other military members may have served in the Office of the Secretary of Defense and the Joint Chiefs of Staff, but I am certain that there is no one who ever served in four major cabinet directorates simultaneously like me, the Joint Chiefs of Staff, Office of the Secretary of State, the State Department, and in Health and Human Services.

Thinking back when I voluntarily deployed into two high risk areas and put my life on the line, the Middle East and South Korea, I may not be here today if I did not have a strong sense of survival and like many veterans had a strong will to return alive and hold my family in my arms again. People would ask if I had any fear at the time. My answer was that military members do not have time to be afraid when they need to focus on accomplishing their mission.

I want to stress, however, that "many Veterans return from combat having combat stress, suffering from Post-traumatic stress disorder (PTSD), a disorder that develops in some people who have experienced a shocking, scary, or dangerous event. Service members are exposed to traumatic events during war. If you were deployed to a combat zone, you may have been in life-threatening situations. Research on Operation Enduring Freedom (Afghanistan War) and Operation Iraqi Freedom (Iraq War) suggests that 1 or 2 out of every ten troops (or 10% to 18%) are likely to have PTSD after they return. In addition to PTSD, OEF/OIF Service members are at risk for other mental health problems. Although studies vary widely in terms of methods used, estimates of depression in returning troops range up to 1 of every 4 (or from 3% to 25%). (178)

"Many Iraq and Afghanistan veterans face a life of disability due to the physical and psychological injuries they sustain in the war zones. Over1.8 million veterans have some degree of officially recognized disability as a result of the wars — veterans of the current wars account for more than half of the severely disabled veteran population. Many additional veterans live with physical and emotional scars despite lack of disability status or outstanding claims. The costs of caring for post-9/11 war vets will reach between $2.2 and $2.5 trillion by 2050 – most of which has not yet been paid.

In comparison to the civilian population, Iraq and Afghanistan war veterans are facing elevated rates of suicide and mental illness, drug and alcohol dependence, car crashes, and homelessness. They and their families also experience higher rates of divorce as well as homicide, child abuse, and child neglect by both parents left behind and returning veterans." (179)

I not only served during Enduring Freedom and Iraqi Freedom, but I served during Noble Eagle (protecting the United States and Canada's airspace and homelands.

There is also an alarming rise in the suicide rates among both active-duty military and Veterans.

"Suicide rates among active-duty military members are currently at an all-time high since record-keeping began after 9/11 and have been increasing over the past five years at an alarmingly steady pace. In fact, some branches of the Armed Forces are experiencing the highest rate of suicides since before World War II.

In 2021, research found that 30,177 active-duty personnel and veterans who served in the military after 9/11 have died by suicide - compared to the 7,057 service members killed in combat in those same 20 years. That is, military suicide rates are four times higher than deaths that occurred during military operations. For military families and parents, whose active duty loved one already sacrifices so much to protect our freedom, this trend is extremely troubling." (180)

I was never told to report for active military duty. I repeatedly volunteered whenever and wherever called upon. After I could volunteer no more, I returned from active duty to an empty home, disconnected from friends, and no social life or special person waiting for me. I hardly saw my children for six years. It was also the same year that the economy and stock market took a nosedive, my significant other of 18 years found someone else, and I was forced to leave my gainful employment because I was harassed and discriminated against by two administrators from my University. Like many Veterans, I became withdrawn and disassociated with life. Luckily for me, I had a loving and caring family.

The sad situation is that we do not seem to be making much headway in curbing Post-traumatic stress disorder and suicide deaths among our active military and veterans.

What helped me to cope with my PTSD was due to my military assignment was to save lives and to protect our American freedoms and way of life. As I always placed my country first, I never had any fears of losing my life and would do it again. My family was also incredibly supportive.

CHAPTER 34

Romance Blossoms

I returned to my elected position and what was left of my civilian career. My former eighteen-year relationship with a young lady was also gone due to my absence. It seemed that I would never fill the void I felt in my life or be able to restart my life.

At the suggestion of my family, I logged onto a dating site to hopefully make new relationships. None of the ladies, however, seemed to light my fire. I became increasingly despondent after many dates yielded no one that sparked my interest. It was only when my two sons, each sitting by my side, encouraged me to give the dating site another chance. Looking at many photos and biographies, I skipped over one because the photo did not immediately catch my eye. My sons pulled the page back and said, "it is only a cup of coffee." Looking again, I saw a small photo of the young lady dressed in biking gear at the bottom of the page that gave her an alluring and attractive look. Her name was Joyce. Unbeknownst to her, her friends listed her on the same dating site as me.

A phone call to her revealed that she did not have the time to actively socialize or date. She was a resolute nurse practitioner and was taking care of a friend that had a terminal illness. The first time I called her; she had no time for even a cup of coffee.

A couple of weeks later, I gave Joyce another call. This time she agreed to meet over coffee. I suggested a movie which turned out convenient for her. When we met up, this little lady that had the aurora of a beautiful and vibrant young girl. When I saw a tear come to her eye for her friend, I knew that she was a special lady with deep compassion and love. Someone that I never thought I would ever find.

After the movie, we spent hours talking at a coffee shop, exchanging stories about our lives. She was wonderful to converse with. Because of my elected office, I was invited to a President Obama election party at a posh club in Pittsburgh. Not realizing that her political leanings was moderate like mine, I invited her to go with me. It was winter and funny how little things are attractive in a person. When I opened the car door and she stepped out onto the snow, her easy-going demeanor caught my attention. The next sight that blew me away was when I gazed upon her petite silhouette standing in front of a huge fireplace. It would be difficult for me to even describe how I felt at that moment.

Being afflicted with PTSD and having served long tours of duty, I was struggling to regain my life. As a result, I almost lost Joyce. I scrambled to keep her in my life. Words that I spoke to her resonated in my mind and what we both once said, "I waited all my life for you to come along." I said it again when I pleaded with her to give me another chance. It took some time for her to trust me. Fortunately for me, she is understanding, compassionate, loving, and extremely loyal.

In the fall of 2020, our family and many of our friends witnessed our marriage. At last, I found my soul mate. We are joined at the hip. We are so much alike, including our birthdays, likes and dislikes. Our passion is hiking, biking, and simply cultivating new friendships and enjoying our huge families and friends. We also share the love of God, family, and Country as well as hiking, biking, and traveling.

This is not the end of my story. It is only the beginning of my next adventures. One such adventure was being placed on the New Hampshire ballot as a candidate for President of the United States. My name appeared on the same presidential ballot as President Trump on their 2016 ballot.

NEW HAMPSHIRE
DEPARTMENT OF STATE

William M. Gardner
Secretary of State

Robert P. Ambrose
Senior Deputy Secretary of State
David M. Scanlan
Deputy Secretary of State

MATT DROZD
Pittsburgh, Pennsylvania

This office has received your declaration of candidacy as a **REPUBLICAN** candidate

for the Office of **PRESIDENT OF THE UNITED STATES**. Your name and address

will appear on the ballot as it is printed above.

To make certain that all ballots will be printed correctly, please notify this office as soon

as possible if any of the information above is incorrect.

Karen Ladd
Assistant Secretary of State

November 17, 2015

State House Room 204, 107 N. Main St., Concord, N.H. 03301
Phone: 603-271-3242   Fax: 603-271-6316
TDD Access: Relay NH 1-800-735-2964
www.nh.gov/sos   email: elections@sos.state.nh.us

As for me and Joyce, I would mimic what Rose said to Jack in the classic movie Titanic, "I will never let Joyce go." When it came time for me to say my vow at our wedding, I emphatically said that we will stay together "through eternity and beyond"!

Joyce and Matt Hiking in Yosemite National Park

REFERENCES

PRELUDE

1. My base guide, A peak in Fort Knox, the most heavily guarded military base, by Ashley Nation
2. Britannica, Military united forces

CHAPTER 1 Persian Gulf

3. Defense Technical Information Center, The Air Force Individual Augmentee Program
4. Air Force Medical Corps, About us
5. Joint Chiefs of Staff, Origin of the Joint Chiefs of Staff, Origins of Joint Concepts
6. North Carolina Weslyn University, about Henry H. Shelton

CHAPTER 2 USS Cole Attack

7. Naval History and Heritage Command, USS Cole Determined Warrior
8. FBI.gov, USS Cole bombing
9. United State Navy, USS Cole (DDG-67), Navy History and Heritage Command
10. Air Force Mortuary Affairs Operation, Dignified Transfer
11. FBI.gov, USS Cole bombing
12. U.S. Department of Defense, The USS Cole is towed away from the port city of Aden

CHAPTER 3 America under attack

13. DoD Executive Agent. Archived from the original on 2013-10-04
14. Britannica, September 11 attacks United States [2001] Also known as: 11/9 attacks, 9/11 terrorist attacks, September 11, Written by Peter L. Bergen Fact-checked by The Editors of Encyclopedia Britannica Last Updated: May 20, 2024•Article History, Terrorist Attack, WTC, Pentagon

CHAPTER 4 Chaos and Uncertainty

15. United States Navy, Attack on the Pentagon

16. US Army News Service, Army leaders share stories of the 911 attack on the Pentagon, by Thomas Brading

17. Historical Office, Office of the Secretary of Defense, 911 attack, History.com-Behind the 9/11 White House order to shoot down U.S. Airliners, it had to be done, by Garrett M. Graff, Dr. Alfred Goldberg, Former OSD Historian

18. Behind the 9/11 White House order to shoot down US liners, It had to be done, History, by Garrett M Graff

19. Office of Secretary of Defense Historical Office, Pentagon 911

20. Six ways uncertainty reigned aboard Air Force One, History, by Amanda Onion

21. The White House, George W. Bush

22. Behind the 9/11 White House order to shoot down US liners, It had to be done, History, by Garrett M Graff

23. Army leaders share stories of the 911 Pentagon attack, Army News Services, by Thomas Brading

24. Marine corps University Press: Escaping atonement in Sunni Islam, death by Jihad for deliverance, by Christine Sixta Rinehart, PhD

CHAPTER 5   Devastation and Carnage

25. Joint Chiefs of Staff, Director Joint Staff

26. Military.com Tiffini Theisen (2023)."What is DEFCON?". Military.com. Retrieved 19 November 2023.

27. www.historycommons.org.,Archived from the original on 2021-07-01. Retrieved 2016-08-02.

28. DoD Executive Agent". Archived from the original on 2013-10-04. Retrieved 2015-02-11

29. United States Navy, National Museum of the U.S. Navy, Little Boy-Hiroshima-August 6, 1945

30. Homeland Security, IED Attack: Improvised Explosive Devices

31. Guantanamo Bay detention camp, History, Location, and facts, by Tina S. Kaidanow and Jeannette L. Nolan

32. The White House, International contributions to the war against terrorism and operation Enduring Freedom, Source-Department of Defense

33. OUSD, Office of the Secretary of Defense, Nuclear weapons employment policy, planning, and NCE

34. George W. Bush presidential library, Marine One. 35-A, When It Comes to Government Planes and Political Trips, Who Pays for a President's Campaign Travel? US News, by Associated Press

35. George W. Bush Library, Marine One

36. When it comes to government planes and political trips, who pays for a President's campaign travel, AP News, by Chris Megerian

CHAPTER 6 Battle of Logistics

37. Britannica, Afghanistan War by Griff Witte

38. U.S. Department of Defense, Combatant commands

39. PBS, Interview with U.S. Army General Tommy Franks

40. U.S. Army, Moving forward with logistics advising in Afghanistan, by Captain Ross A. Powers

41. NPR, In Afghanistan, fighting the battle of logistics, by Tom Bowman

42. Bill Marmon (February 2010)."New Supply 'Front' for Afghan War Runs Across Russia, Georgia and the 'Stans". The European Institute. Archived from the original on 3 December 2011. Retrieved 25 February 2011.

CHAPTER 7 Building a Coalition

43. The White House, George W. Bush

CHAPTER 8 Call in the Calvary

44. Britannica, Afghanistan War history, combatants, facts, and timeline by Griff Witte

45. Military Times, How the horse soldiers helped liberate Afghanistan from the Taliban 18 years ago, by Diana Stancy

46. Britannica, Afghanistan War history, combatants, facts, and timeline by Griff Witte

47. MOTHER OF ALL BOMBS ABC News, US drops 'mother of all bombs' on ISIS forces in Afghanistan

CHAPTER 9 Hunt for Bin Laden

CHAPTER 10 Protecting our Government

CHAPTER 11 Homeland Defense

CHAPTER 12 Heroes not forgotten

70. History, Pat Tillman killed by friendly fire in Afghanistan
71. US Naval Institute, Friendly fire, facts, myths, and misperceptions by Major Charles F. Hawkins USAR 1994
72. U.S. Army, The United States Medal of Honor
73. U.S. Department of Veteran Affairs, National Cemetery Administrations, Medal of Honor
74. Vietnam Veterans memorial fund, Dan Bullock, youngest American killed in Vietnam War
75. Air and Space Forces Magazine, Valor, Skip bombing pioneer, by John L. Frisbee

CHAPTER 13 Wearing Several Hats

76. Under Secretary of Defense for Policy, U.S. Department of Defense
77. Rafferty, Andrew (April 7, 2017). "Here's the kind of security needed to discuss sensitive information". *NBC News*. Retrieved August 10, 2023.
78. McGrath, Jenny (October 23, 2019)."Why Can't You Bring Electronic Devices into a SCIF?". Retrieved August 10, 2023.
79. "White House completes $50 million revamp of high-security Situation Room". September 8, 2023.
80. Columbia University Libraries, Columbia Spectator, By Kathy Gilsinan
81. The New York Times, With empty homes all over the globe, an easy position to take, by Jim Dwyer
82. Convention on International Civil Aviation" 24 March 2012. Retrieved 21 June 2019
83. National Library of Medicine, Preparing for the psychological consequences of terrorism: A public health strategy
84. FBI.gov history, Amerithrax or anthrax investigation
85. Pentagon Force Protection Agency, History of
86. National Library of Medicine, the anthrax vaccine: is it safe" does it work?

CHAPTER 14 Assignment State Department

87. U.S. Department of State, Bureau of Political Military Affairs-State Department
88. Wikipedia, Colonel Charles Wilson

89. Political Military Action Team (PMAT)-U.S. Department of State

90. Britannica, Wahhabi-Islamic movement

91. Department of Justice Office of the Inspector General, Special report

92. U.S. Department of State, Foreign Consequence Management-state.gov

93. Baylor College of Medicine, Vaccine Nation: ten most important diseases without a licensed vaccine

CHAPTER 15 Iraq War

94. Council on Foreign Relations, Iraq, Weapons Inspections: 1991-1998

95. NPR, 20 years ago, the U.S. warned of Iraq's alleged weapons of mass destruction, by Jack Mitchell

96. The New Arab, Kuwait has the highest rate of polygamy, cousin marriages

97. Britannica, Iraq war, Summary, causes, dates, combatants

98. Encyclopedia Britannica, Republican guard, military organization, Iraq

99. Fox News/AP, Kuwait could provide key launching pad for allied ground forces

100. American Red Cross, Summary of the Geneva Conventions of 1949, and their additional protocols

101. Watson Institute, International & Public Affairs, Brown University, Costs of War

102. International Committee of the Red Cross, Convention (II) for the Amelioration of the Condition of Wounded, Sick and Shipwrecked Members of Armed Forces at Sea. Geneva, 12 August 1949.

103. Information on the chronology of the war comes from "Chronology of Operation Enduring Freedom," an internal Human Rights Watch database of press accounts, policy statements, and other information compiled during war.

104. The New York Times, In Kuwait, missile smashes into a mall: Blast hits Iraq market; 50 reported dead, by Thomas Fuller, International Herald Tribune

105. CNN, Arab backlash mounts in Kuwait, Britannica, Iraq war, Summary, causes, dates, combatants

106. U.S. Naval forces Central Command, Manama, Bahrain

107. U.S. Department of State, Security programs for U.S. Embassies and Consulates, Bureau of Diplomatic Security

CHAPTER 16 Hostages

108. AlJazeera.com, About Us | Today's latest from Al Jazeera

109. AlJazeera.com, US hostage beheaded

110. Culture.gov/BH, Al Fateh Mosque

111. Office of the Historian, State, The Iranian hostage crisis

CHAPTER 17, Like father like sons

112. CNN, Bahrain offers exile to Saddam, Wednesday March 19, 2003

113. History.com, Qusay and Uday Hussein killed, July 22, 2003, Wikimedia Commons, Airborne, and Special Forces Uday Qusay raid, 2003

CHAPTER 18, End of a Dictator

114. BAGHDAD, Dec. 30 — The New York Times, On the Gallows, Curses for U.S. and Traitors, Dec 31, 2006, by Marc Santora

115. President Bush Announces Major Combat Operations in Iraq Have Ended" georgewbush-whitehouse.archives.gov. Retrieved February 14, 2023

CHAPTER 19, Cost of Afghan and Iraq Wars

116. Costs of 20 years of Iraq war, Crawford 15 Watson Institute for International and Public Affairs

117. United States Institute of Peace, In Afghanistan, was a loss better than peace

118. U.S. Department of State, U.S. Security Cooperation with Ukraine

119. Watson Institute for International and Public Affairs, Human Costs, costs of War

CHAPTER 20, Wrong Intel

120. NPR, 20 years ago, the U.S. warned of Iraq's alleged weapons, by Jack Mitchell

CHAPTER 21, More command centers

148. Migration Data Portal, Remittances to Afghanistan are lifelines: They are needed more than ever in a time of crisis

149. Hundreds of billions were spent by the US in Afghanistan. Here are 10 of the starkest examples of 'waste, fraud and abuse, CNN World, By Nick Paton Walsh

150. How the U.S. lost billions over nine years in Iraq, CNBC, By David Francis

CHAPTER 28, Afghanistan and Iraq today

151. Pew Research Center, A year later, a look back at public opinion about the U.S. military exit from Afghanistan, By Katherine Schaeffer, AUGUST 17, 2022,

152. Council on Foreign Relations, Instability in Iraq, Global Conflict Tracker, updated February 2024, Instability in Iraq | Global Conflict Tracker

CHAPTER 29, Assignment Korea

153. Smaman Spider, Elwood 5566, shaman spider | Elwood 5566

154. Four instruments: the Dharma sound for liberation, Wikimedia Commons, By Kim Haan-young

155. DTIC, United States Air Force (USAF) Air Expeditionary Force (AEF) https://apps.dtic.mil

156. Liberty in North Korea, The DMZ and North Korea, What is the DMZ

157. Statista, Religion in South Korea, statistics, and facts

158. South Korea passes bill to ban eating dog meat, ending controversial practice as consumer habits change, CNN World, By Jessie Yeung, Gawon Bae, Yoonjung Seo and Marc Stewart

159. Chaplain news from the front, Buddhism in South Korea

160. The Hatted Buddha, The Korean Times, By Yi Woo-won

161. Steemit.com, Stone Pile and Wishes of Common People

162. Study.com, Prayer flags history meaning and use

179. U.S. Veterans and Military families, Watson Institute for International and Public Affairs
180. Concerns Rise Over Military Suicide Rates; Here's How the USO is Trying to Help, USO.org, by Danielle DeSimone

PHOTOS

1. Fort Knox Gold Bullion Depository, An exterior view of the United States Gold Bullion Depository at the United States Army Armor Center, Wikimedia Commons, John Coffman, https://nara.getarchive.net/media
2. Troops of 649th Tank Destroyer Battalion on Infiltration Course – DPLA, National Archives at College Park - Wikimedia Commons, war department, Army service forcesW
3. USS Cole Bombing, Damaged ships, work of a sailor or employee of the U.S. Navy, taken or made as part of their duties. It is in the public domain.
4. MV Blue Marlin work of a sailor or employee of the U.S. Navy, taken as official duties. In the public domain. http://www.dcfp.navy.mil/cgi-bin/, Wikimedia Commons
5. National Military Command Center, media is available in the holdings of the National Archives and Records Administration, Under Identifier NAID 6342760, Wikimedia Commons in public domain.
6. Guantanamo captives in January 2002 Photo by Petty Officer 1st class Shane T. McCoy, Wikimedia Commons
7. Aerial view of the Pentagon during rescue operations-post September 11 attack, by TSGT Cedric H. Rudisill, USAF
8. Air Force One flying over Mt Rushmore, In Public Domain https://web.archive.org/web/20070315005902
9. Copy from U.S. National Archives, RG 77-AEC. Chuck Hansen,The Swords of Armageddon: U.S. Nuclear Weapons Development Since 1945 (Sunnyvale, CA: Chukelea Publications, 1995)Atomic cloud rises over Nagasaki Japan, National Archives at College Park, U.S. National Archives and Records Administration

10. Atomic bombing of Japan, Atomic Cloud Rises Over Nagasaki, Charles LevyUnited States Department of Energy

11. Marine One Whitehouse, nsf/0/a01e7a3af32b559f852565b4007cc1bd? Open Document

12. Australian Army Chinook helicopter in Afghanistan during 2010, Vernell Hall, U.S. Army https://www.dvidshub.net/image, by SFC Sadie Bleistein

13. Public Domain, Turning the Tide, Soldiers on Horseback Wikimedia Commons, https://www.dvidshub.net/image/368802

14. US Navy 011104-M-4912C-001 Service members sign weapons before deployment, Wikimedia Commons By U.S. Marine Corps Photo by Joseph R. Chenelly,

15. MOAB Bomb, U.S. Department of Defense, Wikimedia Commons, Public Domain

16. NORAD Blast-Doors, USAF, Wikimedia Commons

17. The airborne command post battle staff prepare for departure in an EC-135 Looking Glass command and control aircraft during the joint military exercise GLOBAL GUARDIAN, National Archives at College Park, Wikimedia Commons

18. Pair of F-16 Fighting Falcons fly in formation during a Combat Air Patrol (CAP) mission, Wikimedia Commons, In Public Domain

19. Medal of Honor of the United States of America, Alexeinikolayevichromanov, Wikimedia Commons

20. . Pentagon Hall of Heroes, www.army.mil/medalofhonor/valor24, from the U.S. Army

21. Situation Room, President George Bush Library and Museum, White House photo by Chris Greenberg

22. Gracie Mansion Snow, Wikimedia Commons, Jim.henderson

23. Global Medic 15 150614-A-GA303-027, https://www.dvidshub.net/image/2001424/global-medic-15, Pfc. Christopher Martin

24. U.S. Embassy Bahrain 2011 Vacation Asia Middle East, Wikimedia Commons by ShashiBellamkonda

25. Airborne and Special Forces Uday-Qusay raid, by SPC Robert Woodward, USA, Wikimedia Commons, https://www.webcitation.org

26. US Navy 030626-N-0000R-001 Hospital Corpsman decontaminate a simulated victim during a chemical biological and radiological (CBR) drill, U.S. Navy photo by Hospital Corpsman 3rd Class Raolito M. Pambid

27. Abandoned Russian Military Transport, Wikimedia Commons, by Vyacheslav Argenberg

28. Mission Accomplished Banner on the USS Abraham Lincoln, U.S. Navy photo by Photographer's Mate 3rd Class Juan E. Diaz, Wikimedia Commons

29. Korea-Andong-Bongjeongsa-Monk hitting the bell, Wikimedia Commons, by Robert Picasa 2005-07-19-Andong

30. Joint Security Area, Korean DMZ, looking south, Wikimedia Commons, by Jack Upland

31. War Memorial of Korea main building, by Abdar, Wikimedia commons

32. Gyeongsan Gatbawi Buddha, Wikimedia commons, by Barnkim

33. Buddhist Monk Service By Christopher Michel, https://creativecommons.org/licenses Wikimedia Commons

34. Korea Seoul-Blue House Reception Center by Steve 46814 Wikimedia Commons

35. Earth Science and Remote Sensing Unit, NASA Johnson Space Center, Wikimedia Commons, American

36. Soyuz 18 booster, Soyuz 18 booster on the launch pad 1 at the Baikonur complex in Kazakhstan, USSR Audin on Wikipedia

37. Starship SN16, Starship up close, Wikimedia, by Lars Plougmann, Wikimedia Commons, Lars Plougmann

Flag by Noah Wulf, Cover Photo, rds323, Image by Richard R. Schünemann

OTHER NOVELS BY MATT DROZD

RETURN OF THE RUSSIAN CAZAR A fairy tale like story filled with romance and intrigue. Readers will travel through time starting with Czar Nicholas's 1917 abdication of the Russian throne to the present day of 2023 where Russia's President contrives a sinister plot to deceive the Russian people by thrusting an obscure and unsuspecting descendant of Nicholas's into becoming the Russian Czar. The suspense thickens and twists when it is discovered that the heir to the throne is American born who becomes loved by the Russian people. The author's experience in international and military affairs provides the reader with insight as to what may befall Russia's President if he continues to wage war on Ukraine. He voluntarily deployed into harm's way, to protect our embassies and our troops.

For information on his novels and where to purchase them, please visit his web site https://mattdrozdbooks.com

SAVE OUR COUNTRY
Matt Drozd

Save our Country A fictional novel blended with intrigue, romance, and historical facts. A powerful and captivating drama based on extensive research on the process of electing the President of the United States. Readers will begin their journey starting with the author of our Declaration of Independence and ending with the election of an unorthodox candidate as our next President. Along the way, the reader will learn about the different leadership styles of past presidents and the candidates that are now vying for the highest office in the land. The Author has unraveled the mystery of what to look for when selecting the best candidate that will become the most powerful leader of the free world. *Save our Country* is more than an entertaining and intriguing story. It is a call to action, urging the silent majority to make their voices be heard and lays out a road map for political campaigns of independent candidates. It surprise ending only occurred once in our nation's history. Copyright registered @ 2024 by Matt Drozd